The Responsible Contract Manager

Titles in the Series

The Responsible Contract Manager

Protecting the Public Interest in an Outsourced World

Steven Cohen and William Eimicke

Georgetown University Press → Washington, D.C.

Georgetown University Press, Washington, D.C. www.press.georgetown.edu

Library of Congress Cataloging-in-Publication Data

Cohen, Steven, 1953–
    The responsible contract manager : protecting the public interest in an outsourced world / Steven Cohen and William Eimicke.
        p. cm. — (Public management and change series)
    Includes bibliographical references and index.
    ISBN 978-1-58901-214-1 (alk. paper)
1. Public contracts—United States—Management.   2. Contracting out—United States.   I. Eimicke, William B.   II. Title.
    HD3861.U6C64 2008
    352.5'3—dc22   2008002164

♾ This book is printed on acid-free paper meeting the requirements of the American National Standard for Permanence in Paper for Printed Library Materials.

15 14 13 12   9 8 7 6 5 4
First printing

Printed in the United States of America

For
Annemarie, Ariel Mariah, and Gabriella Rose

Contents

Figures

Preface

CONTRACT MANAGEMENT is a critical skill for all contemporary public managers. Managers must learn how to write contract requirements and elicit bids that obtain important services and products at the best possible price and quality. They must learn to work with, manage, and measure the performance of these outside private and nonprofit organizations. This two-way sharing of information is essential to decision making in a networked organizational environment. Managers must also learn how to participate in teams that include both public and private sector partners. In addition, students and practitioners of public administration must place these new management practices in the broader context of representation theory and public ethics. What is the effect of this new public sector on representative democracy? How do we guard against corruption and other potential violations of public trust?

In earlier works we have discussed a variety of mechanisms or tools a manager uses to influence internal organizational behavior and to position the organization in its environment. In this respect, the boundary of the organization is sharply defined. One can tell what is inside the organization and what is outside. The internal dynamics of the organization have the most proximate influence over the organization's work processes and outputs. The organization's environment (along with organizational factors) influence organizational inputs (such as resources) and outcomes. Even when examining change-oriented tools we term "tools for innovators," this boundary between the organization and its environment continues to hold. However, when production is a function of a number of organizations linked together in a network, much of the organization's work is produced outside the organization. Some of this work is produced through informal agreements and a shared mission, and some of this work is the result of a formal, contractual relationship. This book focuses on the formal aspect of the relationship between organizations in a network, the contractual relationship.

The need for information about the organization's environment and internal production capacity remains, but the complexity of the information has grown exponentially. Of course, one could argue that the need for information about a contractor's internal capacity and environment is not as great as the need for information about the "home" organization. In all likelihood, a few pertinent facts about the contractor's capacity and environment will suffice—but which piece of information is pertinent? What does the contract manager need to know to obtain productivity from the contractor?

The type of information needed by government contract managers is likely to emerge only over time as the two organizations learn to work together, in concert with other members of the particular production network. Early in the contract relationship, management must stress communication and learning as each party learns the most critical elements of interaction. From that organization-learning exercise we will need to identify key indicators of organizational activity, outputs, and outcomes. We will also need to learn how to communicate those indicators to each other and verify the accuracy of the data.

In addition to the production process that members of an organizational network take part in, public sector networks are characterized by a unique set of features stemming from their role in implementing public policy. First, as we all acknowledge, policy formulation and implementation are not truly distinct processes. Implementation issues constrain policy design, and decisions made when implementing policy shape the operational definition of policy. The law may set the speed limit at fifty-five miles per hour but that policy may be meaningless if the police only stop people who are going seventy. Second, the acts of private parties implementing public policies under contract to public agencies are public and not private acts. The public agency contracting for this service or good is responsible for the safe, effective, efficient, and ethical production of the good or service. The standards public agencies are held to are different and higher than those applied to private organizations. The level of media scrutiny is also higher than in the private sector.

This means that public managers have a unique burden as contract managers. They must develop practices that ensure the production advantages of networked organizations along with systems of transparency and accountability required of the public sector. This makes an already complicated set of interorganizational relationships even more complex.

In many respects, the lessons of public network management are now being learned out of necessity. In countless informal interactions these lessons are being taught and learned as public and private organization members learn to work with each other on the public's business. Many of the lessons are painful. Most are important, and the purpose of this book is to examine these issues and begin the process of detailing, analyzing, and disseminating the lessons learned by today's network managers. Our focus is on the formal, contractual part of interorganizational relations, but we understand that relations in an interorganizational production network include important noncontractual relationships as well. It is important that the reader understand our perspective on public sector contracting and network management. We do not think that the modern manager has a choice about contracting and drawing on other organizations to help implement programs. Government will continue to contract and contracting will grow. In our view, being for or against contracting is like being for or against the weather. It really doesn't matter.

Effective public managers need to quickly learn how to be better managers of activities in other organizations. We need to learn more about how to influence their behavior. We need to learn how to make these organizations act as extensions of the public sector while maintaining their private character. We need to learn when not to contract. While we acknowledge the reality of increased network management, we still believe we must explore the critical strategic managerial issue of when to do it yourself. Under what conditions is the task best performed directly by your own organization? When should you develop the capacity in-house instead of purchasing it from another organization? The war in Iraq has provided a graphic example of the ethical issues involved in contracting with private parties to provide goods and services in a war zone. It is clear that some work should never be contracted by government to private organizations.

The goal of this book is to explore the practical issues of contract management and to extend the discussion to issues of public ethics, governance, and representation theory. Connecting or linking public views to the work of unelected bureaucrats is difficult enough—how do we now ensure that the work done by contractors serves the public interest?

In addition, we want to be practical and thought provoking. To do that, we present a volume that includes theory, concepts, practical examples, and management advice. We hope to add to the academic literature on public sector contract management and to continue to contribute to the main goal of our collaboration over these past two decades—to enhance the effectiveness of public management and public managers.

Acknowledgments

WE OWE a great deal to many people for helping us produce this work. Christopher L. Busch was the research assistant who helped us revise the work for publication. Juan Fernando Orozco served as research assistant as we prepared the manuscript for publication. Kristin McElroy and Louise Rosen, senior members of Steve Cohen's staff, helped a great deal as well. We are grateful for the guidance we received from Professor Beryl Radin as the manuscript made its way through the review process. Both of us thank Dean John Coatsworth of Columbia's School of International and Public Affairs for his encouragement and support. We also wish to thank Columbia's president Lee Bollinger, provost Alan Brinkley, and vice provost Roxie Smith for supporting Columbia's Earth Institute and School of International and Public Affairs and working to build the academic study of global sustainability at our university. If sustainable development is to be achieved, we need to improve the institutional capacity of governments throughout the world. We wrote this volume in the hope of making a small contribution to this effort.

Steve Cohen acknowledges the support of Jeffrey Sachs, director of the Earth Institute, for allowing him to combine the role of scholar and manager. While it is a little unusual, Steve also acknowledges the support, humor, and insight of Bill Eimicke, coauthor and collaborator over the past two decades. He gratefully acknowledges the love and support of his family: his wife, Donna Fishman; his wonderful daughters, Gabriella Rose and Ariel Mariah; his sisters, Judith and Myra; his brother, Robby; and his parents, Marvin and Shirley. He acknowledges a special debt to his father, Marvin Cohen, a private sector chief executive who couldn't help but teach and communicate a sophisticated approach to management to his argumentative and oblivious older son.

Bill Eimicke acknowledges the inspiration of Steve Cohen, a friend, colleague, partner, and role model. He thanks his wife, Karen Murphy; daughter, Annemarie; and dog, Balsam, for providing the motivation to spend the enormous time to complete this project. He also thanks Nicholas Scoppetta, commissioner of the New York City Fire Department (FDNY), and Salvatore Cassano, chief of department, for giving him the chance to work at the department. And he thanks all the members of the FDNY for reminding him why he remains dedicated to public service.

Part I

The Basics

Chapter 1

Defining Contracting and Contract Management

ORGANIZATIONS THROUGHOUT the world, in the public sector as well as the private sector, are becoming less hierarchical and increasingly part of interorganizational networks. Today's effective public manager must learn to manage people outside of his or her home organization, as well as those within that organization. Some of the relationships between organizations are informal partnerships and interactions, but many are formal and contractual. Developing and maintaining both sets of relationships are important and growing elements of the work of the contemporary public manager. This book will focus on managing the formal relationship between organizations: the contractual relationship.[1] This chapter will address five questions:

- What is a contract?
- How is it used in the public sector? What influences the make-or-buy decision in government?
- How often is contracting used in the United States?
- How do you manage a contract?
- Why focus on accountability and corruption?

What Is a Contract?

The definition of a contract is straightforward: "An agreement between two or more parties, especially one that is written and enforceable by law" (www.merriam-webster.com). Still, as Phillip Cooper has observed: "A contract is a legal instrument. Even so, great latitude is left to the contracting parties to an agreement to have the tools to fashion and implement it. Negotiations resulting in a meeting of minds are the dominant dynamic in most contracting" (2003, 13). While contracts involve negotiations between a buyer and a seller, a great deal of the attention in this volume will be devoted to the issues faced by the buyer, the government contract manager.

It is critical that the contract agreement be specific enough to provide a high quality good or service, but flexible enough to allow for that good or service to be modified to meet the government's evolving needs. A contract specifies the good or service being procured, and typically includes information about

- Price
- Schedule
- The definition of the service or product being delivered
- The amount of service or good being provided

A defining characteristic of a contracted relationship in government is that the contractor is a separate and typically nongovernmental organization. For purposes of this work, a memorandum of understanding or cooperative agreement with another governmental organization will not be viewed as the type of contractual relationship we are analyzing.

The literature of public administration uses the term contracting to describe a number of relationships, and therefore it is important to be clear about the type of relationship we are analyzing. In their excellent analysis of contracting patterns among state governments, Jeffrey L. Brudney and his colleagues (2005, 394) note that

> Despite the apparent heterogeneity of the privatization concept and the various methods for achieving privatization, in the U.S. context especially, this term is usually taken to mean government "contracting out" or "outsourcing" with a for-profit firm, a nonprofit organization, or another government to produce or deliver a service. Although the job of delivering services is contracted out, the services remain public, funded mainly by taxation, and decisions regarding their quantity, quality, distribution, and other characteristics are left to public decision makers (Brudney et al. 2005; compare Boyne 1998a, 475; Ferris 1986, 289).

What is key in Brudney's definition, from our perspective, are the notions of public control, funding, and decision making. The government is the principal and the contractor is simply the agent. The issue of accountability will be a recurring theme of this work, and our definition of contracting leaves no ambiguity about the power relationship we see in government contracting. We understand that those who implement policy hold the power to define policy through administration, but that any exercise of this power by the contractor does not eliminate or diminish in any way government's responsibility for the actions of contractors.

How Is It Used in the Public Sector? What Influences the Make-or-Buy Decision in Government?

Government agencies have always purchased goods and services and have developed relationships with vendors as part of the routine administration of public programs. When discussing the "competition prescription," Don Kettl makes this point when he tells the story of George Washington's complaints about the shoddy uniforms supplied to his revolutionary troops by private contractors. While these relationships with vendors continue, some analysts believe that contracting is different today than in Washington's time. Stephen Goldsmith and William D. Eggers discuss the evolution from simple contracting for goods and services to contracting as a means of establishing and maintaining complex interorganizational networks. "In service contract networks, governments use contractual arrangements as organizational tools. Contractor and subcontractor service agreements and relationships create an array of vertical and horizontal connections as opposed to simple one-to-one relationships. Such networks are prevalent in many areas of the public sector, including health, mental health, welfare, child welfare, transportation and defense" (2004, 69).

In this view, contracting is a part of the organization's fabric, and what Phillip Selznick (1957, 42) termed the "distinctive competence" of the network is indistinguishable from that of the organization. In fact, one key dimension of the value added by the organization is its ability to manage the network it has established.

The make-or-buy decision is made by organizations as they attempt to identify their own unique identity or distinctive competence. An organization may decide that to adequately perform its core function, it must shed other functions. Those other functions still must be performed for the organization to deliver outputs, but now they will be contracted out to other organizations.

Other management considerations that influence the decision to contract might include either the hope for a reduced price or the need for access to new or proprietary technology. Contracting can also in some instances provide higher quality services without a cost increase. The need for presence or capacity in a particular geographic location might also lead an organization to seek a partner or a contractor. Finally, the need to develop capacity quickly can lead a government organization to contract.

In some instances, the purpose of contracting is not to buy a particular good or service, but to develop capacity. Defense and high-tech contracting sometimes involves funding private research and the development of new technologies. Rather than investing in in-house scientific expertise, government decides to partner with a private firm for that purpose. A problem with this type of contracting is that often there are very few firms with the ability to compete for these "high end" contracts. This can lead to sole-source procurements, higher prices, and the appearance of impropriety. In addition, as Patrick Dunleavy has observed, "taking on a contractor may also create dependency on them, as when agencies build up data on one proprietary computer system and then find that major transition costs attach to shifting to an alternative supplier. In . . . these circumstances, effective market competition at the recontracting stage is prevented, and firms taking over government functions have every prospect of making super-normal profits with a particularly heavy cost in social welfare terms" (1991, 246).

Dunleavy also believes that the management preferences and self-interest of government contract managers can provide incentives for non-competitive contracting. According to Dunleavy,

> Policy-level staff are keenest to shift over to contracting where they can deal regularly with a few large corporations which have congru-

ent management structures, are simple to monitor and have higher status and prestige. Large firms can better organize flowbacks of benefits for their official contacts, and they share bureaucrats' well attested preferences for negotiated or selective tendering procedures rather than open competition (Turpin, 1972). But senior bureaucrats have less to gain from privatizing activities in highly competitive markets. Small businesses are constantly shifting, hard to monitor, prone to failure and their performance is highly sensitive to personnel changes. Bureaucrats' preferences thus distort privatization policy, promoting contracting-out where agencies become dependent upon a few oligopolistic suppliers, but resisting it where competitive markets exist (1991, 241).

While we do not find evidence of contractors actually resisting competitive markets where they exist, it is true that the ideological preference for privatization can lead to contracting in noncompetitive markets. Moreover, while there are sound managerial reasons to contract, not all decisions to contract are based on management criteria. Sometimes the decision to contract is based on a political calculus. This might include an ideological preference for the private sector and antigovernment sentiment. It might be based on a desire to manage public relations and make it appear as if the government is not growing. Paul C. Light has written extensively on the "true size of government," and in reviewing the growth of federal contracting he notes that

> the government's hidden workforce has crept to its highest level since the end of the Cold War. According to new estimates by the Brookings Institutions Center for Public Service, which I direct, federal contracts and grants generated just over 8 million jobs in 2002, up by more than 1 million since 1990. When these off-budget jobs are added to the civil service and military head count, the true size of the workforce stood at 12.1 million in October 2002, up from 11 million in October 1999. The true size of government is still smaller than it was before 1990. The end of the Cold War resulted in cutbacks of more than 2 million on- and off-budget jobs at the Defense and Energy departments and NASA by 1999. But according to the center's triennial inventory, based in part on estimates generated by Eagle Eye Publishers, the federal government has added back more than half of that head-count savings. But even as cuts were under way at Defense, Energy and other agencies added roughly 300,000 jobs back into government between 1993 and

1999. In the three years since, civilian agencies have added 550,000 more jobs and Defense has added roughly 500,000 (2003, 80).

While population grows and services must be expanded to meet growing needs, antigovernment ideologues more interested in "starving the beast" than delivering well-managed services force contracting on reluctant public managers. For example: "The 1970s witnessed an antibureaucratic mood that sought to limit the bureaucracy's power through various budgetary approaches, reorganizations, reforms, and spending limitations such as California's Proposition 13. Though not without efficacy and utility, overall such approaches are inadequate to the task. They must be augmented by an effort to maximize the political representativeness of public bureaucracy" (Krislov and Rosenbloom 1981, vii). Nevertheless, this type of contracting is a fact of life in the United States, and it distorts the analysis of make-or-buy choices in many public organizations.

How Often Is Contracting Used in the United States?

While contracting is increasing all over the world, this work will focus on the United States. As Barbara Romzek and Jocelyn Johnston have observed, "[g]overnments at all levels have expanded the range of services they deliver through contracts—from traditional 'make-or-buy' decisions for defense weaponry, highway construction and fleet purchases, to contracting for the ongoing provision of specialized social services" (2005, 436).

At the federal level, contracting increased in the late 1990s after declining at the end of the cold war in the late 1980s. As figure 1.1 indicates, defense contracting strongly influences the overall trends in federal contracting. The general tendency toward increased outsourcing is difficult to find in the data due to the size of the defense budget and its volatile nature over the past two decades.

Federal agencies procured more than $235 billion in goods and services during FY2001, reflecting an 11 percent increase over the amount spent five years earlier (U.S. GAO 2003). Despite the rapid increases in contractual spending, it must be noted that in FY2001, the $235 billion spent at the federal level represented about 10 percent of the entire

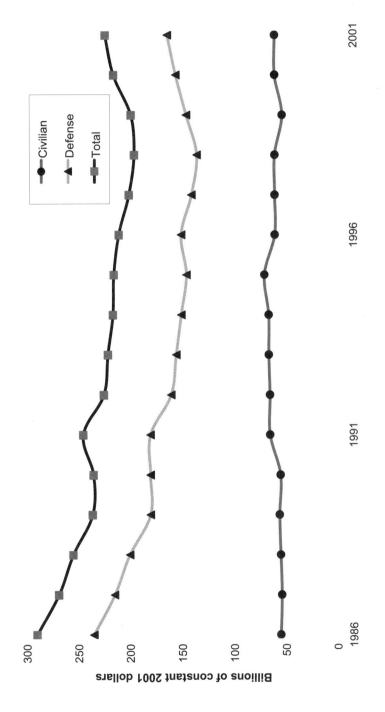

Figure 1.1 Trends in Defense and Civilian Agency Contracting Dollars, 1986–2001

Source: www.afge.org/Documents/CapReport.pdf.

budget. While there are examples of mismanagement in contracting, such as those in Iraq and New Orleans, fears of what H. Brinton Milward and Keith G. Provan (2000, 359) have termed a "hollow state" (without the capacity to manage contracts) are probably premature at the federal level: "Overall, contracting for goods and services accounted for about 24 percent of the government's discretionary resources in fiscal year 2001. However, contract spending consumed between 34 percent and 73 percent of the discretionary resources available to the four largest acquisition spending federal agencies" (U.S. GAO 2003). The analysis by the U.S. Government Accounting Office, now called the Government Accountability Office (GAO), indicates that certain types of spending are more likely to be in the form of contracting than other types of spending. For example, spending for communications equipment and computer equipment and support also tends to be in form of contracts with private parties. According to GAO,

> Further growth in contract spending, at least in the short term, is likely given the President's request for additional funds for defense and homeland security, agencies' plans to update their information technology systems, and other factors. For example, the President's fiscal year 2004 budget request reflects steady increases in DOD's discretionary budget authority, as well as increases in the budgets of other agencies involved in homeland security. Additionally, the President's budget request reflects increased investment in information technology both for new systems and for related support (U.S. GAO 2003).

At the federal level we see some types of contract spending increasing, while other types of spending are either flat or declining. Supplies and equipment purchasing drops while service contracting grows. Of course, some of the supplies and equipment no longer need to be purchased by government contract if contractors are purchasing it for their own use in delivering services. Figure 1.2 shows changes in federal contracting by categories of spending. According to GAO, "the growth in services has largely been driven by the government's increased purchases of two types of services:

- information technology services, which increased from $3.7 billion in fiscal year 1990 to about $13.4 billion in fiscal year 2000; and

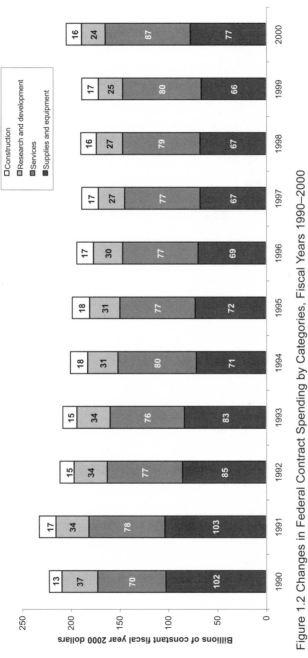

Figure 1.2 Changes in Federal Contract Spending by Categories, Fiscal Years 1990–2000

Source: GAO analysis of data extracted from the Federal Procurement Data System for actions exceeding $25,000; www.gao.gov/new. items/dØ1753t.pdf.

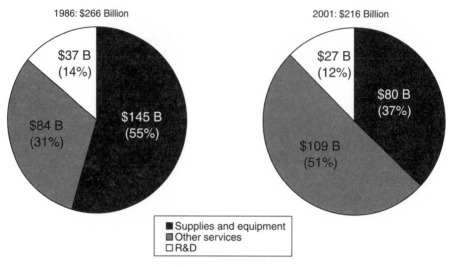

1986: $266 Billion

$37 B (14%)

$84 B (31%)

$145 B (55%)

2001: $216 Billion

$27 B (12%)

$80 B (37%)

$109 B (51%)

■ Supplies and equipment
■ Other services
□ R&D

Figure 1.3 Contracting Activity Has Shifted

Source: www.afge.org/Documents/CapReport.pdf.

- professional, administrative, and management support services, which rose from $12.3 billion in fiscal year 1990 to $21.1 billion in fiscal year 2000" (U.S. GAO 2001).

In the past several years, the growth of contracting at the federal level has followed a pattern of spending growth by the Department of Defense (DOD). The war in Iraq and the war on terrorism that began in late 2001 have resulted in increased spending. According to the White House web site in late 2005, Defense Department procurement grew more than 20 percent from 2001 to 2004. In discussing DOD's increased spending the White House site observed that

> the Department of Defense (DOD) is currently on the front lines of the War on Terror. As of December 14, 2003, there were 12,387 U.S. military troops deployed to support Operation Enduring Freedom in Afghanistan and 125,141 to support Operation Iraqi Freedom. These troops are fulfilling the President's commitment to take the war on terror to the terrorists. . . . Since taking office, President Bush has consistently built defense strength. In fact, in constant 2004 dollars, defense spending has only been higher twice since

World War II—during the Korean War and at the peak of the Cold War buildup. While some of this spending may be attributed to the War on Terror, President Bush committed to and has succeeded in steadily growing the base budget of DOD from $296.8 billion when he took office to $401.7 billion in the 2005 Budget. This 35-percent increase to the Department's base budget helps fulfill the President's commitments and ensures a fighting force that is second to none.[2]

While the picture at the federal level is far from uniform, state and local contracting provides a clearer picture. At the state and local level, data indicate that contracting is increasing. One way to assess this trend is to examine spending trends within cities (fig. 1.3). In many respects, government's funding "funnel" tends to end at the local level, where services are actually delivered. Management trends tend to be more directly related to performance, since performance is more easily observed. If the garbage doesn't get picked up, one doesn't need a major study to learn about the failure—a keen sense of smell will do. The make-or-buy decision may be influenced by ideology, but in the end, reality seems to play an important role.

Nevertheless, since privatization and contracting of services normally entails "significant changes in the form of service provision, either reduced quality standards, or decreased public or consumer control over service provision" (Dunleavy 1991, 241), accountability of the bureaucracy is key. The separation between the "policy level bureaucrat" and the citizen he or she is serving can make it difficult to implement proper contracting of the services. What a policymaker may view as an improvement may in reality be something different. With most funding ending at the local level, it is important to ensure that implementation of contracting at the local level is just as sound as that at the federal level. Often "policy level bureaucrats' welfare is little affected, especially where there is a wide social gap between senior officials and their agencies' clients in terms of class, gender, age or ethnicity—as in most welfare state agencies dealing with the poor, elderly, unemployed, disabled, or homeless. Even in policy fields where bureaucrats themselves consume public services, spatial segregation can recreate a wide social gap between senior officials and clients—as when the schooling, health care or environmental services in run down areas are managed by officials living in more congenial parts of the metropolis" (Dunleavy 1991, 241).

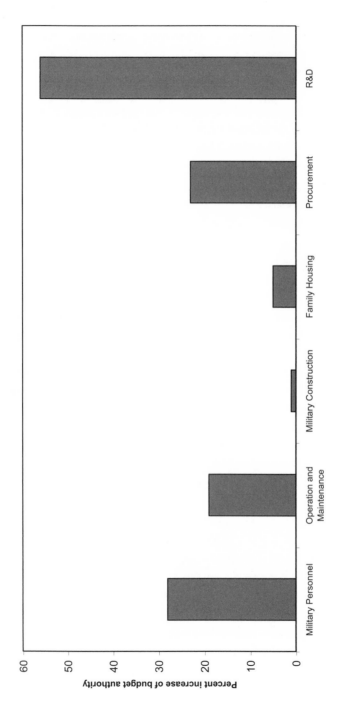

Figure 1.4 Defense Department Spending Trends, 2001—4

In New York City, government contracting has grown dramatically over the past several years. According to the NYC Mayor's Office of Contract Services' annual report on "Agency Procurement Indicators" (2005), contracting increased from $7.3 billion in FY2002 to $9.1 billion in FY2003, and from $9.5 billion in FY2004 to $11.4 billion in FY2005. These data are in absolute and not constant dollars, but with a total budget ranging from $42.7 billion in FY2002 to $46.3 billion in FY2005, contracting has grown from about 17 percent of total city spending to 25 percent. One could argue that most of this increase is in contracts related to increased capital spending, but in fact capital spending during this period was a relatively fixed $6 billion per year. In some areas such as social services delivery, the city has gradually gotten out of the business of providing direct services and now manages an extensive network of nonprofit service providers. This is particularly pronounced in areas such as homeless and foster care services in New York. While most governments still spend most of their funds on direct transfer payments to citizens (such as Social Security and Medicare), personnel, and debt service, governments have seen a gradual growth of contracting in the late twentieth and early twenty-first centuries. There are of course variations in these trends, but when we see a major event like the war in Iraq or the destruction of New Orleans by Hurricane Katrina, we also see a dramatic and rapid rise in government contracting.

From the perspective of management, the issue of contracting and its use as a management tool is most important at the point that goods and services are produced and used. The vast majority of spending at the federal and state levels is transfer payments and grants to governments and individuals. The federal government collects and distributes funds for Medicare, Medicaid, Social Security, and a variety of smaller programs that benefit individuals. They also spend billions of dollars on grants in aid to state and local governments. States in turn transfer most of the funds they collect to local governments. The great exception here is the Defense Department, which contracts for much of the services it provides and all of the equipment it uses. As figure 1.4 indicates, most federal contracting dollars are let by the Defense Department.

Given the tendency to greater outsourcing and increased organizational specialization in the private sector, we expect to see those tendencies reflected in government management now and in the future. Perhaps even more important for government managers, effective management in an era of increased technical, economic, and social complexity requires increased use of this management tool. Contracting is growing, and sophisticated managers are learning how to use the make-or-buy decision to focus their organization on core competencies. Moreover, the strategic use of outsourcing is requiring that modern managers learn how to get some of their work done through the labor of people in other organizations.

How Do You Manage a Contract?

In government, contracting is a highly regulated activity. There are rules on advertising, the bidding process, and the steps that must be taken to review a bid. Once a contract is awarded, there are rules governing the ethics of interaction between government and contractor. Despite these constraints, the normal imperatives of management must hold. Managers must develop and implement organizational strategies that reach into the behavior of organizations contracted to be an extension of the organization. Incentives must be provided to obtain desired behavior from contractor staff members. Informal networks and communication must also be established. Informal contact, in particular, may be difficult in an environment designed to prevent corruption and the appearance of impropriety.

Effective contract management requires a range of management tools that we will discuss throughout this book. Some of those tools relate to contract provisions that provide resources to government contract managers. What we mean by resources are contract clauses that provide managers with

- The ability to define and shape the work of contractors.
- The flexibility to make midcourse corrections.
- The ability to obtain frequent and audited measures of contractor performance.
- Methods for systematically providing performance-based incentives and disincentives—particularly financial bonuses and penalties.

- Procedures for developing and maintaining informal communication from government staff and management to contractor staff and management.

Managing a contractor's work has all the conceptual elements of internal management. It requires strategic planning, leadership, human resource management, financial investment, financial allocation and control, work process analysis improvement, and performance measurement. It also requires that government managers ensure that contractors adhere to many of the same ethical standards that government officials follow. Finally, government contract management requires reporting and control that facilitates contractor accountability to the authority of laws enacted by elected officials.

Obviously, these management requirements are not easy to meet and are often not systematically factored into the make-or-buy decisions of government officials. One of the purposes of this volume is to describe these challenges to government contract management and identify methods for addressing these challenges. As we have noted elsewhere, there are some situations that make contracting so difficult it should not be undertaken. There are also some situations that make contracting so easy and effective that performing the work in-house would be bad management. There are, of course, many make-or-buy decisions that lie between these two extremes. We need to get contract management past the barrier of ideology and myth to a place where problems can be anticipated, analyzed, and managed. Our objective is to think about and discuss contracting as a management tool like financial or performance management. No one disputes that a well-managed organization needs to have a budget and a financial control system. So too should it have a contracting plan and strategy that makes the best possible use of external parties in the production of goods and services.

Why Focus on Accountability and Corruption?

Corruption is not simply a problem in the public sector, as Enron and thousands of other private sector examples demonstrate. However, public corruption is in many respects a more serious issue with greater impact. Government funds are compelled through taxation and not generated through a choice-laden private market. Stealing government funds is stealing from everyone. Stealing private funds is stealing from a select set of private investors. Moreover, society and political stability depend on public trust that the government serves the public interest. If the government is a kleptocracy, what is the probability that private business practices will adhere to the rule of law? Of course, as our parents taught us, stealing is stealing and it is never justified—but some crimes are worse than others. Contracts provide a legitimate conduit for public funds to be allocated to private organizations. Sometimes these contracts are quite large, and performance and accountability measures are poorly developed. When you combine lots of money with poor audit and control, you invite corruption. Large contracts and low visibility can lead to corruption. Sometimes the corruption is not public corruption, but government officials being taken advantage of by private companies. Sometimes government contract officials and project managers are hopelessly outstaffed by private firms and their high-powered legal and financial staffs. Many of these private organizations have profit maximization as their goal, and when they interact with mission-driven public organizations, the potential for misunderstanding is high, as is the possibility of government officials being misled and deceived. The different motivations of the public and private sectors can create a clash of cultures. In this instance, some of it is a clash of culture and some of it is private firms (to quote Plunkitt of Tammany Hall) "seeing their opportunities and taking them."[3]

Private firms' outsourcing functions face similar issues, but the interaction of two profit-seeking firms has different characteristics than a relationship between government and a contractor. The control on private deception with other private parties includes legal contracts enforceable by governments, letters of credit administered by private firms, insurance also delivered by other private parties, the desire for repeat business, the danger of poor public relations affecting a firm's ability to sell to new customers, and that old standby—ethics. The relationship between private parties is conditioned by the mistrust often resulting from intense competition, as well as an explicit recognition of the shared goal of profit maximization. Private firms are under no illusion about the motivation of their suppliers and other partners. If they can succeed at your expense, they will.

A government agency contracting for goods or services is sold these items by vendors who may attempt to demonstrate their belief in the agency's mission. While that belief may be sincere, the underlying factor that motivates the firm's behavior is not adherence to the agency's mission but increased market share, profit, and return on equity. The potential for stealing and other forms of corruption makes accountability and ethics a key dimension of government contract management.

The ideological preference for the private sector has led to some costly management decisions as elected officials seek to mandate the make-or-buy decision. These policy decisions can also lead to the appearance of impropriety. A limited number of vendors are asked to play a role in implementing a program, and these same vendors also turn up on lists of contributors to political campaigns. In 2005, when the Medicare prescription drug plan was implemented, the legislation required offering the elderly beneficiaries of this program a bewildering array of choices of private drug plans—all of whom had higher administrative costs than the government.

The blindness of ideology can lead to subpar government performance, and infatuation with either government workers or the private sector can distort management decisions and impair efforts to hold managers accountable. If a public manager is compelled to favor an implementation mechanism—one that is less cost-effective or efficient—it is difficult to then hold that manager accountable for results obtained under these constraints. A manager confronted with these conditions can of course follow Hirschman's classic formulation of "exit, voice and loyalty" (Hirschman 1970). Such a manager can apply the same framework used to deal with ethical issues to deal with politically imposed contracting decisions. If political interference in management is so profound that the organization is doomed to failure, the manager can go public and take the route of the whistle blower (the "voice" option). If the level of interference is objectionable but more a matter of preference, the manager can quit and move on to another organization (exit), or simply decide to go along to fight another day (loyalty).

In addition to these political and ideological issues, a number of contemporary public administration scholars have conducted a profound debate on the use of "reinvention" management concepts, and they are concerned that "entrepreneurial" public managers are confusing citizens with customers. They question the use of new techniques such as contracting out and are concerned about the impact of public sector entrepreneurship on democratic accountability. This literature is well summarized in Kalu Kalu's 2003 piece in *Administration and Society*, where he notes:

> it is only by understanding how bureaucrats truly relate to their public purpose that we can be able to know to what extent and in what form we should hold them accountable. Accountability in this regard presupposes administrative efficiency, political responsibility, and regard for the law as well as the implicit notion of due process. Whereas the appeal of efficiency in the private sector (profit-driven) is different from its appeal in the public sector (clientele satisfaction), it would thus mean that a bureaucratic administration premised on the values of public entrepreneurship would, at best, create an ontological incongruity between theory and practice. Alternatively, extreme adherence to orthodox administrative values without regard to temporal or generational shifts in the operational environment would resurface the perennial issues of administrative insensitivity, bureaucratic red tape, and procedural anachronism (Kalu 2003, 559).

Kalu cannot solve the dilemma proposed by what is essentially a disconnect between the needs of modern organizational management and the requirements of democratic control of administration. We cannot solve this problem either. We note the concern and believe it is worthy of attention and an effort to overcome it, but we move on—because the trend toward contracting is not going to be stopped by scholars of public administration. Contracting must be understood and adapted to conform to the requirements of representative democracy. Outsourcing is essentially a management technology—just as electricity is a physical technology. Once discovered, it is impossible to undiscover. It must now be controlled—and made safe for democratic use. If you'll excuse the play on words, we need to insulate our democratic institutions from the threat posed by contracting. The use of contracting has been growing steadily for years. However, the transition of contracting into inherently governmental functions, such as fighting wars, changes the scope and importance of contracting. In this context, contracting cannot simply be looked upon for efficiency gains, but attention must also be given to what powers the government is giving to private contractors over the general public.

Conclusions

Management is a craft and not a science. A craft is built on lore, apprenticeship, and a shared aesthetic. While contracting is not a new element of the public management craft, it is a tool that is used with increasing frequency. If the government follows the private sector's trend toward increased outsourcing, we can expect increased use of this tool as organizational differentiation increases. Lower-priced transportation, communication, shipping, and information make outsourcing increasingly attractive to the private sector, and we have no reason to believe that the public sector will be immune to these trends.

We believe the management challenges that government faces when using contracts can be met with care, diligence, and imagination. In theory, the use of contractors extends the reach of government—it extends its areas of expertise and its presence. It can also reduce costs and simplify administration. On the other hand, if it is poorly managed it can lead to corruption and program failure. It can also make it more difficult to maintain representative institutions that link citizens to government. If contracting makes service delivery more difficult to influence, it can impair representative government. Obviously our task is to learn more about this management tool and make it easier for government to manage its private contractors.

Now that we have established our definition of government contracting and outlined the major issues faced by government when contracting with the public sector, we now focus on the fundamental issues of contracting. The remaining chapters in part I place contract management in the context of the major issues and trends in public administration. In chapter 2, we will discuss the ethical dilemmas caused by contracting with the private sector. In chapter 3 we relate contract management to the worldwide trend toward network as opposed to hierarchical management. In the information age with advances in communication, information, and transportation technologies, the requirements for hierarchical command and control in production have been reduced, and this has permitted interor-ganizational production systems more characterized by mutual self-interest, partnership, and contractual agreement. Part I concludes with chapter 4, where we offer a discussion of the problems that contracting presents for accountability to our representative system of government here in the United States. In the mid-twentieth century we saw more and more decision making placed in the hands of unelected technical experts in public bureaucracies. In the twenty-first century we see some of this decision making devolving to nongovernmental organizations delivering public programs under contract to unelected government officials.

The remainder of the volume focuses on practical issues of contract management. How can a public manager make use of this important tool and how has contracting facilitated and impeded public management in several (we hope) typical cases?

Notes

1. We should note, however, that even though the contractual relationship is formal, the management process that is required to administer the work of the contract requires informal relationships.
2. See site content on Department of Defense at the Office of Management and Budget's web page. www.whitehouse.gov/omb/budget/fy2005/defense.html (accessed November 23, 2005).
3. *Plunkitt of Tammany Hall: A series of very plain talks on very practical politics*, delivered by former senator George Washington Plunkitt, the Tammany philosopher, from his rostrum, the New York County Court-House bootblack stand, and recorded by William L. Riordon. New York, A. A. Knopf, 1994.

Chapter 2

What Are the Public Ethics of Contracting?

What Are Public Ethics?

PUBLIC ETHICS is a major concern for those in government and the citizens they serve. Caveat emptor is often good advice when dealing with private markets—do not assume that the other party in the transaction has your best interests at heart, or even that they are being fair or honest. We have and should have very different expectations in dealing with public officials and public agencies. By its very name, public service implies that government employees should place the best interests of their citizens/customers first.

Public service also implies honesty, integrity, equal treatment, due process, and transparency. The venerable public servant and writer Elmer Staats observed that "public service is a concept, an attitude, a sense of duty—yes, even a sense for public morality" (Perry 1993). Public service is not about personal gain; it is about putting the public interest first.

How to know exactly what is in the public interest in any particular situation is more challenging. We continue to find Walter Lippmann's definition of the public interest helpful: "The public interest may be presumed to be what men would choose if they saw clearly, thought rationally, acted disinterestedly and benevolently" (1955, 42). While these general principles are helpful, the practicing public manager needs a guide to public ethics that provides a set of behaviors that public officials must adhere to in the service of the public interest.

In her excellent book *The Ethics Challenge in Public Service* (1991), Carol W. Lewis suggests that public ethics is different from personal ethics in terms of values and guiding principles. To Lewis, ethics is thinking systematically about morals and conduct and making judgments about right and wrong. Public ethics must go beyond thinking to action-based judgments about right and wrong (Cohen and Eimicke 1995, 99).

Lewis provides twenty-one rules of thumb to guide public officials toward ethical decision making. Elsewhere, we have sought to reorganize and consolidate her far-reaching analysis into five principles to guide public contract managers (Cohen and Eimicke 1995, 1996b, 1999b; Eimicke, Cohen, and Perez Salazar 2000; Cohen and Eimicke 2002, 233–34):

1. "Seek justice under the law." In general, the legal thing to do tends to be the ethical thing to do (being mindful of the exceptions of Jim Crow and the Nazis).
2. "Serve the public interest." This is not always easy to do, but most of the time, reasonably obvious.
3. "Ensure through analysis." Competence matters, or as we once observed, "[m]aking a decision without the appropriate level of technical skill and knowledge is a dereliction of duty. Exercising such incompetence at the public's expense is a violation of the public's trust, an abuse of office, and a breach of ethics" (Cohen and Eimicke 2002, 234).
4. "Act with compassion and empathy."
5. "Take personal responsibility for decisions."

We also suggest that if your goal in life is to become wealthy, do not go into government service—find another line of work. We also believe that government officials should not accept any gifts of any kind that could give even the appearance of impropriety. In other words, government service is a public trust that requires a stricter code of behavior than those followed by people in other professions. When we use the term "public ethics" we are referring to the behaviors noted above by those that serve the public.

The issue of public ethics is particularly relevant when government works with private contractors. Private firms are profit seeking, and the culture of the private sector considers the accumulation of riches to be a good thing, a measure of success, and to some degree the mission of the organization. Government is different, and the culture of public organizations is different. In government, the accumulation of riches is looked on with suspicion and is often considered evidence of corrupt behavior. When government relies on private for-profit (as opposed to nonprofit) organizations to carry out its work under a contractual arrangement, these two cultures necessarily interact. In all probability these two cultures will influence each other and possibly clash. The private firm may adopt some of the mission-driven characteristics and risk-averse behavior of government organizations; the government officials might start focusing on the size of their paychecks and the wealth created by the programs they manage.

What Kinds of Corruption and Unethical Behavior Are Associated with Contracting?

A concern regarding the privatization of public services is that it will lead to corruption and unethical behavior. H. George Frederickson equates privatization with the adoption of the enterprise model of service delivery by government and observes that

> the propensity for corruption and unethical behavior increases and organization and structure moves from the governmental model to the enterprise model. As we increasingly privatize governmental activities—as we move from the direct carrying out of governmental services to contracting these services to free enterprise—we increase the propensity for corruption and unethical behavior (1997, 179).

The concerns of Frederickson (also raised by Don Kettl in his landmark book *Sharing Power*) regarding the risks of privatization are legitimate and significant. In the developing world, corruption can be a major concern. A survey of 150 high-ranking public officials and key members from civil society from more than sixty developing countries ranked public corruption as the most severe impediment to development and growth in their countries (Gray and Kaufmann 1998, 7). During the second term of George W. Bush as U.S. president, the Defense Department, Congress, and their private contractors were all damaged by admissions of serious violations of conflict-of-interest laws, accepting payoffs, or fraudulent billing practices (Cahlink 2005, 1; Palmer 2005, 1; Witte 2005, A11; Babcock and Weisman 2005, A01). These are but a few examples of contracting gone wrong.

Corruption can make fair competition impossible, thereby negating one of the strongest arguments for contracting—the efficiency of markets. Corrupt contracting processes waste rather than save public resources. Transparency International suggests that "systemic corruption can add 20–25 percent to the costs of government procurement and frequently results in inferior quality goods and services and uneconomic investments or unnecessary purchases" (2005a, 1).

At the same time, all organizations including government face relentless pressure to do more with less. In many cases, contracting proves to be the most efficient and economical method to get work accomplished. In many of these organizations, government officials have been able to manage the contracting process in a way that avoids illegal and unethical behavior. Contracting can also, however, have an impact on government. Outsourcing work to private for-profit organizations raises questions about democratic representation that should be considered when considering the use of contracting. We will address this issue in chapter 4.

The effective, ethical public manager seeks to identify the ways in which the contracting process may be corrupted, then establishes standard operating procedures to prevent such behaviors whenever possible. When prevention fails, the effective manager has also instituted rigorous monitoring, evaluation, and audit procedures to stop corrupt practices as soon as possible and punish the guilty. To establish these procedures, the manager must first identify the types of corruption most likely to accompany a contracting process. Second, the manager must develop measures designed to prevent such corruption or at least uncover it as quickly as possible after it has occurred.

A common understanding of corruption in government is the use of a public position for private gain. Corruption and unethical behavior associated with contracting usually involve compromising the public interest for private benefit (Gray and Kaufmann 1998, 1). The World Bank describes administrative corruption as "the intentional imposition of distortions in the prescribed implementation of existing laws, rules and regulations to provide advantages to either state or non-state actors as a result of the illegal transfer or concentration of private gains to public officials" (2005, 2). A simple example is when a contractor pays a bribe to influence a person with the authority to award, renew, or change the terms of an existing contract. In such a circumstance, both parties may be acting illegally or at least unethically—one party by offering and/or paying a bribe and the second party by soliciting and/or accepting the bribe.

A bribe is often thought of as a cash payment, but it can also be in the form of a gift of more than nominal value, such as meals, travel, loan forgiveness, donation to a favored charity, hospitality, discounts, valuable services, use of private property, or even inside information regarding a financial transaction. Those improper gifts might also be provided to immediate family members of the person participating in the contracting process (MTA 2005). In some places, gifts for major life events such as weddings or the birth of a child are excluded from a ban on gifts; in other places, they are not (Connecticut Office of State Ethics 2005).

The potential parties to a contract can also behave unethically if they exchange information that would give unfair advantage to one contractor over another (U.S. Office of Government Ethics 2005, 5). This might involve improperly disclosing the operational preferences of the purchaser's staff or even the criteria and point system used to compare the bids. In such a situation, the contracting official might have other business or personal relationships with the prospective bidder. In these circumstances, the contracting agent must consider whether any reasonable person would question the impartiality of the agent in the award process. If there is any doubt, the agent should not participate in the contract development or award process.

A related category of corruption is often characterized as the "revolving door," where a contractor has the capacity to "trade" career opportunities for the contracting agents or members of their families in return for assistance in winning the contract. Whether it just looks bad or is the result of an explicit quid pro quo, most organizations seek to monitor the behavior of their employees regarding the award of contracts and future employment of those employees. Many governments and nonprofit organizations have explicit laws or regulations limiting the right of former employees to work for an organization that received contracts during their public employment. A common limit lasts for one year after separation from the contracting organization (see, for example, Corporation for Public Broadcasting 2004, 5).

A highly visible case of revolving door corruption involved Darleen Druyun, a senior procurement administrator at the Pentagon during the administration of George W. Bush. Druyun moved directly from purchasing major defense products from Boeing to the position of deputy general manager for missile defense systems at Boeing. She was negotiating the terms of her new position while handling a $30 billion tanker lease contract with Boeing for the U.S. Air Force (POGO 2004, 9–10). Druyun and the chief financial officer of Boeing were subsequently fired for this behavior, and Druyun ended up in prison.

In their report "The Politics of Contracting," the Project on Government Oversight (POGO) examined the relationship between the federal government and its twenty largest contractors for the period January 1997 through May 2004. Among the study's most significant and disturbing findings (POGO 2004, 3) were:

- At least one-third of the high-ranking government officials who moved into senior positions for the large private contractors studied had previously been in government positions in which they could influence contracting decisions.
- Two-thirds of the former members of Congress who are lobbying or had lobbied for the top twenty contractors had served on committees that approved funds for their future private employer.
- During the three election cycles covered by the report, the top twenty contractors and their employees made $46 million in campaign contributions and spent almost $400 million on lobbying.

A contract may be sole-sourced based on the contention that one vendor is uniquely qualified to provide the good or service desired. While a certain vendor might have special skills or a very well-designed product, the sole-source process is vulnerable to artificially high pricing and terms favorable to the only vendor participating in the negotiation. In such an environment, kickbacks, gifts, or future considerations to the person awarding the sole-source contract are more likely to occur than during more competitive contracting processes.

In complicated contracting situations such as the outsourcing of a large information technology operation or the operation of a sewage treatment plant or waste treatment facility, the government may hire a third-party expert to advise them. It is not unusual for these third-party experts to have financial relationships with some of the bidders for the contract or even a financial interest in the outcome of the transaction, directly or indirectly. These relationships and interests may not be easily identified. Therefore, it is essential that the government invest in extensive due diligence to ensure that their hired advisors receive only payments for their analysis and advice and demonstrate affirmatively that they have no other financial interest in the transaction (Sclar 2000, 121).

Because a government may be unsure of exactly how to fully specify what needs to be in the contract, it may leave aspects of the contract's requirements open or only generally defined. Contractors will often take advantage of the vagueness, requiring additional payments to do what is not explicitly required in the contract (Savas 2005, 33). This failure to fully define what is required could be the result of genuine uncertainty, but it could also be due to incompetence or it could be a deliberate act to enable a favored vendor to reap the benefits from the changes required after the contract is signed.

One of the major scandals of the post–Civil War era involved the contracting out of mail delivery in the remote western territories of the Rocky Mountains and the Southwest. Contracts were often awarded to friends and family members, which, while ethically questionable, was not illegal at the time. The contracts were awarded at rates approved by Congress but then adjusted dramatically upward by the agency administrator to ensure reliable service. These adjustments increased the value of the contract at least tenfold and frequently by one hundred times the original value. Such extreme abuse was eventually detected and became known as the Star Route frauds, named after the star that was stamped on awarded contracts (Karabell 2004, 95–97).

Political considerations can corrupt the contracting process in the public sector. The decision to contract rather than perform a service with in-house staff can be the result of political influence. Campaign contributors may convince an elected official to bid out services without any analysis justifying the decision (Clynch 1999, 2). Career public servants may be pressured by political appointees to award contracts to those who have supported the current party or person in power. The connected contractor might be qualified and experienced, but the problem is the distortion of an objective, merit-based selection process to meet other objectives.

Corruption can also occur among the contract seekers, with or without the knowledge of the contracting agency. Contractors cooperate to take turns or divide territories, submitting deliberately inflated bids for the contracts or districts that are not "theirs" and winning with comfortably "fat" bids in the areas "given" to them. Large contractors and contractors associated with organized crime can intimidate legitimate, honest competitors out of the competition (Sclar 2000, 48).

More broadly, there is corruption by incompetence. Many government agencies are contracting on a massive scale without necessarily instituting equally dramatic changes in their hiring and training practices. As Goldsmith and Eggers note, "[m]anaging a portfolio of provider networks is infinitely different than managing divisions of employees" (2004, 22). Governments that view contracting as a means of off-loading management headaches and that do not invest in staffing and training for proper oversight can expect waste, complaints, and scandal.

Frederickson goes even further, arguing that government by contract is not even reducing the size of government, but deceptively substituting a private, shadow contractor bureaucracy for the downsized public employees. Not only is the process deceptive, it also raises serious issues of ethics and accountability. As Frederickson observes, "[w]e are making little progress in developing a simple understanding of this new form of public service, let alone ethical systems and standards for it. The simple number of transactions between governments, contractors and subcontractors, will multiply the possibilities of corruption to the point that there will almost certainly be both big and little scandals" (1997, 13).

Ensuring More Ethical Contract Management

If contracting is fraught with so many ethical challenges and risks, should governments, nonprofit organizations, and even private organizations move away from what seems to be the prevailing wisdom of contract whenever possible? Frederickson's answer is a clear yes, for he believes that the efficiencies that contracting may achieve come with a price of ethical compromise that is too high (1997, 13). Although we share Frederickson's concerns, we believe the pressures on government to do more with less are increasing and therefore the potential efficiencies provided by contracting will prove irresistible. Moreover, as the modern economy moves from vertically integrated companies to production networks, government organizations must take advantage of the efficiencies and increased effectiveness that can be obtained through contracting.

Government should not contract merely on the assumption that contractors are better, faster, and cheaper—this proposition must be tested through an objective, analytical, and indeed competitive process. Government should not use private contractors to accomplish tasks it can do as well or better with its own employees. Contracting should not be done merely for ideological reasons or to deceive the public regarding the number of people engaged in doing the government's business.

If contracting makes sense, the government cannot expect private firms to adopt the same culture as a public agency or impose on them the same set of legal and ethical standards that apply to public organizations. To require private organizations carrying out public programs to act as if they were government agencies would likely compromise the economies and efficiencies that justify contracting in the first place. Moreover, the culture and practices of private firms would make it impossible for them to adhere to such procedures. The experience the agency and its employees have had with their work, however, should be remembered when contracting to a private organization. The knowledge that has been acquired through long practice of public policy should be retained despite the different cultures in the public and private sectors. While government should not impose all its rules and regulations on private and nonprofit contractors, it does have the obligation to demand a high level of ethical behavior from its partners.

To determine the ethical standards for government contractors, we must first establish the rules that government officials dealing with contractors should follow. Laws and regulations covering compensation, gifts, bidding procedures, equal opportunity and discrimination, and disclosure must be reviewed and assessed to determine the potential applicability to contractors. Ethical standards, laws, and regulations should be part of the contracting process from the outset, should be part of the negotiation of contract terms, and should be reflected explicitly in the contract document and operating procedures.

Some rules that must apply to public employees in the contracting process cannot apply to their private sector partners. For example, the American Society for Public Administration's Code of Ethics suggests that public officials should not realize undue personal gain in the performance of their official duties. In the private sector, a key motivating tool is additional compensation for behaviors that create additional profit for the firm.

For Joel Fleishman and H. George Frederickson, what is needed is more than fighting corruption; we also need public officials committed to doing good. For them, the key is a selfless public official. Selfless officials can be trusted to exercise judgment and make decisions concerning who benefits and who must sacrifice, without suspicion regarding their motives (Frederickson 1997, 2–3; Fleishman 1981, 82–83). While these principles may be helpful to the public official in acting ethically with a private partner and serving the public interest, personal responsibility and abuse of office have less meaning and applicability to the private partner.

What more can be done to achieve more ethical results from public officials who fail to embrace these ethical principles and from private partners to which the principles only awkwardly apply? Laws and law enforcement are an obvious step and we will address this aspect in greater detail as we proceed. But for many, law enforcement is like closing the barn door after the horse has run off. The damage has been done and we can only hope that the enforcement of punishment deters future corrupt behavior. What can be done to prevent corrupt behavior?

Perhaps not surprisingly, Transparency International argues that transparency is an effective mechanism to prevent corruption (2005b, 1–2). Contract solicitations, evaluations, and selections that are as open as possible to all potential bidders, media observers, interested advocates, and the general public are more likely to be fair, well analyzed, and properly awarded. Transparency has its limits, however. Intelligent but corrupt officials and their contract partners may be able to keep their illicit behavior secret. The contract may be so technical that observers may not be interested or able to effectively monitor the process. Or, to ensure fairness or for security reasons, some processes cannot be completely transparent.

Transparency International also suggests that governments and all bidders on public contracts sign a version of an "Integrity Pact" it has developed (2005b, 1–2). The pact formally commits all parties to refrain from offering or accepting bribes, to refrain from colluding in bidding or contract implementation, and to disclose all commissions and payments made in connection with the contract. Sanctions are also specified, ranging from loss of the contract to blacklisting and criminal or disciplinary actions. At its best, the pact ensures honest contractors of a level playing field and government of the accuracy of the bids it receives. Unfortunately, just as with laws and regulations, honest people will follow the pact stipulations while dishonest people may not.

Regarding bribes, it is true that the dishonest may ignore laws that make bribes illegal. However, in many jurisdictions payments that might have the impact of a bribe are legal. For example, elected officials may legally accept campaign contributions from current and prospective public sector contractors. Corrupt public officials may secretly require those seeking government contracts to make such contributions and even kick back some of the profits from those contracts, as Spiro T. Agnew, disgraced former U.S. vice president, did when he was governor of Maryland (Nadler 2005, 1). On his way out of office, former New Jersey governor James McGreevey, forced to resign for similar behavior, issued an executive order banning campaign contributions by government contractors (Nadler 2005, 1).

Whether it is gifts or bribes, annual financial disclosure filing requirements can be a check on the trading of contracts for personal financial gain. As part of that filing, federal income tax returns can be required. While the completely dishonest person will falsify all documents, the deterrent of multiple chances of discovery and multiple levels of penalties (tax fraud) may keep others from yielding to temptation.

Similarly, there are laws in many places seeking to limit the negative effects of the revolving door between public contracting offices and their contractors. To further discourage improper behavior, we could enact laws prohibiting members of the Senior Executive Service (and similarly situated high-level administrative policymakers at the state and local level) and political appointees from seeking employment with contractors benefiting from their policymaking or rulemaking for at least a year or two upon leaving public service. We could also prohibit former government employees from working in a different division or subsidiary of the division of the company benefiting from their public contracting decision (POGO 2004, 4).

Other methods of limiting the impact of conflicts of interest include recusals, waivers, divestiture, and trusts (U.S. Office of Government Ethics 2005, 5). Recusal requires a public official to withdraw from participation in a contracting decision where there might be personal gain or benefit to a family member or close associate. Waivers can be used on a case-by-case basis to enable officials to participate in a decision where they may have an interest but only where that interest is not substantial, is indirect, and is mitigated by its disclosure. Divestiture can enable an official to eliminate a potential conflict by selling the property that creates the potential conflict. Trusts can manage assets for a public official while they are in a decision-making position such that their actions have no relationship to gains or losses in their investment portfolio.

Corrupt and/or improper contract decisions can result when the officials making those decisions have not been trained in contract solicitation, evaluation, design, or implementation. Many government employees assigned to the contracting process were not originally hired for that task and subsequently receive no training for a complicated and demanding assignment. Rigorous training of those assigned to contract management could help limit corruption and lead to better contracts and contract outcomes (Institute of Public Administration 2005, 1–7; Frederickson 1997, 11).

Stronger laws to protect or even to encourage civil servants who are aware of corrupt practices might also lead to a better contracting process. Those on the inside of the process are most likely to know about corruption in the contracting process, yet these potential whistle blowers are often subordinates of those engaging in the corrupt practices. And the superiors they might be implicating are often politically connected to the chief executive and/or legislative leaders. There must be a secure process that encourages and enables those with concerns about corrupt practices to share what they know with enforcement officials without risking their jobs or creating a chilling environment for those trying to do their jobs honestly.

The process of contracting can also be made less susceptible to corruption. Wherever possible, the government office currently providing the service to be contracted should be permitted to re-engineer itself to meet higher standards of performance and efficiency. San Diego County, California, used this technique effectively for many years (Eimicke 2000).

The county recruited a team of senior civil servants from across the government to serve on a re-engineering and competition committee. The team applied a "yellow pages test" and minimum savings requirement to identify potential targets for contracting, similar to what former Indianapolis mayor Stephen Goldsmith did in the city he led throughout the 1990s. Using outside consultants, the team, and agency personnel, San Diego was able to achieve the desired performance improvements and savings through re-engineering or other internal improvements without moving to a competition or straight outsourcing of the service. When the county did decide to contract out, they were better able to assess the reasonableness and honesty of the bids received since they had already conducted a rigorous analysis of how the service was provided by county employees and/or enabled the county agency to compete directly with private contractors to provide the service. This emphasis on management of the actual work provides a focus on operational issues and builds familiarity with those issues—fostering a more informed and sophisticated make-or-buy decision.

In Indianapolis during the 1990s, Mayor Goldsmith primarily used competition to dramatically improve the quality of city services and cut the costs to taxpayers (Cohen and Eimicke 1998, chapter 8; John F. Kennedy School of Government 1995; Osborne and Hutchinson 2004; Goldsmith 1997; Savas 2005, 50–65). Goldsmith conducted more than eighty competitions to provide city services. He worked closely with public employee unions to give public employees a reasonable chance to win and a path to re-employment if they lost. With public employees winning nearly 40 percent of the competitions, the results seem to indicate the competitions were fair to all. The public payroll was reduced substantially and the city saved more than $400 million over the life of the contracts (Savas 2005, 64).

We could find no allegations that the competition process was tainted by any corruption. In fact, Goldsmith's political career was damaged when he agreed with union employees that their bid was doomed because they had to include the costs of patronage employees from his political party. Once Goldsmith dismissed the political appointees and their salaries could be left off the bid, the city agency won the street repair contract. When Goldsmith later lost his election for governor of Indiana, political commentators observed that many Republican Party regulars supported his Democratic opponent due to the impact of competition on patronage employment.

Cities as different and distant as Phoenix, Arizona, and Bogotá, Colombia, have used competition to improve efficiency and quality of solid waste collection while simultaneously achieving dramatic reductions in the cost of the service (Savas 2005, 67–71; Eimicke, Cohen, and Perez Salazar 2000). And both cities were able to avoid the corruption and associations with organized crime that are often associated with refuse collection. Both cities divided the service into multiple geographical districts and staggered the bidding of each district. In this manner, the public service was not faced with one win-or-go-home competition. The cities ensured that some districts remained public and therefore retained the capacity to take over for a failed or inefficient operator in another district. The cities were also constantly gathering information on costs and innovations in the industry through its public operator, making it better able to assess the reasonableness and honesty of the bids it received for other districts. And by dividing the pie and staggering the competitions, the cities were better protected against one, potentially corrupt, operator taking over the entire city service.

We believe that competition is an extremely effective mechanism to ensure that public contracts are entered into only when prudent and productive and that the process is as resistant to corruption as is humanly possible. However, competition takes time, resources, expertise, political will, and patience. Many governments may lack one or more of these requirements, or they may find themselves under financial and/or political pressures that make more traditional contracting the only available option. In such circumstances, what can public managers do to encourage ethical behavior and discourage corrupt practices among their potential private contract partners? While we find no silver bullet, there are a number of steps that can be taken to influence private firms.

First, the contracting agency can educate bidders on the laws and regulations governing the contracting process and what constitutes ethical behavior. Agency personnel can also exhort and advocate the proposition that private contractors of the government should become guardians and protectors of the public trust. This moral conscience role can be accomplished more effectively if the private contractor is located in or close to the government agency it is serving. Effective public managers will learn to "manage by wandering around" (Peters and Waterman 1982, 121–23) their own offices and those of their contractors, reinforcing the reality that these private firms are doing public service.

Second, in requests for proposals, the government agency can award points to contractors that have a track record of ethical behavior, have strong corporate codes of ethics, and can document a history of rewarding ethical behavior and punishing corrupt behavior on their own. The contract document itself should articulate ethical standards and behaviors and include enforcement mechanisms for violations. The contract could even require the contractor to report overtures for corrupt behavior coming from public employees.

Third, the contract can specify incentives or bonus payments for meeting ethical standards and stiff penalties for violations. Contract renewals can be conditioned on the meeting of ethical requirements. Violations of certain provisions can even specify that the contractor is blacklisted from bidding on all future public contracts for a number of years, or even forever.

Finally, the public agency should independently monitor the behavior of the contractor to ensure ethical behavior. This can be done with agency employees or a third party, such as a private accounting firm, that can be hired to serve as a monitor. While potentially expensive, an outside monitor can help to preserve a positive working relationship between agency and contractor personnel and eliminate the possibility that agency personnel might try to deliberately sabotage the contractor. Inspectors general should also be established as self-guided investigators of potentially corrupt practices.

Conclusions

We would certainly agree with Kathryn Denhardt that "ethics in public administration suffers from the absence of a theoretical framework" (1988, 1).

But as we have noted elsewhere, substantial progress has been made over the past two decades, and the work of Carol W. Lewis (1991), James Bowman (1991), Terry Cooper (2004), John Rohr (1989), H. George Frederickson (1993), and David Hart (1992) provides practical guidance to assist public managers in assessing the ethics of their actions (Eimicke 2005, 366). Acting ethically oneself is difficult enough; ensuring that others do (particularly contractors who don't even work for you) is much more difficult.

Reducing the number of government contracts might reduce the number of opportunities for unethical and illegal behavior. We do not believe that is feasible or even desirable. We agree with Goldsmith and Eggers that "government can in many instances produce more public value through a networked approach than they can through hierarchical methods" (2004, 22).

The tools and techniques suggested in this chapter can help public managers and private contractors operate together more effectively and ethically. Ultimately, it is the responsibility of the public manager to ensure that ethical standards are understood and observed. To do so, public managers will need to develop a set of skills that are helpful in managing internal hierarchies but are essential to effective management of a network of outside contractors.

Effective public network managers will need to develop their negotiation skills to establish workable agreements with private partners that also follow the public sector's standards of ethical behavior. Public managers will need to improve their communication and listening skills to make sure that private partners understand the standards and that the public manager hears when the private vendor is raising concerns or subtle warning signals.

Public network managers must become expert consumers of information technology and performance management tools so they can effectively monitor the activities of off-site contractors and provide incentives for ethical behaviors and penalties for actions that do not meet government standards. Clearly, there must be performance measures for ethical behavior and those measures must be highlighted as critically important to the private contractors.

Unethical behavior by government officials, alone and in partnership with private contractors, has occurred since the founding of the United

States and will no doubt be with us as long as we are a nation. The increase in government contracting increases the risk of unethical behavior, but we believe the risk is worth the reward of better government services at a lower price. Government is already doing a better job of managing these networks of service providers and ensuring the ethical behavior of its own employees and those of its contractors. It remains one of the great challenges for public managers in the twenty-first century, but with proper training, attention, and application of the proper management tools, it is a challenge we believe can be met.

Having defined contracting and identified the key management challenges confronting the effective public contract manager, we turned to a discussion of the ethical dilemmas posed by public sector contracting. We now turn to the role of contracting in the modern world of network management. The management environment of contracting has been substantially influenced by the growth of outsourcing.

Chapter 3

What Is Network Management?

PUBLIC-PRIVATE PARTNERSHIPS are no longer limited to a series of individual contracts or informal interactions between government and a single private organization. Rather, what is evolving is a complex set of episodic and ongoing relationships among an array of public, private, and nonprofit organizations, each playing a specialized but interlocking role in implementing public policy. Some of these relationships are formal and contractual and some are not. Government is moving away from the hierarchical model that predominated during the twentieth century toward a more fluid continuum of organizations collaborating to meet the needs of the public. The relationships between government, the private sector, and the nonprofit sector are not just defined by contracts and privatization, but also by these two sectors playing a larger role in providing services that were previously in the domain of government. While our focus is on contractual public, private, and nonprofit relationships, we acknowledge the importance of the numerous informal contacts and standard procedures that allow multiple entities in the network to serve the public and provide important services.

Globalization and advances in communication, transportation, and technology have created problems and demands that are larger than generally experienced only a few decades ago. Goldsmith and Eggers (2004) use the example of homeland security to illustrate that dealing with terrorism requires both a global scope and cooperation and a simultaneously customized, local response capacity. This new network management "bears less resemblance to a traditional organization chart than it does to a more dynamic web of computer networks that can organize or reorganize, expand or contract, depending on the problem at hand" (Goldsmith and Eggers 2004, 8). The relationships between the various government and private organizations in efforts dealing with terrorism are not always defined entirely by contracts, but some tasks are in the interest of the private sector to perform. For example, a private firm's security force and its practices are a clear part of the network of organizations delivering homeland security services, even though they may have no contractual relationship with government. Information exchange between security forces can be critical, but it is not provided in exchange for fees in a formal relationship. It is provided in exchange for goodwill that might later result in reciprocity.

While reliance on networks is increasing, important questions regarding the proper use of this tool must still be answered. Crucial questions regarding network management concern funding, operations, and results (Kamensky, Burlin, and Abramson 2004, 7). How are networks funded— who raises the money and how is it divided? What is the chain of command, and how does it function during both routine and crisis situations? When outcomes are positive, who gets the credit? And when things go wrong, who is responsible for making things right (see the response to Hurricane Katrina, for example)?

It is most important in a representative democracy that appointed public managers and their private partners manage in a way that serves the policies and directions established by our elected leaders. Networks do not and should not attempt to govern (Cohen 2006, 233). On matters of justice, security, public health and welfare, and life and death, the reliability, due process, and accountability of government hierarchies may well be preferable to the speed, efficiency, flexibility, and creativity of networks.

The United States military action in Iraq in the early years of the twenty-first century has demonstrated the advantages and dangers of relying on private networks to carry out public purposes. To improve speed, control costs, and minimize the number of troops (particularly part-time National Guard members), the Defense Department has relied more on private contractors than at any time in our history. Contractors have taken over the majority of support functions previously performed by uniformed troops and have even become involved in intelligence, politics, public information, propaganda, and police functions to the extent that "the line between military personnel and contractors during the war has become blurred" (Goldsmith and Eggers 2004, 13).

As we noted previously in our chapter on the ethics of contracting, effective network managers must negotiate agreements with private partners that follow the public sector's standards of ethical behavior as well as allow for proper oversight and communication between partners in the network. In most circumstances, it may be sufficient to enforce these standards through performance measures connected to financial incentives and penalties. However, as we saw at Abu Ghraib prison, the damage to human rights, human dignity, and our national reputation and conscience cannot be erased by financial penalties or even the termination or permanent expulsion of a contractor.

As Brint Milward observes, the developers of management by network include terrorists, drug dealers, and anarchists (Milward and Raab 2002, 5). The risks of corruption and fraud raised by H. George Frederickson (1997) and Donald Kettl (1993) under government by contract are exacerbated in a government network. Network management, while clearly allowing for a more flexible mechanism to respond to citizen concerns and needs, also dampens the control of government over those exercising influence over policy that has an impact on the public. Under a purely contractual relationship there is a clear legal relationship allowing for more government control over its contractors. In a network with multiple partners, the legal connection begins to evaporate. If part of the network is contractual and part is not, government control over the network may also be difficult.

Given all these issues and challenges, it should be clear that public management, and thereby government networks, cannot mirror private management and private networks. In the private sector, financially beneficial outcomes dwarf all other measures of success. In government, outcomes are important, but so are the distribution of benefits, equal access, due process of law, and public participation. In the private sector, a series of partnerships that improve efficiency and profitability but decrease transparency and accountability might be attractive. In the public sector, a partnership of that type might not be attractive or legal.

In this chapter we will examine why organizations are moving away from the traditional model of bureaucracy and hierarchy to the more flexible and fluid structure of managing through series of contracts, partnerships, and collaborations. We will look at the differences between purely private networks and those that include or are managed by government. For the networks that involve public partners, we discuss the central issues of accountability and ethics. Finally, we look at the roles and responsibilities of the effective network manager. What is different about managing a network instead of (or in addition to) an internal hierarchy? What new skills, performance measures, incentives, and methods of control are needed? How can we maximize the benefits of governing through networks while effectively controlling the risks?

Why Are We Trying to Reduce Bureaucracy in the Public and Private Sectors?

Hardly a day goes by that we do not bemoan some consequence of bureaucratic organization—the paperwork and red tape associated with applying for a student loan, the lines at the Department of Motor Vehicles, the documentation required to close on a house purchase, or the frustration of trying to book a flight for your spouse using frequent flyer miles. We have all called a large public or private organization and been unable to speak to a person, trapped in an automated telephone answering system that seems designed just to get rid of our call. And there is always a policy set by some nameless executive that specifically prohibits the person we can speak to from helping us, as much as they might want to do the right thing.

Bureaucracy wasn't always a bad word. Indeed, the bureaucratic model helped governments and the emerging large private organizations meet the challenges of industrialization and urbanization that characterized the twentieth century. There is no clearer or more authoritative voice in favor of bureaucracy than the respected sociologist Max Weber. As Weber saw it, "[t]he decisive reason for the advance of bureaucratic organization has always been its purely technical superiority over any other form of organization. The fully developed mechanism compares with other organizations exactly as does the machine with the non-mechanical modes of production. Precision, speed, unambiguity, knowledge of the files, continuity, discretion, unity, strict subordination, reduction of friction and material and personal costs—these are raised to the optimum point in the strictly bureaucratic administration" (Gerth and Mills 1958, 214).

For some time (albeit in different versions), the bureaucratic model provided the pathway to success. Rockefeller, Morgan, Carnegie, Siemens, Du Pont, and Sloan used the principles of bureaucracy to build extraordinarily large and profitable private businesses (Drucker 1999). Elihu Root used bureaucracy's hierarchy and command and control to organize the U.S. Army into the dominant military force of the twentieth century. And Franklin D. Roosevelt built the "big, bureaucratic government" to overcome the Great Depression and defeat fascism during World War II. In our view, it was large-scale, vertically integrated bureaucratic hierarchies that created the economies of scale and mass production needed for the wealth-generating machine we called industrialization. For the first half of the twentieth century this model worked, and to a great degree it works today. However, as technology developed (satellite communications, the Internet, superhighways, containerized shipping on huge cargo ships, air freight, super and personal computers, cell phones, bar codes, etc.), the global economy encouraged organizational specialization and discouraged vertical integration. The make-or-buy calculus changed. Moreover, in the post scarcity, post industrial information age we now find ourselves living in, standards of efficiency, effectiveness, and customer services were raised. People expected instant gratification and were less willing to accept slow, nonresponsive organizations.

Advocates of what is now referred to as the "New Public Management" essentially argue that bureaucracy's reliance on laws and regulations resulted in standardized goods and services, a kind of one-size-fits-all, and a narrow definition of accountability limited only to compliance with rules and procedures (Page 2005; Barzelay 1992). By the 1980s, voters were demanding smaller governments, lower taxes, customized services, and a customer orientation from service providers. Technology and private sector performance began to convince the public that they could have the costs and quality benefits of mass production without the standardization of the industrial age. Henry Ford once said that the consumer could have any color Model T as long as it was black. Then the competition decided to offer automobiles in every color of the rainbow, and "one size fits all" began to end. The New Public Management seeks to respond to the public's emerging demands by focusing on performance measurement, customer service, decentralization, outsourcing, and accountability measured by results (Behn 2001; Kettl 2000; Page 2005).

The reinventing government movement of the 1990s, as articulated by David Osborne (Osborne and Gaebler 1992), argued that the bureaucratic model served us well in a world where "tasks were relatively simple and straightforward and the environment stable" (Osborne and Plastrik 1997, 17). But bureaucracy was too slow, unresponsive to customers, and incapable of changing to meet a world experiencing a technological revolution, globalization of markets and politics, and filled with educated workers and consumers. Bureaucracies could not win the new wars such as in Vietnam, could not anticipate or cope with a multinational oil cartel like OPEC, deal with global warming, or provide the poor with the dignity of a job instead of a demeaning handout.

Osborne provided the distinctly antibureaucratic blueprint for the Clinton-Gore National Performance Review (NPR) reorganization of the federal government. Indeed, Osborne would later codify many of the principles and lessons of the NPR in a book titled *Banishing Bureaucracy: The Five Strategies for Reinventing Government* (Osborne and Plastrik 1997). The first report of NPR to President Clinton by Vice President Al Gore set out four core strategies—cut red tape by streamlining the budget and procurement processes, decentralizing personnel policies, and eliminating regulatory "overkill"; putting customers first by bringing choice and market competition to public service delivery; empowering employees by flattening hierarchy, decentralizing decision making, and holding employees accountable for results; and cutting back to basics by shrinking the number of public employees and organizations (Gore 1993).

While the NPR had some direct lasting impact in the form of welfare reform, decentralization of decision making, and contracting out of government services, it has more significance as a signpost of change. Some theorists suggest that the reinventing government movement has "emerged as something like a new orthodoxy within public administration" (Spicer 2004, 354) and has "the potential to become a dominant approach to public management" (Rosenbloom and Kravchuck 2002, xiii). While President George W. Bush may have de-emphasized reinvention after his election in 2000, these management reforms continue in the federal government anyway and are thriving at the state and local level (charter schools, Internet-based motor vehicle bureaus, housing and homeless services run by community-based nonprofit organizations) and in countries around the world.

As Peter Drucker describes it, two fundamentals upon which the bureaucratic model rests—that people who work for an organization are full-time employees of that organization and that these employees are subordinates with minimal skills doing what they are told to do—are no longer always true: "[A] large and steadily growing minority—though working for the organization are no longer its full-time employees. They work for an outsourcing contractor. . . . They are temps or part-timers. Increasingly they are individual contractors working on a retainer for a specific contractual period. . . . Even if employed full-time by the organization, fewer and fewer people are subordinates. . . . Increasingly they are knowledge workers . . . and knowledge workers are not subordinates; they are associates" (1999, 18).

What does this mean in practice? For Jack Welch, former CEO of General Electric, it meant making the organization chart as flat as possible— "managers should have ten direct reports at the minimum and 30 to 50 percent more if they are experienced" (Welch 2005, 116). In essence, former vice president Al Gore and Jack Welch had a similar strategy—flatten the hierarchy, decentralize decision making, and manage by results.

While hierarchy is being reduced and modified, it is far from being eliminated. Peter Drucker called the notion that hierarchy might end "blatant nonsense" (1999, 11). In all organizations, someone must have final authority, and, particularly in times of crisis, decisions must be made with little or no participation and followed virtually without question. And while the Clinton-Gore team eliminated forty thousand federal managers between 1993 and 1998, they added sixteen new titles at the upper levels of government and simply reclassified first-line supervisors into team leaders (Light 2001, 100).

Some view these attacks on bureaucracy as more than an argument over the best form of organizational structure. They see it as "part of a larger cultural contest over the way terms such as 'public interest' and 'public service' are to be understood in this new century" (Considine and Lewis 2003, 131). But while critics seem to agree on the inadequacies of the old bureaucratic model, there is no consensus on what should or will replace it (Considine 2001; Moe 1994).

The world of today is materially different from the world of bureaucracy's heyday in the mid-twentieth century. New models are emerging, out of necessity and by design. For Margaret Thatcher, Ronald Reagan, and the antigovernment advocates, the model was privatization—the smaller the government the better. For Osborne and the reinventers, the model was innovation—streamlined and more effective government.

Today, we see increased emphasis on contracting out and a broader strategy of managing public services through networks. Contracting out and network management are not synonymous, but our view is that networks include both informal and contractual linkages. We consider the contractual links as equivalent to the steel frame of a bridge—the key relationships upon which the informal and noncontractual relationships are built.

Network management is potentially superior to simple contracting out and more extensive "privatization" strategies, since it may offer the flexibility and choice provided by market mechanisms while retaining greater control and clear accountability for the government and the governed. According to Mark Considine, "[t]his 'network governance' paradigm ... suggests a possible breakthrough in public administration and organization theory by providing a means to tackle problems in a multidimensional and locally flexible way. It forges a new path between bureaucratic centralization and privatization and as such may be regarded as the emerging model of public organization for the twenty-first century" (2005, 1).

We also agree with Robert Agranoff that it is "time to go beyond heralding the importance of networks as a form of collaborative public management and look inside their operation" (Agranoff 2006, 56). It is time to get past the assumption that networks are good because they are new, or at least recently discovered, and begin to examine how networks operate and how well they perform. One of the first observations that is emerging from the field is that networks are not replacing the traditional hierarchies but working through them and between them. Indeed, Agranoff found that managers still spend most of their time working in the traditional hierarchy (2006, 57).

Managing homeland security presents an interesting example of the challenge of networking local first responders into the national intelligence, military, and border control agencies. Unfortunately, as Elaine Kamarck concludes, our initial response to the challenge was to create a huge, traditional bureaucracy—the Department of Homeland Security (Kamarck 2004)—which failed to perform adequately in the face of its first public challenge, the impact of Hurricane Katrina on the city of New Orleans and the surrounding gulf coast region. Interestingly, the absence of a major terrorist event in the United States in the years that followed September 11, 2001, may be attributable in part to the effectiveness of a network of federal agencies, local first responders, private companies, and nongovernmental organizations and international partners, both public and private.

In *Governing by Networks*, Goldsmith and Eggers (2004) provide several examples that illustrate how networks can be more effective than traditional bureaucracies. The list includes several clear success stories—the IRS's e-file initiative; CARES, the information technology system that supports Wisconsin's widely praised W-2 welfare-to-work reform initiative; and the extensive contract and partnership network developed by the Golden Gate National Recreation Area in California's Bay Area. Several others on this list of prime examples seem less significant or cannot be characterized as successful—the Coast Guard's modernization of its deepwater fleet and NASA's Jet Propulsion Laboratory design cycle reform. While the contracting decisions have been made, there is no evidence yet to document better outcomes. Still others are viewed by many as failures— the Department of Defense Acquisition University curriculum revision (emphasizing the need to move away from arm's length relationships with contractors) and the contracting out of the Iraq war (see chapter 9).

The U.S. Department of Defense has been working for more than a decade to transform itself from a command-and-control hierarchy into a digital "netcentric" organization (Thompson 2006, 619–22). While such a vision is possible, many doubt its feasibility in a large public organization (Thompson 2006, 620; Hill and Lynn 2005). Separation of powers, particularly as it relates to budget making and financial decisions, makes private-sector-style, smoothly functioning, supply-chain networks highly difficult to replicate in the public sector.

While large public organizations (particularly military and quasi-military ones) may find it difficult to create the highly integrated and decentralized network structure that private organizations such as Wal-Mart and Procter & Gamble have achieved, "public managers operate in collaborative settings every day" (McGuire 2006, 33). But, as McGuire and others have noted, there are various degrees and types of networks; indeed, networks may benefit from coordination achieved through a central core organization (McGuire 2006, 36).

When we examine examples of successful and less-than-successful partnerships, it is clear that public and private organizations behave differently as network partners. Wisconsin's successful welfare-to-work network was damaged by instances of private partners using public funds for parties and lobbying activities (Goldsmith and Eggers 2004, 39). Criticism of the Iraq war contracting has escalated because contractors often refuse to provide even basic information to the media about how they are spending public funds (Martin Smith 2005). If governing by network is the future, we must better understand the differences between public and private organizations in networks and develop mechanisms to ensure public-sector-style transparency.

How Are Public and Private Organization Networks Different?

Private organizations pioneered network management under the name of supply chain management. A supply chain is a network of production locations and distribution channels that transforms raw materials into finished products and delivers those products to customers. While it is easier to describe the supply chain for manufactured products, service organizations also utilize supply chain management (Ganeshan and Harrison 1995).

Supply chain management involves planning, implementation, operation, and control of the process of creating and delivering a product or service to a customer. The scope of supply chain management is similar to the domain of total quality management, with suppliers at one end of the chain and customers at the other end. The task of managers in between is to turn those supplies into products and services that meet or exceed customer definitions of quality at the lowest possible cost (Cohen and Eimicke 1998, 49–64). At its best, supply chain management attempts to bring the benefits of a vertically integrated firm to a production and distribution process where each step is operated by an independently owned entity. In a typical supply chain process, the efficiency and effectiveness of the process can be influenced by the location of facilities, what is produced where, how inventories are managed, and how goods and services are transported through the production process.

When the Internet became pervasive and relatively uniform during the 1990s, the potential of supply chain management increased dramatically. It became possible to connect suppliers, producers, distributors, retailers, and consumers into one seamless flow of low-cost communication. The real potential lies in visibility and transparency of information, and therein lies a major challenge: "The supply chain in most industries is like a big card game. The players don't want to show their cards because they don't trust anyone else with the information. But if they showed their hands, they could all benefit" (Worthen 2002, 1). Visibility and transparency are key elements of any successful public venture. Competitive private companies are naturally predisposed to keep their processes and profit margins private. Clearly, transparency and open access to information will be a challenge in networks involving public and private members.

A visible private sector illustration of the potential benefits of supply chain management is the partnership of Procter & Gamble and Wal-Mart. These two giant corporations built a computer network that enables Procter & Gamble to monitor the inventory at Wal-Mart's distribution centers and sales at the checkout counters and to ship what it determines is the proper amount of product. Invoicing and payment is automatic. Customer service is maximized, as is efficiency and profit for both partners.

What makes supply chain networks so attractive and generally effective is that there is a common set of measures for success. The network participants share an interest in low price, rapid delivery, high quality, and profit. In each case, the measure is easy to define and evaluate. Problems are also obvious and, once identified, often easy to fix. Partners may differ on the fair share of costs and benefits but not on the desired outcomes. As noted supply chain expert Martin Christopher puts it, "[t]hus the focus of supply chain management is upon the management of relationships in order to achieve a more profitable outcome for all parties in the chain. This brings with it some significant challenges since there may be occasions when the narrow self interest of one party has to be subsumed for the benefit of the chain as a whole" (2005, 5).

Networks involving the public sector are seldom so simple, particularly when private and nonprofit organizations are involved. Public networks generally deliver services, the outcomes of which may be difficult to measure and may take years to determine—education, job training, and environmental protection, for example. Additionally, measuring success can be made more difficult because of differing ideas about transparency between the public and private sectors. It gets even more difficult because partners in the network may have different measures and definitions of success as well as incentives that may encourage different behaviors.

The welfare-to-work reform of the mid-1990s is a good example. The overall objective seems clear—to move welfare recipients from welfare dependency to work. However, as we look at the networks designed to carry out the program, measures of success, incentives, and even outcomes become less clear. For the lead agency, local departments of social service, the desired outcome was the transformation of welfare-dependent women with children into self-sufficient working mothers with well-adjusted children.

To reach that objective, social service departments contracted with nonprofit and for-profit job training and job placement organizations, education organizations, child care agencies, and drug treatment organizations. Most job training and job placement organizations were paid to place participants in jobs as quickly as possible. They often received additional payments for retention but seldom for retention beyond six months.

These placement organizations had an incentive to refer participants to child care agencies since the lack of adequate child care was a major obstacle. However, they had little incentive to refer participants to education or drug treatment organizations. While the participant might need those services and those services would probably enhance the prospects of the participant's achieving long-term self-sufficiency, the incentive for the job placement organization was to record and be paid for six months of work as quickly as possible.

The education and drug treatment organizations may have shared the long-term objective of self-sufficiency, but their focus and incentives centered on raising the participants' level of education or helping them overcome an addiction. In both cases, these network partners may oppose immediate job placement. Some of the mission-driven nonprofit job placement agencies may see education as a more important immediate need for the participant, not rapid movement into employment (even if that hurts the nonprofit financially). Even some of the social workers employed by the local social service agency may believe that education is a better immediate "occupation" rather than work and push the partici- pant/client in that direction.

It is relatively easy for Procter & Gamble and Wal-Mart to agree that selling as much soap as quickly as possible is an excellent outcome. How- ever, it is easier to make a beer that "tastes great and is less filling" than to "end welfare as we know it." Few government programs have as simple an outcome or as complete agreement with their network partners on goals. Public and private organizations face several other major challenges in working smoothly together in networks.

All networks face challenges in the areas of capacity, coordination, com- munication, transparency, and oversight. Managing networks is different than managing an internal bureaucracy, particularly a bureaucracy popu- lated by career civil servants. According to Mathur and Skelcher, "[n]etwork governance reshapes the role of public administrators, positioning them as responsively competent players in a polycentric system of governance rather than neutrally competent servants of a political executive" (2007, 235).

Private organizations have to make the transition from internal man- agement to network management, and there is a financial incentive/im- perative to make the shift. Private organizations often have the resources for training and recruitment of new talent, and they are not constrained by civil service rules and regulations. Private managers can be trained in the new skills required, rewarded for success, or punished or terminated for failure, and new managers could be freely recruited from other firms.

Government civil service provides no obvious career path for talented project and network managers (Goldsmith and Eggers 2004, 49). Out- sourcing and retirements are also reducing the management population at all levels of the U.S. government. And our "age of permanent fiscal crisis" may be limiting government's ability to recruit and/or train effective net- work managers (Osborne and Hutchinson 2004).

Communication difficulties challenge all organizations, networked or not. Networked organizations face the additional hurdles of multiple loca- tions, several different cultures, incompatible information technology sys- tems, and sometimes deliberate withholding of important information when partners perceive they are in competition with one another or sim- ply to protect bureaucratic turf. Communications challenges can be worse for governments with severely constrained resources, which often result in outdated and limited information technology hardware and software. Further, the desire of private entities to protect information they may view as proprietary hinders communication and transparency, something for which government should strive. The flow of information can also be stymied in the opposite direction as governments may face legitimate legal and regulatory constraints in sharing information with partners.

Coordination is a key element in the success of any network, public or private. Coordination becomes more difficult if the network includes multiple public agencies, for-profit firms, and nonprofit corporations. In most networks with public participation, the coordination function is the responsibility of the government since public funds generally support the network and the participating public agency is therefore accountable to the citizens for proper use of tax dollars. With a network designed to serve a single customer, network partners must understand one another's standard operating procedures so they can effectively respond to the actions of their partners. Users of the service provided by the network should not be subjected to dealing with what could simply become multiple bureaucracies. Unfortunately, funds to support this critical coordination function and implementation of standard operating procedures are usually limited, public managers lack training and experience in network management, and if there are multiple public agencies from different levels of government involved, there will also be jurisdictional disputes to overcome.

Finally, there is the challenge of oversight and accountability. As Beryl Radin noted in her assessment of the Government Performance and Results Act (GPRA), the fragmentation of decision making between the executive and legislative branches, the decentralization of authority to program levels, and the devolution of federal authority to the states and localities make it increasingly difficult to hold any one individual or agency accountable for the performance of the system (Radin 1998, 307–16). Federalism is not a factor in purely private networks. Accountability and oversight become even more complicated when collaboration between public and nongovernmental agencies is also involved (Page 2004, 591). One of the major benefits of involving nongovernmental actors in addressing public policy problems is providing them the discretion to be creative in developing different approaches and overcome the constraints of large command-and-control bureaucracies. Unlike contracting, the participants in a network are not under a legally binding agreement to perform a specified service for a set price. Rather, the network could be viewed more as a collaborative effort that may be funded in part by government but is less well-defined than a contractual relationship. Services that are outside the defined agreement between the partners in a network are being performed and are one of the advantages of the creation of a service network. The challenge is to ensure accountability in this more free and flexible operating environment.

Advocates of the reinventing government movement and the New Public Management make the case for accountability for results (Osborne and Hutchinson 2004; Kamensky and Morales 2005; Page 2004; Behn 2001; Kettl 2000). The idea is simple—hold agencies, networks, and individual collaborators accountable for outcomes, not for following procedures or obeying the rules. In practice, measuring outcomes for each collaborator may create debate over the most appropriate indicator of achievement. Data to support the indicators may be lacking or of suspect reliability. And intermediate indicators for individual collaborators may not cumulate to accurate measures of the ultimate outcomes of the network desired by the public and stakeholders.

Another potential difficulty when measuring public sector performance is that the indicator can often be "gamed." This may be counterproductive, particularly if the indicator itself is a poor measure of the desired outcomes. For example, the use of raw test results in education can distort effort (teaching to the test, focus on the margin, deselecting marginal or failing students) such that the overall educational outcome can be worsening while the performance measure shows improvement (Wilson 2003). Similarly, in the health sector, measures focusing on the quantity of patients treated in a given period can reduce the focus on quality of care. This can have significant negative impacts on patients such as the elderly, who have a longer recovery time. Finally, sometimes public organizations cannot agree on the results that should be produced. It is difficult for results-oriented management to function under such conditions of extreme uncertainty.

Managing a network of public and private organizations by results is meaningful only if it enables the system to improve its performance (Page 2004, 600; Kamensky and Morales 2005, 12; Osborne and Hutchinson 2004, 189–90). While this is a substantial challenge, research in the field indicates progress is being made. Page's study of local human services collaboratives found that "analysts can measure a collaborative's capacity to be accountable for results on a continuum" (2004, 601). Iowa's "charter agencies" provide several examples of successful performance agreements between the governor and legislature and several state agencies (Osborne and Hutchinson 2004, 237–39). And we also make note of Baltimore's CitiStat approach to combine agency output data with geographic information to engage the public and improve performance, neighborhood by neighborhood (Kamensky and Morales 2005, 13, 465–98; Osborne and Hutchinson 2004, 163–89).

Ensuring accountability in networks involving public and private collaborations is a complex enterprise. The recipe for success varies and it cannot be codified in a scope of work in a written contract. This is particularly true in some of the most important policy processes such as the response to natural disasters. As Waugh and Streib describe it, "[t]he response to natural disasters is, in large measure, an ad hoc affair involving nongovernmental actors, governmental actors, and emergent groups that often become well organized and long lived. Nongovernmental organizations will respond with or without government approval. Volunteers will arrive with or without an invitation. First responders will self-deploy" (2006, 138).

Success requires judgment—selecting the right collaborators; choosing indicators that are meaningful and broadly accepted; being flexible; accepting no excuses; trying something new when the old formula begins to fail (Goldsmith and Eggers 2004, 155).

Judgment and decision making are distinctly human enterprises. The success of networks is largely dependent on the network manager, just as it is for less complex organizations. To better understand how networks work, we need to look at the behavior of their managers.

What Do Network Managers Do?

The real-world practice of network management is moving much faster than the descriptive and analytical literature about it (McGuire 2002, 599). That said, a number of academics and practitioners are actively engaged in creating a body of knowledge around the network manager—what it is, what it does, how it does it, and how it differs, if at all, from the non-network manager. In our view, much can be learned about effective network management using the manager as the unit of analysis.

The public network manager is accountable for the satisfactory delivery of goods and services with and through networked settings. According to McGuire, public managers cannot dictate action through the network, but they are nonetheless responsible for its performance (2002, 600). Consi-dine and Lewis observe that network managers, or process owners (as they call them), "take charge of the supplier-customer chains in order to shorten them" and link program objectives to an individualized system of service delivery, using flexible technology for mobilizing resources and success-fully combining public and private initiatives for service improvement (1999, 472).

The effective network manager must also manage the everyday opera-tion of the network, becoming knowledgeable about exactly what is going on along the interfaces. But to be effective, the network manager must be able to connect the day-to-day with the big picture of the network's de-sired outcomes and performance measures (Goldsmith and Eggers 2004, 164). To be successful, network managers must master a range of skills and knowledge well beyond the traditional POSDCORB—planning, orga-nizing, staffing, directing, coordinating, reporting, and budgeting (Gulick 1937, 3–44).

Network managers must also become proficient at activating, synthesiz-ing, framing, arranging, stabilizing, and integrating (McGuire 2006; McGuire 2002; Goldsmith and Eggers 2004). Activating involves bringing together the people, organizations, funding, and authority necessary to put the network in operation. Synthesizing involves building the relation-ships and smoothing the rough edges between participants so the network can operate as smoothly and seamlessly as possible. Framing means docu-menting participants' standard operating procedures and then creating bridges and coordinating mechanisms so that the network members un-derstand and respond properly to each other's actions and behaviors. Ar-ranging involves the creation of a plan that sequences the work of individ-ual network participants into a process that will produce the product or service desired by the customer. Integrating is similar to conducting an orchestra. Network managers must meld, blend, modulate, and mesh the work of individual members into a value-added process. Stabilizing refers to continuous calibration of the network process so that the network operates at the highest level of efficiency and a minimal level of error. The informal contacts and agreements between network partners that will allow the network manager to accomplish these tasks are essential and are difficult to define in a memorandum of understanding or contract that may have helped create the network.

The literature on network management is in its early stages. The aforementioned activities are offered for consideration, not as a conclusion. However, as the research of Considine and Lewis suggests, "networking does in fact appear to be based on a coherent cluster of work strategies" (1999, 475).

An effective manager in a traditional, hierarchical organization not connected to a network might not be an effective or happy network manager. Effective traditional managers may be comfortable in developing and communicating standard operating procedures, enforcing rules and regulations, monitoring performance, and reporting results. Their focus is primarily on their organization's internal workings and their role is primarily as a supervisor. Effective network managers will spend more time focused on activities external to the organizations that employ them. They will deal primarily with peers and superiors in other organizations. Effective network managers need to be good at negotiation, facilitation, conflict resolution, and mediation. They will spend much more time dealing with teams instead of hierarchies. Managing a network requires more informal communication and understandings than does managing a hierarchy. In fact, the growing importance of informal organization and communication in hierarchical organizations indicates that elements of network management are entering management in all types of organization. Call it the impact of the Facebook-LinkedIn generation on organizational life. Effective network managers must be good at developing and managing contracts, but they must also be good at negotiating the uncharted terrain of informal interorganizational relationships.

Effective network managers must be flexible, they must be good listeners, and they must pay attention to communication flows and accuracy. They must be good at providing feedback and building feedback loops that lead to improved communication and performance. They must be comfortable with an ever-changing work environment and constant problem solving.

Effective network managers are willing to deal face to face and talk with a wide range of superiors, subordinates, and peers spanning the boundaries of the network. They cannot limit their interactions to the Internet and e-mail. And, like Peters and Waterman's managers in the 1980s that searched for excellence within organizations, these managers must manage by wandering around their own organizations—physically and virtually—as well as the organizations of their partners and collaborators.

Network managers must also be expert contract managers. They must be willing and able to anticipate issues and negotiate well-functioning contracts. They also need to learn how to modify contracts when necessary and find ways of operating within the scope of existing contracts. They must learn the rules of the game, know what they don't know, and learn how to use experts who know what they don't know.

To attract and enable this new kind of public manager, government will need to invest more in training on team management, project management, risk assessment and risk management, negotiation and conflict resolution, contract management, and communications skills. This does not require a massive expansion of government employees, but managers with a different understanding of management. The manager must take a more holistic approach to the network than would be appropriate for managing an internal hierarchy. The informal contacts between network partners are as essential as is the agreement underlying the network. This new kind of public manager must be able to work not within the bounds of a network's founding agreement, but within the bounds of the network itself, something much more difficult to define or chart.

Conclusions

Governing through networks has the potential to provide higher quality public services at a lower cost, just as supply chain management has enabled the private sector to deliver better products at lower prices and still make a healthy profit. And there is a growing body of literature to indicate that in the future public managers will need the skills necessary to collaborate effectively (Bingham and O'Leary 2006, 165). At the same time, we do not believe bureaucracy, hierarchy, command-and-control, and traditional management techniques will disappear any time soon. Networks connect, complement, and enhance our existing organizational structures and procedures. Managing in both worlds will require creative, talented, and energetic public managers who are committed to ongoing training and learning.

We have defined contracting, discussed the challenges it presents to public ethics, and assessed its relationship to the growing phenomenon of interorganizational networks. We conclude this discussion of the environment of government contracting with an analysis of the impact of contracting on our system of representative democracy and on the treasured value of government accountability to the public. While in graduate school in the Vietnam- and Watergate-influenced 1970s, we both found ourselves working on the difficulty of connecting average citizens to the increasingly complex and bureaucratized work of government. As government's work grew in technical complexity, the public's ability to influence that work seemed to decline. Controlling unelected bureaucrats seemed an impossible task. With the growth of contracting in the twenty-first century, the people implementing the government's programs seemed one further step from public control.

In the next chapter we ask you to take a step back from the issues of contract management that we have just addressed, and will resume in chapter five, and explore with us the fundamental questions of representation and accountability. In our view, these issues must be understood if we are to *begin* to assess the impact of contracting on the institutions of representative democracy. What is representation? What are the mechanisms available to the public to influence the actions of government? How does contracting influence representation and citizen-government linkage?

Chapter 4

Ensuring Accountability and Democratic Representation in Government Contracting

IN A REPRESENTATIVE democracy the behavior of private parties under contract to government should be under the control of public officials accountable to the citizens they serve. Ensuring accountability to the public is made more complicated because the public officials supervising the contractors are appointed rather than elected. And who are contractors accountable to? This chapter explores these fundamental issues of representation and the issue of citizen-bureaucracy linkage, connecting the preferences of the public to unelected leaders and the private contractors who work for them.

Many discussions of privatization and contracting out note the threat that private contractors pose to our system of accountability. We share that concern and decided to provide a detailed analysis of this issue. We ask four fundamental questions: 1. What is accountability? 2. Accountability to whom and what? 3. How does the public influence the work of its government—how is "linkage" performed? 4. How does the growth of private contracting influence this system of representation and linkage? If we are concerned about the impact of contracting upon representative democracy in America, we need a profound understanding of our system of representation, starting with the definition of representation itself.

This chapter is meant to provide a close examination of the underlying issues of government accountability. It examines the logic and reality of representation and analyzes the institutions that influence the public policies made by unelected government officials and the private contractors that work for them. This inquiry is at a different level of analysis than the rest of this volume to provide an in-depth treatment of the fundamental issue of accountability.

Representation

We begin, then, with the issue of representation. When we discuss contractor accountability, we need to ask the question: accountable to what or whom? We believe that the answer to that question is: "accountable to the system of democratic representation and its elected officials." To understand what we mean by representative system, we must first understand the concept of representation. Representation is a complex and multidimensional phenomenon. Various scholars have seen fit to interpret it in strikingly different fashions. According to Charles A. Beard and John D. Lewis, the origin of representative government can be found in Europe in the Middle Ages.[1]

Beard and Lewis document four phases of the development of representative government in England. The first did not provide for representation of people, but of estates, "nobility, clergy, landed gentry, and burgesses of towns" (Beard and Lewis 1932, 231). These early legislatures met to ratify the king's taxes and did not actually legislate in the modern sense.

During the second phase of development, the tax-approving assemblage gradually became a lawmaking body. The "estate representatives" eventually began to discuss their common problems and grievances. When they came to agree on a preferred solution to the problem at hand, these representatives would draft a petition and present it to the king. If the monarch approved the petition, it became law. The king could not casually dismiss these petitions, "since the parliament held the purse strings [and] it could often compel the king to consent" (Beard and Lewis 1932, 232). In the third phase, the estate representatives achieved primacy over the monarch, thus forming the constitutional, or limited, monarchy.

The connection between democracy and representation is one that contemporary scholars find quite natural. There are, however, nondemocratic aspects to the historic and modern concepts of representation. In fact, as a move away from direct democracy, representation can be seen as intrinsically antidemocratic.

The legitimacy of the representative's power in this relationship, as we understand it today, derives from the representative's accountability to those represented. The power relationship may be explicit or implicit, mutual, exclusive, or possibly a variable subject to fluctuation over time. There are many perspectives regarding the power relationships involved in each view of representation, which we will explore in the following analysis.

Why does this matter for our purposes here? Let us assume that contractors must be accountable to elected representatives. Let us also assume that the policy perspectives of representatives vary and the very definition of representation itself varies. Obviously, this means that the operational definition of accountability is far from simple. Representation is not simply adherence to popular will, and accountability is therefore not simply responsiveness to the views of the public.

Representation as Authority

To Thomas Hobbes, representation is the mechanism by which individuals escape the ungoverned state of nature, that theoretical hell on earth where life is nasty, brutish, and short. As a result of the social contract, each individual gives up his or her right of self-government to a sovereign power in order to escape the state of nature. This sovereign represents the individual in the sense that the individual accepts the decisions of the sovereign as if they are the individual's own decisions, as binding decisions.

The Hobbesian concept of representation is the authorization of a sovereign to act in place of each individual member of society; that is, representation "is authority, the right to make commitments and incur consequences for another" (Pitkin 1967, 8). The representative acts and the represented is bound by these decisions and is responsible for their consequences as if they themselves had been the actor. The difficulty with this view of representation is that if it is followed to its logical conclusion, all government is representative government (Pitkin 1967, 8).

In the contemporary view, the representative is given the authority to act in place of the represented.[2] There is an aspect of the modern sense of representation in which the decision maker (or representative) is legitimately permitted discretion when making decisions. The representative is permitted to act without instructions when he or she is unsure of his or her constituents' opinion (or no opinions exist), and in certain situations is accorded authority to act contrary to the opinions of his or her constituents on matters of conscience. The modern view maintains, however, that constituents have the right to hold the representative accountable for his or her actions and revoke the grant of authority entrusted to the representative, while the Hobbesian view permits no such revocation of authority.

Representation as Accountability

This view defines representation as the formal arrangements that follow and potentially terminate representative activity, as "accountability, the holding to account of the representative for his actions" (Pitkin 1967, 11).

Accountability is not simply intended as a means of punishing representatives for taking wrong positions, but as a stimulus for eliciting from representatives behavior that is responsive to the needs of the represented. The difficulty with the accountability position is that this notion of providing stimulation for right behavior does not necessarily follow from the definition of accountability. Representation is an ongoing activity, not merely a set of mechanical or formal structures. When we think about administrative accountability and extend that notion to government's private contractors, it is frequently this aspect of representation that we are referring to. The accountability view of representation leaves a measure of power in the hands of the represented. According to this view, if the representative is willing to be elected to office only once, that representative can do as he or she pleases. Hence, the power relationship can be described as follows: in the short run, the representative is in the dominant position, but due to their ultimate veto, the represented have the last word and in the long run hold greater power. Clearly, the represented hold greater power in this view of representation than in the authorization view. Nonetheless, the public's leverage is periodic and latent rather than continuous and present.

Descriptive Representation

During the American Revolution, John Adams argued that a representative legislature "should be an exact portrait, in miniature of the people at large, as it should think, feel, reason and act like them" (Pitkin 1967, 60–61).

Much of the literature in "representative" bureaucracy appears to be based on this conception of representation. Norton E. Long argued that the unelected federal bureaucracy was more "representative" than elected legislators because the social and economic status (SES) level of the bureaucracy was closer to the national average than was that of elected officials (Long 1952).

Descriptive representation is also the theoretical basis for those advocating the use of sampling and survey techniques to represent the mass public (Swabey 1969, 90). Representation is thus simply reproducing the views of the public and incorporating these views into the decision-making process. Similarly, advocates of proportional representation schemes are actually advocates of descriptive representation. Proportional representation is simply a form of sampling.

Descriptive representation does not require or imply public control of the activities of representatives. All that is required is that representatives have attitudes and attributes that are similar to those of the public. Hibbing and Theiss-Morse's research into the attitudes of the American public with respect to representation and policymaking, *Stealth Democracy* (2002), suggests that descriptive representation is in line with the desires of the electorate who want "a system that is instinctively in touch with the problems of real Americans" in which "representatives would understand the concerns of ordinary people simply because they are ordinary people themselves and because they spend time among other ordinary people" (2002, 131).

Symbolic Representation

Symbolic representation is perhaps one of the more abstract and difficult-to-grasp aspects of representation. Examples of representative symbols include a nation's flag or its head of state (representing the nation's unity), a corporate logo (represents the image of the company), and the "ban the bomb" or peace symbol (representing pacifism).

Since an object such as a flag can be a symbolic representative, it is difficult to conceptualize the power relationship between representative and the represented. Nevertheless, power remains an important dimension of this aspect of representation. The group that controls and manipulates the central symbols of a society controls society. In the United States, the influence of capitalism manifests itself in the symbols Americans accept as signs of success.

Although ultimately each individual perceives a symbol privately, perception is structured socially. Because symbols are in part interpreted emotionally, the danger of manipulation is great. Still, this sort of manipulation has its limits. If a recession is going on, no amount of manipulation will convince people that good times are imminent.

Representation as Responsive Stewardship

Responsive stewardship is a representative role that considers each aspect of representation as legitimate in varying degrees and that attempts to balance the various elements in order to establish a meaningful link between citizens and government. This notion of responsive stewardship is strongly influenced by the incisive analyses of Hannah Pitkin. According to Pitkin, "[p]olitical representation is primarily a public institutionalized arrangement . . . what makes it representation is not any single action by any one participant, but the overall structure and functioning of the system. . . . The representative system must look after the public interest and be responsive to public opinion except insofar as nonresponsiveness can be justified in terms of the public interest" (Pitkin 1967, 221 and 224).

The question then arises: What standards can be utilized to judge the responsiveness of the representative system and thereby judge a key factor contributing to the representativeness of that system?

It should be expected that at times it will be difficult to assess whether a public's wish is detrimental to life-support requirements. Analysis will need to explore the general thrust of a particular issue and try to keep in mind the limitations inherent in our categorization scheme. Despite these difficulties, such a categorization of citizen wishes is essential if responsiveness is to be meaningfully evaluated. This of course has impact on our assessment of bureaucratic and contractor accountability. We would not want these unelected officials and contractors to meet public needs that were detrimental to society. An example of a wish that is detrimental to long-term systems maintenance would be the desire Americans appear to have for large, gas-guzzling automobiles. Such a wish need not be responded to by a representative government because it endangers ecosystems and economic system maintenance. An example of a wish that may be irrelevant to system survival might be citizen lifestyle preferences (e.g., collective vs. individual, extended family vs. nuclear family, urban vs. rural living, etc.). Those preferences affect the character of society but need not affect its survival.

Normally, when government responds to the citizenry, it is reacting to the exercise (or fear of the exercise) of citizen power. For representative government, responsiveness and the authority to assure stewardship are equally critical, and achieving the balance that brings about the maximum responsiveness while simultaneously assuring stewardship is the main difficulty encountered when attempting to maintain a healthy representative system.

The second way government receives messages is more "painful." Citizens force government to listen to their views. Luttbeg identifies three of these "coercive" models of political linkage. They are the rational activist model, the political parties model, and the pressure groups model (1974, 3). Citizen-government linkage is a prerequisite of responsiveness, which in turn is a central component of the concept of representation. Linkage mechanisms range from coercive to noncoercive. Each type of mechanism is helpful if representation is to occur, but a key requirement for a responsive political system is the presence of ongoing and organized coercive mechanisms that articulate mass demands. There are two polar types of organization imaginable: (1) mass-based political parties and (2) interest-based voluntary organizations (interest groups). Group and pluralist theorists have claimed that most significant interests in society are represented in decision making by organized interest groups. In recent years, the Internet has allowed interest groups to recruit and maintain organizational presence at lower cost. Organizations such as MoveOn.org and others have begun to redefine the form of traditional interest groups.

A second stream of theorists has disputed the claim that mass representation can be achieved through interest groups (Schattschneider 1960; Cobb and Elder 1972; Bachrach and Baratz 1963). Pressure politics is oriented to achieving the aims of special interests. Party politics, on the other hand, is oriented toward securing the common interest. Pressure politics attempts to privatize conflict and reduce the scope of its contagion. Again, the Internet may be providing interest group politics with a lower cost and possibly less elite-driven model.

A major arena of conflict in politics is the political agenda-setting process (Cobb and Elder 1972). Demand articulation is a central component of this process. The two different modes of coercive organized linkage exhibit strikingly different tendencies regarding which (or whose) demands are articulated. The pressure system of organized interest groups pursuing special interests is a demand articulation system heavily skewed toward the "haves" elements of American society. Schattschneider proclaimed in his now famous statement: "The flaw in the pluralist heaven is that the heavenly chorus sings with a strong upper class accent. Probably about 90% of the people can't get in the pressure system" (1960, 34). While it is too early to tell, mass and interactive communications technology may be changing the fee charged for entering the pressure system.

Nonetheless, the representative system's ability to respond to the wishes of the public can be seriously compromised by reliance on any exclusionary method of demand articulation. For this reason, the status of a society's party politics or, more generally, the status of mass-based groups organized to pursue the common interest is a key determinant of a political system's responsiveness. Government-sponsored and legally required citizen participation programs are not, of course, coercive, mass-based linkage mechanisms. Therefore, by definition their potential for engendering political responsiveness must be seen as extremely limited.

The second aspect of the multidimensional conception of representation is stewardship. Stewardship, or the survival of society, is the central purpose of government. Although scholars concerned with effective decision making in government have pointed out the dangers of too much citizen voice in governance, students of representation have paid less attention to the need for effective governance as a prerequisite for meaningful representation.

We take the perspective that responsiveness is only one aspect of representational activity, and a second aspect is the ability of representative policymakers to deliver policy outputs responsive to public demands. When analyzing a representative system, it is important to first identify the authoritative decision makers in a political system and then assess the responsiveness of these decision makers to the wishes of the public. Much of the study of representation has focused on the responsiveness of legislatures. Yet important policy decisions are made every day in the executive branch, particularly its unelected component: the administrative bureaucracy. The concern, of course, is that policymaking may now be devolving even further, from the appointed government officials to unappointed private contractors. Regulation writing in federal executive agencies has taken on many aspects of lawmaking, and the twentieth century witnessed a remarkable increase in the amount of policy formulated in these agencies. An analysis of the representativeness of the political system ought to include an assessment of all major arenas of policymaking activity. Such an analysis should attempt to assess the ability of the representatives/decision makers to actually provide for stewardship. In so doing three basic questions should be asked: Can the system govern? Who governs? Are the governors responsive to the wishes of the public?

Linkage to "what" is a central and often unexamined question in the literature of representation. Decision-making studies and representation studies emerge from different streams of literature, and the two phenomena are only rarely studied simultaneously. Because our definition of representation includes a concern for stewardship, we are in effect compelled to examine the locus of decision-making power and the capability of the political system to make authoritative decisions. The bureaucracy is a key locus of governmental policymaking; can these unelected officials control the actions of their private, contracted agents?

The Rise of the Policymaking Bureaucracy

Although the media often focus their attention on the actions of elected leaders, the major change in national-level power over the past seventy-five years has been the rise of the policymaking bureaucracy. This phenomenon has not gone unnoticed by students of American politics. As far back as 1934, a Brookings Institution study reported that rules and regulations published by the administration "cover altogether eight or ten times as many pages as the acts passed by Congress. Furthermore . . . the decisions of the various authorities which exercise administrative judicial powers are several times as numerous as the recorded decisions of all the federal judicial courts" (Blachly and Oatman 1934, 11).[3] Although administrative decisions did not always have the scope of the decisions of the president, Congress, and the courts, the aggregate impact of bureaucratic decisions was impressive, even in the first half of the twentieth century.[4]

In an article in the *American Political Science Review* in 1956, Herbert Kaufman wrote that the bureaucracy had become an independent source of decision-making power in the American political system.[5] Kaufman observed that

> in thirty years, the number of federal civilian employees has more than quadrupled. If power were measurable, the federal bureaucracy's power would probably turn out to have increased by an even greater factor. Governmental policy is now formulated in administrative regulations and orders, as the growth of the Federal Register vividly attests; judicial proceedings before administrative agencies probably exceed in quantity those before the courts. . . . All this is handled by administrative officials under the very broadest of mandates from Congress and the President. Much of our legislation originates in administrative agencies (Kaufman 1956, 50).

The ascendancy of the policymaking bureaucracy can generally be attributed to the governance demands of a complex, industrialized society. The nature of political system inputs or demands has undergone a radical change in (at least) the past century, and the nature of governmental activity has changed along with these demands. The tasks of government are increasingly complex, interconnected, technological in content, and massive in scope and volume (Peters 1978, 16). These tasks result in an increased need for scientific and managerial expertise. They require a large-scale, full-time, organized effort if they are to be addressed meaningfully. As a result, elected leaders increasingly have come to rely on bureaucratic organizations in the policymaking process. In turn, over the past quarter century, these unelected bureaucrats have come to rely on expertise and labor from the private sector.

Policymaking in America's complex socioeconomic environment is less often the relatively overt, value-expressing, grand policymaking that sets broad social direction and more often nuts-and-bolts decision making—technical decisions designed simply to keep things going. Bureaucratic organizations with clearly delineated areas of distinctive competence are usually best-suited to make these technically complex, detailed decisions. By focusing their efforts narrowly, bureaucratic organizations are able to specialize and develop the expertise needed to deal with complex issues. As the world gets even more complex, these unelected bureaucrats have in turn come to rely on the expertise lodged in private, nongovernmental organizations. The converse of these administrative and contractor strengths are legislative and executive weaknesses.

The president, by directly commanding a team of bureaucrats (The Executive Office of the President) is perhaps a more effective decision power competitor for administrative agencies, but even the president's ability to direct the bureaucracy is limited (Allison 1971; Neustadt 1976, 1990). Institutions dependent on elections are characteristically less stable than bureaucracies. Tenure is uncertain, and bureaucrats can drag their feet or time policy decisions to achieve the reaction preferred from elected officials. While contractor-bureaucrat competition exhibits different features, the contractor's presence in the field and control over the details of implementation give it substantial leverage in its power relationship with unelected officials.

Bureaucratic expertise and information are two sources of bureaucratic power. As private parties assume outsourced administrative roles, the power relationship is modified. On the one hand, unelected officials have lost their monopoly. On the other hand, if they maintain control of their contractors, their influence can be magnified many times over.

Related to the issue of expertise is bureaucratic control of information. Administrative agencies provide much of the information that forms the basis for public policy decisions. This information helps define public policy problems and set the parameters for feasible solutions. This gives the bureaucracy substantial influence in policy formulation. It is especially noteworthy because bureaucracies provide much of the information that legislatures receive on agency activities. Administrative bureaucracies define the reality that surrounds a particular policy, and those who define reality have an advantage in the race to control reality. This chain of information control for our elected leaders becomes even more attenuated when the implementing agencies are nongovernmental contractors. The growth of the Internet and World Wide Web makes it more difficult for agencies to retain a monopoly on information, and this new media will likely have impact on the role of information on the power equation in our society. While it is too early to measure this impact with any precision, we see a clear growth in the role of nongovernmental organizations in collecting, analyzing, and disseminating policy-relevant information.

Another important source of bureaucratic power is the administrative power of implementation (Powell 1967, 12; Rourke 1976, 18). In the final analysis, it is bureaucratic actors who make public policies real. Bureaucrats have a power roughly analogous to the power a laborer always has vis-à-vis a boss, or an army private to his or her commander: the power to withhold human effort.[6] This power of implementation is therefore a power of discretion (Rourke 1976, 18). Much modern legislation has become quite vague, often leaving a substantial degree of discretion to administrative agencies (Dimmock 1936; Landis 1938; Leirson 1942; McConnell 1967; Lowi 1969, 1979). Marshall Dimmock has termed these vague enactments "skeleton legislation." Such legislation is both an effect of bureaucratic power and a cause of a certain type of bureaucratic power, namely the discretionary power of implementation. While the U.S. Congress has attempted to enact more specific legislation over the past quarter century, it is poorly equipped to deal with the complexity of modern societies and economies.

There are three basic styles of discretionary power: (1) routine, (2) emergency, and (3) rule-setting.[7] Routine discretionary acts are those simple acts of discretion carried out by low-level governmental officials in their daily work. Although these decisions seem trivial at the systemic level, they are often critical matters for citizens interacting with bureaucrats. Emergency discretionary power results from bureaucrats acting beyond specific mandates in matters critical to public health and welfare. Finally, discretionary power comes from the process of putting flesh on the bones of vague or skeleton legislation (rule-setting discretion). Power over the rules that guide the implementation of public policy is the most important source (or variant) of discretionary power (Dimmock 1936, 48–51). This is discretion at the upper reaches of administration, as distinguished from other types of implementation power that often exist at the lower levels of the bureaucratic hierarchy. Much of the information and analysis used in this policymaking by unelected officials is collected, analyzed, and reported by private contractors—in many cases giving them significant influence over policymaking.

It seems clear that the bureaucracy and its army of private contractors have considerable power to influence and create public policy. Although it is certainly a complex and value-laden issue, the dangers of this administrative power will now be discussed.

The Dangers of Bureaucratic Power

As Carl Friedrich once observed, "the core of modern government . . . [is] a functioning bureaucracy" (1937, 44). Put another way, the major actors operating at the heart of the American political system are unelected officials. This has been extended to networks of public and private unelected officials in an increasingly complex set of market- and nonmarket-based relationships (Olsen 2006). The presence of unelected government and nongovernmental players may be a difficult notion to reconcile with a theory of governance that maintains that government ought to be democratic, or of and by the people.

According to Dwight Waldo, "[i]f administration is indeed the 'core of modern government,' then a theory of democracy in the twentieth century must embrace administration" (1952, 81). In the twenty-first century, Waldo's analysis must be extended to include the power of private organizations under contract to government. Although it is impossible to imagine that a democracy could exist in the modern era without an administrative bureaucracy and its private contractors, it is possible to imagine that bureaucratic power could subvert and destroy democratic institutions. As policymaking becomes more complex, the pressure increases for a professional style of governance to respond to public problems. Increasingly, citizens come to be considered incapable of controlling political decisions. The growth of expertise in governance has been beneficial and has enhanced government's capacity to deal with contemporary problems. The enhanced capacity brought by private contractors has only extended the expert reach of the bureaucracy.

Nevertheless, we acknowledge that there are significant costs involved in utilizing expertise. As Frederick C. Mosher notes, "[t]he danger is that the developments in the public service of the mid-century decades may be subtly, gradually, but profoundly moving the weight toward the partial, the corporate, the professional perspective, and away from the general interest" (1968, 210). Mosher's critique focuses on the results of bureaucratic rule; a second danger is simply the fact of bureaucratic rule.

Assuming democracy is a cherished value, the spectacle of unelected officials ruling society must be considered a significant cost to democracy. The possibility that this authority could be further devolved to private contractors is truly terrifying for those of us committed to a democratic form of government. Unless administrative and contractor decision making is somehow directed by the citizenry (either directly or through its representatives), there is no democracy in a modern state. According to William Eimicke, "[n]o matter how democratically we recruit our administrators, it is nonetheless true that administrators are not democratically responsible or controllable" (1974, 33). Eimicke further observed that "[t]he conflict between the need to administer professionally and the desire to maintain democratic control is difficult to reconcile" (1974, 33).

Although Eimicke correctly notes the difficulty of applying democratic direction to professional/administrative decision making, there is no reason to believe that it is impossible to subject administrators to democratic direction and control. Although bureaucrats cannot be voted out of office, their behavior can be controlled in other ways: they can be rewarded, punished, or simply made irrelevant. The public and its elected officials are potentially capable of directing and controlling bureaucratic behavior. The complex nature of the policy areas dominated by bureaucratic decision makers makes it a difficult task, but certainly not an impossible one. The power of expertise can be challenged by the establishment of competing institutions of expertise. Finally, as indicated by Anthony Bertelli and Laurence Lynn, self-control of bureaucrats is also possible through professional and managerial responsibility "that incorporates accountability, judgment, balance, and rationality" (2006, 31). The entire story of accountability is not simply one of balanced power, but of responsible bureaucracy.

Assessing the Performance of Citizen-Bureaucracy Linkage Mechanisms

Controlling bureaucracy is particularly difficult because some degree of bureaucratic policymaking freedom is useful and beneficial. One reason bureaucracies are established is to remove some decision-making responsibility from overworked elected leaders. In the abstract, we think it proper to foster political control of value-dominated decisions and bureaucratic control of technical, value-securing decisions. In reality, such a neat division is nearly impossible to operationalize. Some discretionary power must be granted to a bureaucracy. Discretionary power will nearly always be extended to the point that significant, substantive policy decisions will be made by these unelected officials. With private contractors increasingly acting on behalf of unelected officials, the extension of policymaking into the private sector is inevitable. This ever-attenuated "accountability" chain is only as strong as its weakest link and is a key challenge to democratic control presented by contracting. Because of this, political control of bureaucracy and public bureaucratic control of contractors is a prerequisite of democratic government. Political leverage is needed to guide and structure bureaucratic policymaking and to coerce bureaucrats into performing tasks demanded by the public (Hyneman 1950).[8]

Political linkage. This notion of leverage can also be conceptualized as an element of political linkage, as the process of obtaining responsive policymaking. Linkage is achieved within a variety of power relationships. In Norman Luttbeg's (1974) terminology, linkage can either be coercive or noncoercive. In other words, it can be an expression of citizen power (coercive) or governmental beneficence (noncoercive). In addition to the issue of leverage, political linkage has a number of important dimensions. The three we consider central are: (1) Whose demands are being incorporated into policymaking? (2) How are demands being communicated to policymakers? and (3) What impact do these political demands have within the policymaking process and on policy outputs?

Citizen-bureaucracy linkage. Citizen-bureaucracy linkage is the attempt of citizens to elicit responsive bureaucratic behavior or to control and influence that behavior. As figure 4.1 indicates, citizens have a wide variety of means available to affect bureaucratic behavior and the work of private contractors. Linkage is achieved via a complex assortment of processes. Linkage is either direct or indirect. Direct linkage is any linkage not filtered through the formal controllers in figure 4.1. Most direct linkage results in nonbinding but often critical informal constraints. When citizens attempt to directly influence bureaucracies, they must rely on persuasion rather than formal command. Students of American politics understand, however, that political parties and interest groups can be very persuasive, and bureaucracies often take citizen views into account when making policy. Indirect linkage is linkage that is filtered through formal controllers (Congress, the president, and the judiciary [including administrative tribunals]). Indirect linkage can result in either formal controls or informal constraints on bureaucratic behavior. Most direct linkage is mediated through political parties, interest groups, and other active linkage mechanisms.

Citizen participation programs legally mandated by law in specific government programs are passive forms of linkage between citizens and bureaucracy that are highly dependent upon citizen activism for their operation. Agencies set the ground rules and seek input, but active citizens normally provide this input. If political participation literature is applicable to this issue-specific participation, then it is reasonable to expect these active and involved citizens to be disproportionately drawn from the upper socioeconomic class. Since most citizen participation programs only permit citizens to advise bureaucrats, it is reasonable to expect that the impact will be limited.

Nearly fifty years ago, Charles E. Gilbert identified a dozen component values of the concept of "responsibility" (Gilbert 1959).[9] Gilbert was able to identify five distinct traditions within the literature of responsible bureaucracy. He defined these "schools" of thought according to the emphasis each placed on certain "avenues" they relied upon to foster bureaucratic responsibility (Gilbert 1959, 382). His schema of administrative relationships of control was based on two dimensions: (1) internal-external (within the bureaucratic hierarchy vs. outside of the bureaucratic hierarchy) and

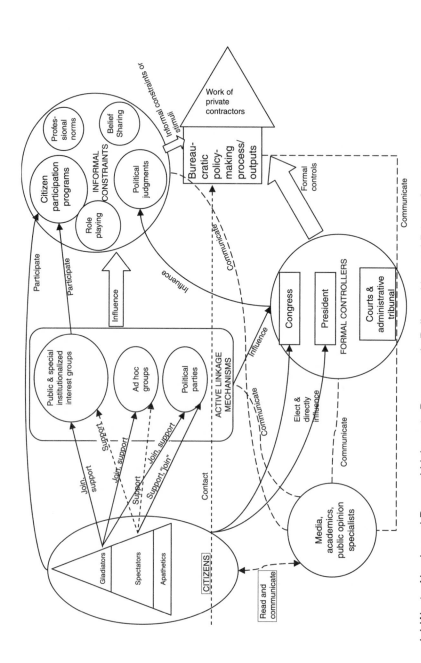

Figure 4.1 Wants, Needs, and Demand Linkage to Bureaucratic Policymaking and Private Contractors

	INTERNAL	EXTERNAL
FORMAL	Internal/Formal	External/Formal
INFORMAL	Internal/Informal	External/Informal

Figure 4.2 Schema of Administrative Relationships of Control
Source: Gilbert 1959.

(2) formal-informal (legal-authoritative control vs. informal, nonbinding constraints). Figure 4.2 illustrates his conceptualization. These two dimensions are the organizing concepts of the analytic framework presented in figure 4.1. Though both informal constraints and formal controls have the ability to affect bureaucratic behavior, each affects that behavior in a different way. Formal control is highly visible and quite effective for setting goals.

The ever more important means-related decisions are often supplied by the force of informal influences. Formal control implies a power relationship. Influence requires persuasion, while control utilizes compulsion. Although each method of affecting behavior is important, it is often more advantageous to possess the power to control. This is because it is best to have both control and influence, and by definition those that control also influence. The threat of control itself tends to facilitate influence.

The internal/external dimension is perhaps less visible in figure 4.1. Along this dimension, we believe the most advantageous position for affecting bureaucratic behavior is internal. Examples of internal influencers or controllers are the president, appointed officials, professional norms and beliefs, and politics.

The analytic framework also illustrates the intermediary role in linkage played by political parties, public and special interest groups, and ad hoc political groups. The information-communication role played by academics, pollsters, and the media is highlighted. Although many Americans do not participate in the activities of active linkage mechanisms, the framework also points to citizen-bureaucracy linkage mechanisms that are mass-based. These mechanisms are indirect linkage achieved through the process of selecting and influencing elected leaders and direct linkage through direct contact with bureaucrats.[10]

The framework conceptualizes citizen participation programs as one component of a system of linkage. These programs are the main direct form of communication with unelected administrators and their private contractor staffs. Each component of this system has inherent strengths and weaknesses as a link between citizen and bureaucrat. However, as components of a system, inherent weaknesses in one area can be mitigated by strengths in other areas. If citizen participation programs do not permit certain types of influence on bureaucratic policymaking, perhaps this is because other components of the linkage system (Congress, for example) are expected to perform that particular type of linkage function.

Applying Gilbert's schema of administrative relationships of control (see figure 4.2) to existing literature, we see five avenues of citizen-bureaucracy linkages: (1) internal/formal, (2) internal/informal, (3) congressional (external/formal and informal), (4) judicial (external and internal/formal), and (5) external/informal. For linkage to the acts of private contractors and for accountability to flow from the acts of private contractors, the connection must "come through" the decisions and acts of unelected public officials. The citizen-bureaucracy linkage we are about to discuss is a necessary but not sufficient condition of contractor accountability to the public.

Citizen-Bureaucracy Linkage via Internal/Formal Mechanisms of Control

Internal/formal direction and control of the bureaucracy is exercised by the president and his executive office. This approach views the federal bureaucracy as a single, huge formal organization, with the president on top of a massive organization chart. It focuses on his formal channels of command and mechanisms of control over the bureaucratic actors who are considered his subordinates. Formal hierarchy featuring political control at the apex of the formal organization is relied upon to constrain and motivate bureaucratic decision making. Linkage is achieved through the selection and influence on the political actor at the head of each administrative organization, and ultimately through the election of the president. In addition, linkage is achieved between elections due to presidential sensitivity to public opinion polls and other indicators of citizen demand.

While presidential control over bureaucratic decision making is substantial, it is more often through the exercise of influence and not through commands. The president may issue orders and command individuals to carry them out, but this can be a costly enterprise (Neustadt 1976, 1990). The president's power is chiefly the "power to persuade," and he has enormously persuasive resources available for his use. Some of these resources stem from his position in the federal hierarchy. He appoints cabinet officers, judges, and other personnel.[11] The Office of Management and Budget (OMB), though itself a bureaucracy, is housed within his executive office and is reasonably responsive to his priorities. The presidential budget is prepared by OMB, and although it is modified by Congress, it is nevertheless "the most important influence on actual appropriations" (Mainzer 1973, 86). The president can use his budgetary power to stimulate bureaucratic compliance with his policy goals. The president can also influence the bureaucracy with his reorganization authority and through skillful use of the "presidential" personnel in his executive office.

Although its control of the bureaucracy is incomplete, the presidency remains a uniquely situated institution of linkage between government and the mass public. The president has a national constituency and is normally sensitive to public opinion. Although the degree of presidential influence on bureaucracy and the degree of public influence over the president are open to debate, the existence of these relationships of influence are generally unquestioned.

Citizen-Bureaucracy Linkage via Internal/Informal Mechanisms of Influence

Internal/informal constraints on bureaucratic policymaking are what John Gaus has termed the "inner check" on bureaucratic discretion (Gaus 1936, 40). These normative restraints are those "mechanisms within the bureaucracy and within individual bureaucrats that can serve as a guide to administration in the public interest" (Peters 1978, 227–28). Peters terms normative restraint "the cheapest form of control we might obtain, and in the end the most efficient in that it can prevent grievances rather than merely correcting them ex post facto" (1978, 228).

One source of internal/informal influence is said to stem from the "representativeness" of the bureaucracy (descriptive representation). That is, the socioeconomic status and attitudinal disposition of the mass public is thought to be closer to bureaucratic decision makers than to elected decision makers.[12] A second limit on "internal" behavior is the shared professionalism of certain bureaucratic actors (Friedrich 1968, 418). Another type of internal check on bureaucratic policymaking results from bureaucratic role playing. Like the delegate-type representative, the bureaucrat acts according to public preferences, even though he or she does not favor the action he or she is taking. Finally, the political judgments and reactions of bureaucrats constrain and influence bureaucratic policymaking. In Washington, D.C., informal contact with congressional or presidential staff helps a bureaucrat understand how particular policy decisions are likely to be perceived "up on the Hill" or "over at the White House."

It is difficult to determine how effective these internal/informal influences are in incorporating public preferences into bureaucratic policymaking. When coercion and overt manipulation are applied, unless the actor's attitude is changed, control is likely to be temporary. If linkage is to occur via internal/informal mechanisms, bureaucrats must be (1) aware of citizen preferences (direct linkage) and/or (2) aware of the preferences of elected leaders.

Generally, this form of linkage lacks a coercive component, and therefore the predisposition of the bureaucrat is the sole motivator of responsive behavior, which limits the capability of this avenue of linkage in one respect. However, a linkage-facilitating predisposition need not be directed toward the specific policy being proposed. If the internal/informal link is based on bureaucratic role playing, then the bureaucrat need not agree with the policy to be implemented, but only believe that he or she ought to play the role of responsive public official and give the public (or its representative) what it wants. While we see a great many examples of public officials playing this role, we have not seen much evidence that these norms extend to contractors. Nevertheless, such an issue belongs at the center of our research agenda.

Citizen-Bureaucracy Linkage via Congressional Control and Influence

Congress both controls bureaucracy (external/formal) and influences it informally (external/informal). The link between citizen and bureaucrat is indirect, but the public does exert some influence over congressional decision making. Stokes and Miller and Sullivan and O'Connor found that representative-constituent linkage, though less than perfect, does exist on certain issues (Stokes and Miller 1962, 531–46; Sullivan and O'Connor 1972, 1256–65). Legislative control of bureaucracy, the other component of this indirect linkage mechanism, while substantial, appears to be diminishing.

Congress has a number of devices for controlling bureaucratic activities: (1) the general power to set policy by statute, (2) review, investigation, audit, and oversight, (3) legislative veto, (4) personnel review, and (5) the power of the purse. Each of the formal powers available to Congress provides a measure of control over the bureaucracy, but the exercise of these powers is subject to limits. For example, Congress sets general policies, and that legislation is a major influence on bureaucratic behavior. However, legislative mandates are often vague and lack clear standards of enforcement (Lowi 1969, 1979).

Legislation is often simply a compact bargained between various interest groups. Bureaucracies are expected to transform these almost incoherent statutes into concrete programs. When Congress enacts vague legislation that requires bureaucrats to use a broad measure of discretionary authority to implement the law, Congress is abdicating its policymaking function. While Congress has attempted to enact more specific mandates in recent years, they only have a limited ability to keep up with an increasingly complex world.

Bureaucrats have the expertise to achieve the policy outcomes legislators want, and they therefore have significant leverage in bargaining with Congress. Congress has the legitimacy of the popular mandate. The importance of legitimacy should not be underestimated. In most cases, the bureaucrat's belief system includes a notion of the elected official as "on top" and the expert "on tap" (Friedrich 1968). Congressional power over the bureaucracy, therefore, is exercised through informal channels of influence as well as formal mechanisms of control.

Citizen-Bureaucracy Linkage through Judicial Control

Although the courts are not structured to serve as linkage mechanisms, there are several avenues of citizen influence on judicial decision making. Because judges are either elected or appointed by others who are elected, a type of citizen-bureaucracy linkage occurs during the election process. In addition, linkage occurs through individual citizen and class action suits brought against bureaucratic agencies.

A difficulty with court review of bureaucratic decision making is that these cases often involve highly complex and technical matters. Since judges generally lack the technical expertise to fairly judge these matters, administrative tribunals have been created. These quasi-judicial boards issue binding decisions and thus control bureaucratic behavior. Administrative tribunals are typically housed within the bureaucracy and only deal with one general type of issue.

Despite the advantages of administrative tribunals in complex or technical situations, there are some significant difficulties with courts, particularly the courts of the judicial branch, as controllers of the bureaucracy. The judicial process is slow and expensive, and it cannot deal with large numbers of cases. Courts are not effective in preventing wrongs, and they have limited power to enforce their decisions.

Citizen-Bureaucracy Linkage via External/Informal Influence

External/informal influence over bureaucratic behavior is highly dependent on active mechanisms of linkage (see figure 4.1). The direct involvement of political parties, interest groups, ad hoc movement groups, and citizens in bureaucratic decision making are forms of external/informal influence and linkage. The link is external because the involved organizations and individuals are not part of the agency's hierarchy and informal because the input provided by these groups and individuals is nonbinding advice.

External/informal linkage mechanisms have inherent weaknesses as linkages. First, they generally require active citizen participation. Americans tend not to participate in politics, and those that do participate are usually drawn disproportionately from the rich and powerful. Second, external/informal mechanisms have no formal authority over bureaucracies. As outsiders, those attempting to influence government through this avenue of linkage have to make special efforts to gain information on agency activities, and they must also take initiatives to gain meaningful access to agency policy formulation.

Unlike political parties, community-based groups, and interest groups, citizen participation programs are passive mechanisms of linkage. Citizen participation programs are generally not citizen controlled. Hence, citizen participation programs are external to the agency, are nonbinding, and are agency controlled. While political parties, community-based groups, and interest groups raise their own funds and staff their own secretariats, the resources utilized by citizen participation programs are controlled by government.

Taken together, these factors create a discouraging picture of the potential of formal, government-sponsored citizen participation programs as a citizen-bureaucracy linkage mechanism. At the same time, citizens do have some leverage over bureaucrats. Many participants in these formal programs have an independent, organized base of support outside government. Moreover, internal bureaucratic norms may discourage interfering with the efforts of citizen participants. Finally, many government officials want to be responsive to public demands. In many respects, the bureaucratic norm of wishing to be responsive may be the surest force ensuring effective linkage.

Citizen Participation Programs and Citizen-Bureaucracy Linkage

Participation seems to be an appropriate way to legitimize the exercise of power of unelected government officials in a democracy. The weakening of national political parties, movement politics, and representation through the blogosphere also appear to have contributed to the rise of this new linkage mechanism. During the nearly half century of growth of the citizen participation movement (Langton 1978; Roberts 2004; Weber 2000), the role and function of direct participation by the public in the decisions of unelected administrators and their contracted staffs have become important factors in the accountability of contractors in the American representational system.

Linkage and the Accountability of Contractors: Is the Chain of Accountability Stretched Too Thin?

Connecting the public to unelected officials is an issue that has received limited attention from public administration scholars—Friedrich, Waldo, and Gilbert in the 1940s and 1950s, Cohen and Eimicke in the 1970s. With the growth of the modern, outsourced economy, we again face this issue of citizen-bureaucracy linkage—but now we are yet another step removed from democratic legitimacy. The decisions set in public policy are increasingly carried out by private organizations that answer to their shareholders, boards of directors, or trustees rather than to elected public officials.

This chapter has explored the nature of linkage of citizens to unelected officials. Now, this analysis must be extended to the private firms working for these unelected leaders. To what degree can the linkage connecting the public to unelected government officials also connect the public to the behaviors of private contractors? More importantly, to what degree can the public hold private contractors accountable for their actions—either directly or indirectly through communication with elected and unelected government officials?

The problematic nature of citizen linkage to unelected officials is addressed in part through direct communication between the public and the bureaucracy. It is also addressed through the strong sense of responsibility and public ethics that is typical in American public service. This internal norm in government is a deeply ingrained element of government's organizational culture. Perhaps some of these same communication techniques and sense of public ethics can inform private contractors of public preferences and inspire them to pay attention to them. However, contractor behavior should be even more constrained than the acts of unelected government officials, since whatever actions they take must be approved or at least known by government officials.

In the end, we are not inclined to count on the norm of responsiveness to public demands and public service ethics to spread to contractor staff members. In our view, the key to accountability of contractor behavior is control by unelected government officials. In other words, an accountability chain is necessary. The chain begins with the public and its elected executive officials. Those elected executive officials are responsible for the work of their unelected employees and the contractors these unelected officials hire. When Rudolph Giuliani was mayor of New York City, a contractor with the city's Human Resources Administration placed a young girl into foster care who died at the hands of her guardian. Initially, the mayor attempted to assign blame to the contractor. While the contractor was at fault, the media and the public held the mayor accountable. He came to agree with this position and created a new agency exclusively focused on foster care. This agency re-engineered the foster care contracting system with new reporting requirements, more effective management controls, and better procedures for quality control.

The accountability chain is not a linear additive function. While additional links in the chain can increase the probability of a weak link, it only takes one weak link to eliminate control and accountability. There is nothing automatic about a vertically integrated, internal chain of command. Direct orders can be disobeyed. The issue is one of performance measures, reporting, and an organizational culture that understands the responsibilities involved in a public trust. We believe that the overall probability of establishing such accountability is lower when government contracts a function. When life-and-death issues are involved and extreme levels of accountability are required, contracting should be avoided. Most of the time, such extreme accountability is not needed and the issue then becomes one of establishing a set of performance indicators and management processes adequate to ensuring appropriate contractor performance.

Integrating Contract Management and Democratic Governance Principles

Overall, this chapter should provide the reader with an understanding of the difficulty of connecting modern government activity to democratic controls. Contracting increases the difficulty of establishing effective public-government linkage, but there are techniques that government can use to enhance linkage and accountability to the work of unelected officials and their private contractors. Developing and implementing these techniques are issues of governance and management that can be analyzed and addressed.

Our operational definition of representation for this work is responsive stewardship. Representative government is a core value in the United States. The cry "taxation without representation is tyranny" is incorporated into the collective memory in early childhood. It may be that the legitimacy of representation in government is so deeply embedded in the American political culture that policies formulated without it must fail.

What is the connection of representation to accountability? Our concern is that contractors not simply do what they think is permissible. Accountability is far more than simply doing what their contracts specify. Accountability requires that contractors act as the agents of a representative system where the directions they receive are designed to both respond to public views and ensure that government functions effectively. It is accountability to the spirit of the contract as well as the letter of the contract.

When the public's work is contracted out, it should be conceptualized as a representative chain that starts with the public and extends to elected leaders, then to unelected government officials, and finally to private parties that have entered into contracts with governmental units. While the cultures of the public and private sectors may be very different, private firms that accept public funds must also accept the responsibility of being the agents of the public. Just as private firms need not "go public" and can avoid SEC regulation by deciding not to raise capital in the public marketplace, so too can a firm forgo doing business with government. However, if that firm decides to do business with government, it becomes a private firm that is part of our system of democratic governance. It is in that way part of this system of accountability. To enforce this accountability, it is government's responsibility to actively monitor, measure, assess, and manage the work of its private agents.

After defining contracting, part I attempted to place contracting into context. We began by discussing the ethical dilemmas posed by government use of and interaction with private organizations. In chapter 3 we discussed the relationship of government contracting to the world of outsourcing and network management. Finally, in this chapter we discussed the challenges posed by contracting to the American system of representative democracy. We consider these analyses critical to the more instrumental and practical parts of the book that follow. We are, as always, driven by the need to improve the professional practice of public management. In our view, the responsible and effective public contract manager must have a deep appreciation of the ethical and accountability challenges posed by contracting. This is needed to inform the practice of contract management, the subject we now turn to.

Notes

1. Pitkin appears to place its first political use in the thirteenth and fourteenth centuries. Fairlie appears to agree with Beard and Lewis. See John A. Fairlie (1940, 238).
2. Fairlie (1940, 237) suggests an idea similar to a proposal by John Milton for a perpetual Parliament, which, once elected, would not be responsible to the electorates.
3. Also see Landis (1938, 10).
4. This phenomenon has been the subject of numerous analyses. V. O. Key (1942, 146) observed considerable administrative influence in legislative policymaking, as well as the substantial power of the bureaucracy to decide policy issues on its own, and correctly predicted that "the influence of administrative hierarchies is likely to grow." Long (1952, 810) wrote, "The bureaucracy is in policy, and major policy, to stay; in fact, barring the unlikely development of strong majority leadership, the bureaucracy is likely, day in and day out, to be our main source of policy initiative." Boyer (1964, 2) termed the growth of administrative policymaking "the outstanding legal development in this century."
5. Also in Altshuler (1968). Kaufman makes this point on page 85 in the Altshuler edition.
6. Although the laborer and soldier do have this power, it would not be prudent to ignore the fact that the "boss" has substantial resources with which to terrorize the laborer or soldier into obedient behavior. Likewise, political actors have weapons for securing bureaucratic compliance.
7. Dimmock (1936) originated this typology of bureaucratic discretion.

8. For a discussion of direction and control of bureaucracies, see particularly pp. 38–39.

9. See pp. 375–78. Gilbert identified the following values: (1) responsibility, (2) flexibility, (3) consistency, (4) stability, (5) leadership, (6) probity, (7) competence, (8) candor, (9) efficiency, (10) prudence, (11) due process, and (12) accountability.

10. This latter process has been termed "particularized contacts" by Verba and Nie.

11. The number of appointments made by presidents is only a small percentage of the total federal bureaucracy.

12. An excellent exposition of this idea appears in Long (1952, 808–18).

Part II

When Do You Contract, When Don't You Contract, and How Do You Find the Right Contractor?

Chapter 5

When Should You and
When Shouldn't You Contract Out?

THE FIRST contracting issue that public managers must face is the make-or-buy decision. This chapter focuses specifically on that issue. The issue of contracting out is one part of the role of the modern network manager. The manager asks: To what degree do we do this in-house? To what degree do we try to mobilize our network to take on this task? If we decide that the work should not be done in-house, is a contractual relationship needed? In our view, network management is an essential tool of the effective public manager (Cohen and Eimicke 2002). Learning when and how to obtain goods and services to help achieve your organization's mission is a key to success in an increasingly competitive and complex public marketplace. Without contracting, networking, and the use of market forces, you may hire too many people, use those people inefficiently, spend too much, and not be able to produce the highest quality goods and services. The profit motive of the private sector helps to ensure that the most efficient number of employees is hired and that they are used in the most efficient manner, helping to temper what could otherwise be an inefficient public sector. Sometimes the private sector can be brought in through a policy reform that provides them with incentives. We leave a discussion of that aspect of network management for another day and will focus this work on government contracting. Contract poorly or inappropriately and you will spend too much, not be able to produce the highest quality goods and services, and possibly fuel corruption.

Contracting is a complicated process. Managers must learn how to write contract requirements and elicit bids that obtain important services and products at the best possible price and quality. They must learn to work with, manage, and measure the performance of these outside private and nonprofit organizations. This two-way sharing of information is essential to decision making in a networked organizational environment. Managers must also learn how to participate in teams that include both public and private sector partners.

This chapter begins by acknowledging these realities, then explores the critical strategic managerial issue of when to do it yourself. Under what conditions is the task best performed directly by your own organization? When should you develop the capacity in-house instead of purchasing it from another organization? The most striking recent example of this issue took place in the early days of the war in Iraq. This war involved an ex-traordinarily large number of private contractors in the war zone, probably more than at any other time in recorded history. Yet at certain times dur-ing the war, private vendors refused to deliver services that might have placed their employees directly in harm's way. More problematic has been the presence of contractors in combat situations. This issue reached a cri-sis when the Blackwater security firm killed seventeen Iraqi civilians in September 2007. The contractors argued that they were acting in self-defense, but the central issue for this analysis is the work that brought them into harm's way and whether that work should have been done by U.S. troops. In addition to the issue of military policy and practice, there were also allegations of systematic overcharging for products such as gaso-line and abuse of prisoners by employees of these contractors.

One of the reasons for the high level of contracting by the Department of Defense (DOD) was a desire to keep the number of U.S. troops as low as possible. Contracting allowed DOD to provide services privately in-stead of using military personnel in some traditional support functions. The military deployment could then appear to be smaller than it was, cre-ating an image that was sought for political benefit.

There are, of course, many other examples of contracted efforts that do not succeed and are replaced by development of in-house capacity. Our objective is not to argue against contracting, but rather to enhance our understanding of the factors that limit it.

We strongly believe that contracting is a tool that managers must learn how to use effectively and that it is an important method for improving organizational performance. As Peter Drucker (1999) notes, a substantial and growing minority of the people who do the work of most organiza-tions work for an outsourcing contractor. The scarcest commodities in organizational life are the time and brainpower of the organization's management. It is important for top management to take great care in allocating that time and choosing areas of focus.

What are the political, strategic, organizational, financial, cultural, and other factors that make it difficult to contract out a function? Are there any patterns to contract failure that can be identified and known in advance? Our goal is to give managers faced with make-or-buy decisions a more sophisticated tool for making this key strategic decision.

The Make-or-Buy Decision and the Development of Distinctive Competence

In a private organization the make-or-buy decision is mainly a matter of organizational strategy: What type of organization do we want to be? Chester I. Barnard (1938) wrote that the development and maintenance of distinctive competence is the core definitional decision that management must make in any organization. This involves addressing the following types of questions: What do we do around here? How should we do what we do around here? What skills and competencies should we develop in-house, and what should we rely on vendors to produce?

An example of the make-or-buy decision is the decision made by many universities to outsource much of their food preparation. Most top universities are known for achieving world-class performance in the classroom and the research laboratory. In the kitchen, they need help. Private, outside vendors have been brought in at many universities, and food service has improved almost immediately. In making this decision, universities are deciding not to allocate scarce management time to managing food operations. They are making decisions about the areas of distinctive competencies they choose to develop and those they choose to purchase in the marketplace.

Making or buying is not the only way an organization makes decisions on distinctive competence. For example, IBM sold off its PC business to focus on servers, and U.S. Steel has evolved into a company mainly focused on energy. New York City's fire department has increased its focus on medical response, and the U.S. Environmental Protection Agency (EPA) has increased its emphasis on the human health impacts of environmental pollution. All these changes in emphasis are achieved outside of any consideration of the make-or-buy decision.

This chapter focuses on the relationship of the make-or-buy decision to the development of distinctive competence. Organizations can also make broad strategic decisions to develop new capacities due to emerging trends and opportunities. Such issues are important in defining organizations, but they are outside the scope of this work.

The decision not to contract, to make rather than to buy, is, at its heart, a decision to retain and emphasize an area of distinctive competence. An organization must ask itself the question: What work is so central to who we are and what we do that we must maintain the ability to do it ourselves?

One issue contracting poses to an organization is whether the organization should retain enough expertise in the functional area to properly manage the work that is contracted out. In this sense, the organization maintains enough competence to manage, if not perform, the function. The decision to contract is not an "on-off" switch for the development of in-house capacity, but rather a continuum. The competence needed to manage a contractor may or may not differ from what is needed to directly manage the work. Municipalities around the world have attempted to accomplish this by contracting out certain services by district, while keeping at least one district directly served by public employees. This was the case with solid waste disposal in Bogotá, Colombia, and Phoenix, Arizona (Osborne and Plastrik 1997; Eimicke, Cohen, and Perez Salazar 2000). Or, as Steel and Long concluded from their study of road maintenance and construction by Oregon counties, "it is important for counties to maintain an independent capacity to provide maintenance, improvement, and construction of roads to insure both least cost and quality service" (1998, 250).

The decision to contract a piece of work rather than perform it in-house affects the organization and the capacity it retains. So, in deciding to contract, it is essential to project the impact of contracting on the organization. One reason an organization develops distinctive competence is to compete for and obtain resources. An organization gains market share in the private sector, or missions and turf in the public sector, because it does something better than anyone else and can convince customers or elected officials to "purchase" its outputs. A danger with overcontracting is that an organization can lose its capacity to deliver outputs by becoming too reliant on the work of other organizations. These other organizations can develop quasi-monopolies and raise their prices and/or lower their quality and reliability. They can also become competitors. Over time they may be able to obtain their own resources without relying on the funds provided by your organization, or they may offer to take over the policymaking and coordination functions that you perform.

Therefore, the issue of contracting must be viewed in light of the issue of organizational capacity. It may well be that an organization seeks to get out of the direct business of delivering service and simply wants to set policy and manage contracts. In the 1980s, nearly all the homeless shelters in New York City were run directly by government. In 2004, the reverse was true—most of the homeless population lived in shelters run by nonprofit contractors for the city. The direct management of these facilities is no longer a core function of the city's government. The nonprofit contractors deal with the problems related to day-to-day shelter operations, while the city agency addresses overall policy issues. While implementing policy through contractors and networks can be difficult, freeing capacity needed to run the day-to-day operations of service provision enables the organization to focus its resources on creating sound public policy.

Why did New York City choose to get out of the direct homeless service business? As in many other circumstances where government opts for nonprofit service providers, the decision is often "guided by both ideological and utilitarian considerations" (Schmid 2003, 308). The advocates and media generally view nonprofits as mission driven and thereby more likely to do a better job of delivering social services than civil servants could. The contracting mechanism can also enable the public manager to "bypass bureaucratic constraints that would apply if they delivered the service directly" (Sharkansky 1989; Framer 1994; Schmid 2003, 308). In fact, many observers view the trend to contract with nonprofits as a means to use public funds more efficiently and make services more responsive by moving services and decision making closer to the consumer through the use of community-based nonprofit organizations (Bingman and Pitsvada 1997; Else et al. 1992; Hanly 1995; Ryan 1999). Overall, the city's altered capacity in assistance to the homeless did not impair service delivery and was, in the end, seen by practitioners as a positive development.

In sum, contracting out services changes the nature of the organization's own work, and it may have a positive or a negative impact (or a little of both). Before deciding to contract, an organization must determine if it is willing to accept this change in capacity. A negative impact on a capacity that the organization wishes to retain and develop is the first reason not to contract.

Contracting and Accountability

The fact that the New York City Department of Homeless Services does not directly run its own shelters may make it more difficult for them to control what goes on in the shelters, but it does not shield them from responsibility for actions that take place there. By separating policy formulation from implementation, there is a possibility that the control of implementation becomes more difficult. Government agencies must be certain to retain the capacity to manage the work of contractors and must ensure that contract provisions permit effective management. In situations where the contracted organization holds a monopoly, effective management is nearly impossible.

Making a service available through the private marketplace is not the same as providing a government service. Government administrators must be authorized by law before they can act. An elected legislature and executive must provide authority and resources before a government agency can perform a task. Those that authorize this work are responsible to the electorate for its effective performance. Those that perform this work are responsible to the elected officials who authorize it.

The chain of accountability stretches from authorization to actualization. The "chain of command" typically will include people in many different locations. The degree of administrative discretion can vary widely, as can the definition of the work being performed. When government uses a nongovernmental contractor to perform a task, the chain of accountability may be broken. On the other hand, if accountability is the degree to which a worker can be held responsible for the performance of a task, the issue of accountability may not be so clear-cut. If a government worker is a life-time, permanent employee of the government, it may be difficult to punish that worker for failure or provide a reward for success because of civil service protections, rules, and lifetime tenure. A contractor, on the other hand, could be subject to both termination and bonus clauses. The increased motivation could also be used to ensure that the contractor reports results and accepts direction from the public. In contrast, a government worker might simply ignore the public.

Therefore, the issue of accountability in many functional and program areas may be ambiguous. Other times, the issue may be quite clear. Furthermore, there very well may be program or functional areas where the issues of accountability are so profound that the work truly must be performed by government officials in a direct and meaningful chain of command. Issues of intelligence, national security, and law enforcement are prime areas that require further exploration.

Issues of chain of command and accountability are less important when we are trying to find out why a park bench was not painted than when we are trying to find out who allowed a terrorist into the country. Speed and a clear chain of command may be a matter of life and death. The ethical and moral authority to place an employee in harm's way is another example of a management function that does not belong in the private sector. While some tasks may involve some degree of risk, such as working in a location where weather or other conditions may pose danger, this is different from a war situation in which a worker might be shot at. In all cases of private work, workers can and must be given the opportunity to remove themselves from risk. In the case of work that is performed by government, such as fire and police protection or military service, the situation is reversed; those on these front lines can be punished for desertion or dereliction of duty if they refuse to face danger.

A more complicated situation arises when government contracts with nonprofit organizations to provide critical human services, such as home health care and foster care for children. Here, government officials are challenged to "hold nonprofits accountable without micromanaging them" (Buchanan and Snyder 2001, 13). The issue of accountability is one that recurs whenever we examine contracting. No matter what other issues are raised in a case of contracting, accountability seems to emerge as well. As a general rule, a reduced ability to ensure accountability in an area where accountability is critical is a second reason not to contract.

Contractors without Capacity

When an organization finds itself without the capacity to perform a task, it often makes the assumption that this capacity exists elsewhere and can be purchased. In the case of some military equipment contracts, the agency knows that the capacity does not exist and pays a contractor to develop this capacity. For example, to develop new weapons systems, the capacity purchased is the research and development infrastructure needed to build that new system. The military has decided that private firms are better suited to develop and maintain that capacity. The government then attempts, with a history of mixed success, to prevent the contractor from selling the capacity to foreign governments.

We are not arguing that one should not contract in the hopes of developing new capacity. The way that the military explicitly contracts to develop new weapons systems may very well be the best option available to develop such cutting-edge technology. Our concern arises when a contract is let out of desperation in the hope that the contractor can fix something the government has failed to provide. Cause for concern is heightened when an agency thinks the contractor knows how to do something when in actuality the capacity has not even been developed. The classic case of this type of contracting was the New York City Parking Violations Bureau under then mayor Ed Koch in the 1980s. The city let a contract for a handheld computer device that would permit parking enforcement agents to write and print tickets on the spot and download the records to a mainframe computer. The "prototype" that was delivered to the city was a plastic box with nothing inside. As a result of the scandal that followed, the Queens borough president killed himself, and a number of other people went to jail.

A less dramatic but more significant example of this phenomenon has been the contracting of the management of a public school system. In some cases this is a positive affirmation of a desire to improve quality. In other cases the elected leaders of a jurisdiction have given up the direct management of this critical governmental function in the hope that a private firm could do a better job. The resources to do the job may not be available, or the community may be in such a state of disarray that educators are asked to perform tasks that should be performed by families, religious institutions, or other parts of the community. Contracting under these circumstances may create unrealistic expectations and may simply not work.

The decision to buy a capacity or product that has yet to be produced is inherently risky. The capacity may never develop, or it might develop in an unexpected fashion. The organization that develops the new capacity might then have a monopoly and may decide to charge an exorbitant price for the service or product. The strategic issue for the organization relates to the options available. What alternatives does the organization have to access the capacity it requires? How critical is development of this new capacity? Is there any way to develop this capacity in-house?

If the organization must contract to develop a new capacity, it should also develop a contract instrument that allows it to own what it has paid to develop. The organization should also ensure that an effective method is developed to assess contractor performance. In the absence of such a tool for performance measurement, an organization could end up with the portable computer bought by New York City's Parking Violations Bureau—the empty plastic case.

Critical and Noncritical Functions—Under What Conditions Can a Task Not Be Delegated?

One would assume that there are some functions so central to an organization's functioning that they should not be contracted out. For example, one might assume that a university cannot contract out instruction and an army cannot contract out fighting. However, we have examples of both forms of contracting. A fashion company like Calvin Klein not only contracts out clothes manufacturing, it also contracts out for design work. The organization's distinctive competence has evolved into branding and marketing, and it mainly performs communication and quality control functions. Similarly, the military in Iraq has contracted out security functions that are traditionally the preserve of their own soldiers. Finally, universities are increasingly entering into consortium arrangements with other schools to provide instruction in areas they do not wish to cover.

The core function of an organization can change over time as an organization's strategy changes. Often, strategic change is a response to new technologies as well as a change in society or in patterns of economic consumption.

When Shouldn't an Organization Contract?

There is no universal rule of when to avoid contracting other than a connection to organizational strategy and the presence of contractor capacity. An organization should not contract if capacity it deems essential is impaired or if the quality of a good or service will deteriorate below acceptable standards. We also suspect that in situations when an extremely high level of accountability is required, vertically integrated command-and-control hierarchies are more appropriate than contracted network relationships. The need for high levels of accountability tends to be common in life-and-death situations and in performing criminal justice functions.

Politically sensitive issue areas that require a high degree of confidentiality or the ability to modulate a response action to a fine degree of variation are also examples of situations where contracted relationships might be unwise. The difficulty that command communications have when penetrating complex hierarchies and the problems faced by expert advice as it works its way up the chain of command are well-known management dysfunctions. Diane Vaughan identifies this issue in her analysis of the Challenger space shuttle disaster when she discusses the difficulty that lower-level but expert staff had in influencing decision making (1996). In his classic treatment of the Cuban missile crisis, Graham Allison discusses President John Kennedy's concern that his instructions to naval officers for modifications in standard naval interdiction and blockade procedures would be ignored or misunderstood (1971). We have no reason to believe that contracted relationships would eliminate these problems. In fact, we suspect they would be exacerbated by the added impediment of organizational self-interest and distinct organizational cultures.

As we mentioned earlier, our deepest concern about the decision to contract is that some ideologically oriented decision makers have a bias toward the private sector—or to the public sector—that colors their thinking about this issue. The decision to contract is complex and requires a clear analysis of costs and benefits. In no case is the make-or-buy decision a cost-free one. Something is always gained and something is always lost. The issue is: Are the gains more important to the organization and its mission than the losses?

Let us return to the issue of accountability as a rationale for avoiding contracting. In chapter 9 we will discuss the problems of military contracting in the war in Iraq, and we mentioned this issue in chapter 2 as well. Military action requires a clear chain of command and requires military discipline when orders from that chain are not obeyed. History tells us that military discipline breaks down during times of great stress but is essential for operating during such times. The need for immediate decision and response and for a clear and direct relationship to public authority leads us to avoid interorganizational relationships and communication during war. This is difficult when services branches like the army and navy must cooperate. The addition of private organizations to this already challenging work environment makes it difficult to develop and maintain this type of discipline.

In addition to this issue of coordination, there is also the issue of the legitimacy of private action. If government, duly constituted, takes the life of a person under its jurisdiction, that is tragic, but in all likelihood it is a legitimate and legal act of government. A private organization is not authorized to take someone's life or liberty. Moreover, such authorization of private acts without the ethical rules and political norms regulating government's behavior opens the door to illegitimate acts by private parties. These are therefore instances when contracting should be avoided if at all possible.

Similarly, if there is a pattern of corruption and contract abuses in a particular program, it might be appropriate to perform contracted tasks in-house until the corrupt practices are eliminated. Of course, the opposite could happen: A dysfunctional pattern of payoffs by corrupt government officials can be disrupted by having private contractors replace public officials in implementing a program.

Developing a Contracting Strategy

Just as a manager decides the mix of skills and the level of experience needed within an organization to implement programs, so too should a manager develop a strategy for deciding when and what to contract. Not all these decisions follow goal-seeking rational patterns. Sometimes there is an opportunity to hire someone with a unique mix of skills, and you build your organizational capacities around the strengths and weaknesses of that individual. This can influence the mix of internal staff and contractor capacity that you put together. Sometimes you identify capacity in a contractor's organization that you would like to own within your organization—and we see many examples of parts of a contractor firm joining the government. At other times you find that the contractor refuses to join your organization, although that is your preference, and the only way to access that talent is through the private organization.

The obvious first step in developing a contracting strategy is to inventory all the capacity you need to implement your program. With that inventory in hand, you are then ready to decide which of those capacities you prefer to own and which you prefer to buy. There is a tendency for certain types of capacity to develop in the public sector and other types to develop in the private sector. Some capacities tend to be found in the nonprofit part of the private sector, while other capacities are more frequently found in the for-profit sector. These are tendencies and not absolute laws. Sometimes a capacity you would expect to find in the government happens to be present in a private firm. Sometimes you will find the reverse to be the case. A contracting strategy will take advantage of these opportunities and not allow preconceived notions to interfere with the development of needed capacity.

The development and accessing of capacity will change over time, and a contracting strategy should reflect this dynamic dimension of capacity building. Sometimes you incubate a capacity internally and then you devolve it to private firms. The development of the Internet followed this course. It began as an internal Defense Department project with heavy government leadership and implementation. It then became a contracted-out government function and eventually became a regulated private activity.

Conclusions

We are not against contracting. We think that in many cases it is a good way to deliver public services. Contracting is, however, a tool—a means and not an end. Just because we have a hammer doesn't mean we need to find a nail. There are situations when contracting should be avoided. One should avoid the mindset that contracting represents more advanced or sophisticated management. There are situations where bringing in outsiders is appropriate and necessary. There are also situations where contracting is a bad idea. In this chapter we introduce the notion that the make-or-buy decision should be left to managers and, wherever possible, removed from political decision makers, not an easy goal to accomplish. However, the key is to bring contracting into the routine toolbox of the effective public manager. Political people don't typically try to influence the accounting system or the human resource management process used by the agency. The objective here is to routinize contracting and promote the concept that the make-or-buy decision is a routine management practice, not worthy of the attention of elected officials.

With this chapter we have begun our focus on the "nuts and bolts" of contracting. The first obvious contract management issue that public managers face is the make-or-buy decision. Our treatment of this issue began by delineating government functions that should generally not be contracted. We hasten to add, however, that most of government's work does not involve the need for extremely high levels of accountability or raise issues of life and death. For most government organizations, the make-or-buy decision is one that is amenable to analysis and strategy. While most government operations *could* be contracted out, that does not mean they *should* be contracted out. The next chapter makes the assumption that you have decided to contract out a service or function. Once that decision has been made, the public manager must identify potential contractors. In chapter 6, we ask: How do you find the right contractor?

Chapter 6

How Do You Find the Right Contractor?

IN OTHER CHAPTERS and other places (Cohen and Eimicke 2002, 143–56), the wisdom of contracting out is questioned by a number of major scholars, particularly because of its impact on democratic government (Milward 1994; 1996; Milward and Provan 2000). Unfortunately, the decision to contract is sometimes based solely on ideological belief that whatever can be privatized should be privatized. A more thoughtful argument for contracting out government services is that competition will sometimes lead to better public goods and services at lower cost.

As we discussed in chapter 2, governments that fully embrace the competition principle may decide it is feasible and desirable to permit government agencies to compete with private contractors. Former Indianapolis mayor Steve Goldsmith won the Innovations in American Government award for his public-private competition program in the 1990s (Osborne and Hutchinson 2004, 149–57). A key element in Indianapolis's contracting effort was its reliance on a yellow pages test—if there are five or more companies listed under a particular product or service in the community's yellow pages, then that community should consider either a competition or outsourcing (Goldsmith 1997, 13–27).

Despite the concerns regarding the hollowing out of the state, the high and often hidden transaction costs in contracting, and concerns about accountability and failures of performance of the magnitude of the United States war in Iraq, we expect that the contracting out of government services will not only continue but will expand at an even more rapid pace. The challenge facing most public managers is not whether to contract but how to contract most effectively. Facing this reality, it is essential that managers learn to do a better job of finding the right contractor.

Finding the right contractor is not as simple as it sounds, as anyone who owns an older home learns when a pipe breaks, the roof leaks, or the water heater stops working. The process becomes much more complicated when a manager of a public organization must find a contractor. A wide array of laws and regulations comes into play, most very well intentioned and designed to ensure open competition, fairness, honesty, accountability, and security. The effective contract manager complies with these process protections and also comes up with a contractor that does the job well.

In this chapter we will look at a variety of methods that public agencies use to find the right contractor. We will then discuss the methods of ensuring contracting capacity, oversight of the contractor, and contractor accountability. Next, we will examine techniques for measuring and improving contractor performance. Finally, we discuss the rapid growth in government contracts with nonprofit organizations.

Identifying a Broad Range of Eligible Contractors

Most governments have formal requirements for advertising the availability of government contracts. Historically, these legal requirements mandated the publication of solicitation in official government publications and often in major area newspapers and relevant trade journals. Increasingly, business trade is done over the Internet, and government is rapidly catching up to the private sector in "e-commerce."

As government expands the scope and volume of contracting, it is going beyond advertising to a more proactive outreach to encourage contractors to bid on government contracts. In New York City, the Department of Small Business Services (NYCDSBS) has established a Procurement Outreach Program (POP) that helps businesses develop the capacity and expertise to identify and bid on federal, state, and city contracts. The POP staffers offer a monthly training seminar, "How to Sell to Government," which includes a question-and-answer session and the distribution of information packages on mayoral agencies and independent agencies (NYCDSBS 2006, 1). There is also a citywide site with a wide array of information for new and existing vendors aptly titled "sell to NYC" (NYC .gov 2006).

At the federal level, the U.S. Small Business Administration (SBA) offers a similar business-friendly, web-based outreach and education site called Contracting 101 (U.S. Small Business Administration 2006). The site provides basic information on how government buys goods and services, describes the various forms of solicitation, and links the reader to sites listing all procurement opportunities in excess of $25,000 (www .FedBizOpps.gov) and the rules and regulations for the federal procurement process, the Federal Acquisition Regulation (FAR). In October 2001, the federal government shifted from the more traditional, historically print-based solicitation in the Commerce Business Daily (CBD) to the web-based FedBizOpps.

Governments use a variety of methods to select contractors. The most common techniques are a sealed bid and a request for proposals (RFP). A sealed bid is used when the product or service is relatively easy to define, is widely available in the marketplace, and both the unit cost and total contract amount are modest (total purchases of less than $100,000). Since quality is assumed to be standard, the sealed bid is awarded to the lowest bidder. The sealed bid must be received by a specific deadline. All bids are opened in public and recorded. The contract is awarded to the lowest bidder that meets all the specifications of the bid.

Sealed bids are relatively easy and inexpensive to administer. The procedure works well for "off the shelf" items such as office supplies, cleaning products, and simple food items. Sealed bids are less useful for complex services such as day care, home health care for the elderly, complex equipment for law enforcement or the military, or computer hardware and software.

Requests for proposals, or RFPs, are used for purchases of higher amounts ($100,000 or more) and/or when the product or service is technical, approaches vary widely, or the government is not exactly sure about the best approach. The RFP will set out what problem it seeks to solve or what need it seeks to meet, then ask those interested in bidding to tell them what they think is the best approach, balancing price and level of performance. As government contracts out more services and requires complex technological solutions, the RFP is being used ever more frequently.

To avoid charges of favoritism and to enable intelligent choices among what might be significantly different proposals, RFPs should include a predetermined scoring system so that bidders are aware of how their proposals will be judged. The government agency must also assemble a knowledgeable staff to independently score the proposals and a predetermined methodology to choose among the bidders with the highest scores. RFP bids can be negotiated after submission, but again the government agency involved must take care to ensure that fairness is assured, in fact and in appearance.

When government is even less certain of what it needs to solve a problem or meet a need, it may issue a Request for Qualifications or a Request for Quotation (RFQ). A response to an RFQ cannot be accepted as a bid and lead directly to a contract but it can help to educate the government agency about its need and establish the qualifications of the responding organization to obtain a contract through a subsequent sealed bid, RFP, or negotiated or sole-source procurement.

Negotiated or sole-source contracting is generally discouraged in the public sector because the appearance of favoritism is so hard to avoid. Sole-source contracting may be used when there is only one supplier of an essential commodity or service—a medical device, a weapons system, a medication, or a special security system—or in an emergency circumstance such as a flood or terrorist attack where lives are a risk. A negotiated contract might also be used when a delay in acquiring the product or service might result in substantial cost overruns for a larger construction project or weapons system.

To ensure the widest possible distribution of its notices of solicitation, governments may develop lists of bidders. Organizations interested in competing for government business fill out an enrollment application and are placed on a mailing or e-mail list so that they automatically receive notification of solicitations for government contracts. In certain circumstances, where work is complicated, technical, and predictable, government agencies may develop prequalified lists of vendors. Those on the prequalified list might apply for construction projects, auditing, maintenance and repair, road work, and snow removal.

Governments may also make special provisions to ensure that small, locally based businesses and businesses owned by minorities and women have access to public contracts. These provisions may include preference for subcontracts from larger contracts, exemption from bonding requirements, prompt payment guarantees, and technical assistance. Government wants to buy the highest quality at the lowest possible price but it may also want to ensure that local citizens and businesses that provide its taxes and revenues have a reasonable chance to participate in the business opportunities provided by their government. Governments that are fully committed to a transparent and competitive contracting process will reach out to a broad range of stakeholders concerning the decision to contract and in assessing the efficacy of contracts after they are awarded.

Ensuring Capacity, Oversight, and Accountability

Finding the right contractor is the first step in effective contracting. Government and vendors must then have or develop the capacity to manage the contracting process (Brown and Potoski 2003, 153–64). Capacity includes the ability to find the right contractor, to negotiate contract terms, to monitor the work in progress, to reward performance, and to evaluate outputs and outcomes. Government has always been in the procurement business, but the amount of contracting, particularly for services previously provided by government workers, has been increasing since the 1980s. Unfortunately, the expansion in the number and complexity of government contracts has not been "balanced with a major investment of resources in the development of good public management" (Sclar 2000, 157). In particular, contract management is in need of greater attention by public managers.

While Sclar (2000) is pessimistic about the prospects of public contract management capacity catching up with pressures to increase contracting, the research of Brown and Potoski (2003) suggests that governments can and do adjust their contract capacity when confronted with problems such as poor outcomes, high transaction costs, or stakeholder opposition. Whether optimistic or pessimistic, scholars generally agree that government contract management capacity is critical to positive contract outcomes and that contract capacity needs to be strengthened (Kettl 1993).

Capacity to contract involves several components. First, government must have staff members with the skills and capacity to answer the make-or-buy decision. For some, this is as simple as the yellow pages test used in Indianapolis: Are there at least five private firms offering the good or service in question listed in the local telephone book? For others, this capacity must also extend to the ability to make a judgment regarding the efficacy, appropriateness, and even the ethics of contracting. We have sometimes referred to this process as the functional matching analysis—services are more optimally delivered by certain sectors such as justice by government, health care by nonprofits, and consumer electronics by the private sector.

Capacity also involves the resources, expertise, and experience to manage the contracting process. This includes choosing the best bid process—lowest price, sealed bid, sole source, or request for proposals; a transparent and defendable mechanism for selecting the winning bidder; and a legal team to draft and reach agreement on the actual contract. Many governments may have capacity to perform each of these tasks but not in sufficient depth to handle a significant shift to contracting out of service delivery.

Finally, capacity must also encompass the ability to evaluate contractor performance. Evaluation goes beyond simply monitoring the activities of the contractor to ensure they deliver the services they bill for. Evaluation addresses the question: "Did we really achieve the results and get the benefits we thought we would gain from contracting out?"

For all three aspects of capacity, there is reason for serious concern. Government is motivated to contract out by the expectation that it can save money and reduce the public employee headcount. As contracting out continues to increase, it is possible that government will be less and less able to ensure positive outcomes. Research by Brown and Potoski suggests that governments that invest in contracting capacity are not immune from problems, but they are "better positioned to avoid these threats and to prevent full-scale contracting disasters" (Brown and Potoski 2003, 162).

A number of practitioners and scholars also agree that government managers can address this capacity gap by working collaboratively with a wide range of contractors, suppliers, customers, advocates, and intermediaries (Goldsmith and Eggers 2004; Brown and Potoski 2004). To participate in this network, government will need to recruit or develop people with collaborative skills. This will require new training and recruitment strategies and a redefinition of what it means to be a public employee (Goldsmith and Eggers 2004, 178).

Goldsmith and Eggers suggest that the public sector needs to downsize and upsize simultaneously—substantially reducing the number of public employees at the lower and middle levels while adding more highly skilled experts and managers at the top (2004, 186–88). These new additions will need skills in team management, risk assessment, the use of cutting-edge technology, and the willingness to lead change. They will also need a range of skills that are quite specific to government contracting and discussed at the end of this chapter.

This kind of fundamental change in the culture of public employment is neither simple nor easy. In a rush to reduce the size and cost of government, the importance of holding contractors accountable has often been neglected. In many cases, it is assumed that performance-based contracts will automatically ensure accountability, but all too often this has not been the case (Romzek and Johnston 2005). This is not to say that accountability is impossible or even unlikely to be achieved. For example, Virginia's Commonwealth Competition Council has been continuously improving its comprehensive process since 1995 (McMahon, Moore, and Segal 2003).

On the other side of the accountability challenge, congressional hearings during the summer of 2006 focused on the "consistent poor contract management" at the Department of Homeland Security (DHS) throughout its history (Miller 2006). A report prepared at the request of Representatives Tom Davis and Henry Waxman found that thirty-two contracts worth $34.3 billion had "experienced significant overcharges, wasteful spending or mismanagement" (U.S. House of Representatives Committee on Government Reform 2006, i). In 2005, more than 50 percent of DHS contracts were awarded without full and open competition. It is worth noting that while contracting increased by 189 percent, the acquisition workforce increased only 20 percent. The DHS inspector general also questioned the supervision, qualifications, and ethics training of the department's contracting officers (U.S. House of Representatives Committee on Government Reform 2006, 6).

In their study of social services contracting, a large and ever expanding area of government contracting, in Kansas, Romzek and Johnston found that public managers were quite adept at writing contracts that enabled them to determine whether or not contractors were meeting their obligations (2005, 446). Unfortunately, they found poor performance in performance data collection, even though performance measures were clear and well-defined in the contract. The authors conclude that the complexity of the contractor networks and associated technologies hindered rather than enhanced accountability. When appropriate performance information was available and sanctions were called for, they were seldom applied. Romzek and Johnston suggest that this is partially the result of political influence but perhaps more importantly reflects the absence of an adequate supply of alternative suppliers (2005, 446).

Goldsmith and Eggers agree that measuring and tracking performance remain major challenges for public management (2004, 145). However, they cite numerous examples of how technology has enabled governments to assess both the performance of overall networks and individual members. Among the best practitioners identified in their work were Wisconsin's Department of Workforce Development, Arizona and Ohio's Departments of Motor Vehicles, Oklahoma's Community Rehabilitation Services Unit, and New Mexico's Department of Transportation.

Brown and Potoski's study of refuse collection contracting in the Columbus, Ohio, metropolitan area found that public managers can effectively manage the market and the network supporting it through a range of monitoring and benchmarking activities (2004, 656–68). Their study found that managers learned about more effective penalty clauses from neighboring contracting governments, were able to recruit new bidders from nearby districts, and learned about contractor reliability through informal contacts with managers from other governments.

What these authors conclude is that ensuring accountability of government contractors, particularly in a networked environment, is more art than science. We consider contract management, like all management, to be a craft. No contract can provide for all eventualities. The most apparently logical performance incentive can have unintended negative consequences. Shifting of risks can cost more than sharing the risk. The effective public contract manager must remain flexible, work with contractors on a daily basis to improve work processes, and use the power of discretionary contract renewal as the ultimate performance incentive.

Measuring and Improving Contractor Performance

In our view, performance measurement is critical to contract management—"contractual relationships with private and nonprofit firms provide the surest way to punish poor performance: contract termination" (Cohen and Eimicke 2000c, 102). A properly designed performance management system can help a public manager decide whether it makes more sense to contract or to perform the task in-house. If contracting is the decision, then performance management can help make the best choice among competing contractors. An effective, real-time performance measurement system can allow contract managers and contractors to recalibrate resource allocations, assignments, and strategy. If the measures are accurate and on target they can help modify contractor behavior.

At the federal level, contracting has moved from a support activity into a primary management function. Lawrence Martin attributes this shift to a confluence of five major factors: a general acceptance of privatization and contracting out, an explosion in service contracting, a substantial downsizing in the federal workforce (now exacerbated by the retirement of the baby boom generation), the Government Performance and Results Act (GPRA) requiring annual agency performance management reports to Congress, and the performance-based contracting experiment by the Office of Federal Procurement (Martin 2003, 88–91). While performance contracting is growing rapidly at the federal level, state and local governments have been using performance contracts in a variety of forms for more than a decade (Martin 2002).

Performance contracts need not be extremely complicated but that does not mean they are easy to design or employ effectively. At a minimum, performance contracts must include objective performance standards, rewards for superior performance, and penalties for failure to meet a minimum baseline (Osborne and Hutchinson 2004, 180–81). Contractors can share in savings achieved for the government, receive a portion of revenues increased, and/or be rewarded for high customer/citizen satisfaction or for delivering the product or service more quickly than anticipated. Conversely, they can be punished for failing to meet the minimum requirements of the contract.

We recognize that contractors will use their influence with elected officials to "cut red tape" and minimize the "interference of rule-driven bureaucrats." Politically connected contractors will try to avoid complying with contract provisions they previously agreed to but now find "onerous" and use friendly legislators and staff members to apply pressure to government contract managers and monitors. And when contract re-newal time rolls around, the contract manager is sure to receive many phone calls and e-mails from elected officials and "interested citizens" expressing unbridled support for even the worst-performing contractor. The wisdom of involving a broad range of stakeholders throughout the contract process becomes most valuable in these circumstances. The ef-fective contract manager can draw on the unbiased feedback from a wide range of knowledgeable and involved stakeholders to resist political pres-sure to renew a poorly performing contractor.

The Growth in Contracts with Nonprofit Organizations

Lester Salmon uses the national response to the tragedy of September 11, 2001, to tell the story of opportunities and challenges facing the nonprofit sector as a partner in public service in the early years of the twenty-first century (Salmon 2003). As Salmon documents, more than 70 percent of Americans contributed a total of more than $1.3 billion to more than two hundred charitable organizations to assist in the relief efforts following September 11. While these nonprofit organizations were enormously suc-cessful in the mobilization stage, they encountered substantial problems in program delivery, coordination, timeliness, and even transparency and credibility (Salmon 2003, 3).

At the same time, welfare reform and the government mobilization to deal with emerging problems such as homelessness and AIDS would not have been possible without the work of nonprofit organizations (Miranda and Andersen 1994; Kettner and Martin 1994; Savas 2002). Nonprofit or-ganizations in the United States employ about eleven million paid workers and attract close to six million full-time volunteers (Salmon 2003, 8). Non-profit organizations deliver a substantial portion of the nation's health and hospital services, AIDS and homeless services, higher education, day care, and classical arts. The fastest-growing area of nonprofit activity is con-tracts with government, even when welfare-reform-related contracts are excluded. As Steven Rathgeb Smith comments, "[n]onprofit service agen-cies receiving government contracts are now part of the nation's public service system" (2005, 388).

While government contracts now make up a substantial portion of the work and revenues for nonprofit organizations, for-profit organizations are becoming increasingly involved in areas previously the sole domain of nonprofits. For-profit businesses are buying up nonprofit hospitals and competing for government contracts for job training, child care, welfare-to-work, operating elementary and secondary schools, and even helping ex-offenders re-enter society (Frumkin 2002). Peter Frumkin suggests that nonprofit organizations, in competing with for-profits for government contracts, face significant challenges, including smaller size, limited access to outside capital, less access to political power, limited capacity to hire the best and the brightest, and certain normative constraints (2002, 4–12).

It is the normative constraints that Frumkin believes may pose the most important obstacle for nonprofit organizations, particularly as government moves increasingly to performance-based contracts. He suggests that for-profit firms will do whatever is necessary to get these contracts, meet the terms, and earn their profits, regardless of the long-term consequences for the clients. Nonprofits will often face the unattractive prospect of abandoning their work with low- or no-return, special needs clients in order to receive contract funding. There may be times when an organization's mission and its financial viability will be on a collision course.

The reality that better may not always be cheaper places the public contract manager in the crucial position of choosing the proper criteria to use when soliciting and awarding government contracts, particularly in the field of human services. For-profit firms may have an advantage on price, but nonprofits may be better able and more willing to stick with and ultimately really help the hard-to-serve and those most in need. Unfortunately, studies comparing the performance of for-profits and nonprofits in terms of quality and cost are limited and inconclusive (Frumkin 2002, 14; Sanger 2003).

With data on performance and quality inconclusive, politics, fairness, and the ever-present pressure to do more with less in government will inevitably lead many public contract managers to focus on cost as the only certain, uniform, and therefore fair basis for award. This is a frightening prospect in areas such as health care, long-term care for the elderly, child and adult day care, and mental health services. All too often, the only good for-profit care in these areas is the highest, not the lowest, cost option. If for-profits drive nonprofits out of these areas with minimum pricing and then fail to provide even minimally acceptable care, government may be stuck taking back these services, spending all it "saved" and more. As Sanger notes, "when caseloads decline and easier-to-place clients are scarce, the for-profits are likely to move on to other human service areas where they can increase their market share, economies, and profits" (2003, 106).

To overcome this, public program and contract managers should consider factors other than cost when setting criteria for contractor selection. Points should be awarded for documented past success in delivering quality outcomes, as measured by other governments, customers, and/or independent third parties. In fields where success has been difficult to achieve—foster care, substance abuse treatment, and prisoner re-entry, for example—points could be awarded for innovative approaches that might lead to new best practices (Frumkin 2002, 16). Government can also break up the workload into large and small assignments, divide workload by geography and give preference to some community-based providers, reward experience in the field and in the community, and/or reward collaborations between for-profit and nonprofit providers.

Not all observers are so concerned about the importance of maintaining a balance between for-profit and nonprofit providers in the distribution of government human services contracts. Savas makes the case that vouchers can introduce more competition and choice for clients of social services but that such systems are difficult for nonprofit organizations because nonprofits are usually short on working capital and therefore prefer the more steady stream of funding that contracts generally provide (2002, 90). For Savas, "[i]t is easy to argue that the preferred program should emphasize client outcomes rather than agency interests" (2002, 90).

Vouchers are an appealing solution in theory. Vouchers enable a class of citizens (often those with low incomes) to purchase socially desirable or necessary goods in the marketplace. Unlike government subsidies or grants, vouchers put resources in the hands of the consumer rather than the supplier of the good or service. For example, to ensure that poor families have enough food, government can buy food directly from farmers and give it to the poor. In a voucher system, government provides poor families with a prefunded "credit card" they can use to purchase the food they desire at the same supermarkets as other citizens. The supermarket then brings the "credit card charge receipts" to the specified government agency for reimbursement. Grants and subsidies are supplier driven and meet the needs of suppliers first and consumers second. Vouchers give consumers the power to exercise choice in a competitive marketplace.

In practice, from school vouchers to job training programs, voucher programs have encountered serious problems. Vendor fraud is an ongoing problem. Government seldom funds vouchers to a level sufficient to give clients access to the higher-tier or even middle-tier providers. Quality standards are difficult to specify for many social services. For food services, vouchers can work very well. The food stamp program has been a clear success. For job training and vocational education, the history of vouchers is filled with stories of high student debts, poor education, and no jobs at the end of the process. Savas contends that vouchers solve the problem of standards because voucher recipients can make their own choices. The experience in vocational education leads us to question this argument.

Conclusion

The contracting out of government services has been expanding for more than twenty-five years, coinciding with an international movement toward privatization ignited by Margaret Thatcher and Ronald Reagan. The supply of available contractors has increased dramatically over that time, aided by the rapid expansion of the Internet and related concepts of "e-commerce" and "e-government." Today, the challenge for the effective government contract manager is less about finding potential suppliers of goods and services and more about developing systems to ensure that contractors deliver the best possible goods and services at the lowest possible price.

This challenge of ensuring contractor performance is relatively simple when purchasing goods such as office supplies, computers, or even food services. What makes government contracting so complex today is that human services such as child care, elder care, job training, education, and even security services—generally considered the core functions of the public sector—are now being contracted out to for-profit and nonprofit agencies. Finding the right contractor is complicated by potentially conflicting objectives for government contracting—cheaper may not be better or faster, and better may end up costing more. Finding the right contractor begins with reaching consensus among a broad range of stakeholders on the objectives for the services to be contracted. Next, the effective contract manager must find appropriate methods to measure contractor performance. Finally, the contract manager must identify effective incentives and penalties to ensure that the contractor achieves the desired outcomes.

Part III

How Do You Manage Contractors?

Chapter 7

Managing Contracts
*The Skills You Need and What Can Go Wrong—Twenty
Common Problems in Contracting*

THERE IS an emerging literature on the use of contracts by government and the private sector. Network management is becoming a way of life throughout our public and private economy. A great deal of scholarship has been devoted to analyzing the decision to privatize and to providing advice to decision makers about how and when to contract out (Avery 2000). Murem Sharpe has written that contracting out has become a normal response to economic change in the private sector and that workers have learned to adapt to this new world (1997). George Boyne has analyzed the outsourcing decision by local governments in an effort to understand the influence of fiscal stress, market structure, and politics on the make-or-buy decision (1998b). Osborne and Gaebler (1992) noted the usefulness of contractor competition in improving the effectiveness and efficiency of government organizations, an argument also made by John Rehfuss (1991) when he compared contracting out in the United States and Great Britain.

A wide variety of scholars are skeptical about the benefits of contracting out (Harrison and Stanbury 1990; Hirsch 1995; Sclar 1994, 2000). Sclar questions the assumption that contracting leads to cost savings, citing transaction costs and the absence of competitive markets for most of the work performed by government (2000). Others note that while contracting out can save money, it will only do so if a private market exists for the services being purchased (Rehfuss 1991; Johnston and Romzek 1999). Jonas Prager, like Sclar, notes that contracting out should only take place after government analyzes the cost of letting contracts and monitoring performance. Globerman and Vining (1996) also cite the importance of analyzing transaction costs. Prager considers it essential that direct government provision of service be carefully analyzed as an option when considering contracting programs.

Scholars have also analyzed the effect of contracting on government effectiveness and legitimacy. This literature has been best summarized and analyzed in Brinton Milward's pathbreaking work on what he terms "the hollow state" (Milward 1994, 1996; Milward and Provan 2000). Gilmour and Jensen have written of the need to redefine our formal concepts of government accountability to deal with the facts of increased privatization (1998). Bardach and Lesser raise the issue of accountability to particular parties versus accountability for results (1996). In their view, before developing accountability mechanisms one must decide to whom management is accountable and for what government is accountable (Bardach and Lesser 1996). While concerns about the hollowing out of government are important and worrisome, increases in contracting activity are widely reported (McDavid and Clemens 1995; Greene 1996; Light 1999). A number of observers have discussed the need for more sophistication in government contract management (Johnston and Romzek 1999; Romzek and Johnston 1999; Gooden 1998). Whether one favors or opposes contracting out, its growth is indisputable. Those of us in the business of advising and training public managers must learn to understand this management tool and teach public managers how to use it more effectively. The focus of this chapter is to get specific about the obstacles that public managers must overcome to be better contract managers.

We have written elsewhere about a "functional matching" approach to privatization and the different attributes and motivational advantages of each sector for different tasks (Cohen 2001). Simply put, government organizations must be used when authority relationships are at the center of the task, such as police and regulatory functions. Nonprofit organizations seem best suited to functions such as health care that have a strong, mission-driven dimension. Private organizations are best when material incentives are needed to assure high-quality task performance.

We foresee that public managers will continue to assign functions to nongovernmental organizations. As we noted elsewhere (Cohen and Eimicke 2000a, 2000b) and throughout this volume, the trend toward multisectoral public service delivery creates several critical and difficult operational problems that must be addressed. Public managers must become effective contract managers and need to learn how to:

- Find out what their contractors are doing.
- Develop and implement systems of contractor incentives.
- Get a fair price for services.
- Develop the skills needed to negotiate performance-based contracts.

The importance of performance measurement to managing contractors has received a great deal of attention, as scholars have sought to identify the conditions that lead to successful outsourcing (Cohen and Eimicke 2000b; Wulczyn, Orlebeke, and Melamid 2000; Campbell and McCarthy 2000; Heinrich 1999; Panet and Trebilcock 1998). While we are optimistic about the ability of government to enter into productive and successful contractor relationships, we think that the new era of privatization requires a substantial increase in the sophistication and managerial skills of government managers.

Contract Manager Capabilities

The capacity to contract is a critical skill for twenty-first-century public managers. It includes an understanding of all the fundamental and innovation tools of management deployed within organizations, plus a range of techniques for extending the manager's reach outside the organization. The fundamental tools include strategic planning, human resource management, information and performance management, financial management, political and media relations, and leadership. The innovation tools include re-engineering, quality management, benchmarking, team management, and contracting. A contract manager, like a manager focused on internal management, must have the skills to address the following issues: (1) What is the work? (2) What skills do we need to perform these tasks, and where will we find those skills? (3) How do we ensure that the work is done effectively but at the lowest possible price? (4) How do we know the work has been completed? (5) How do we know that the outcomes we've produced are the correct ones?

1. What is the work? In this case, the contract manager must know what he or she doesn't know and be able to tap into technical expertise about the issue being contracted. The RFP, contract, incentive clauses, and mandatory performance indicators require that the contracting official either have experience managing the work being contracted or have access to someone who has that type of experience. There is no adequate substitute for subject matter knowledge. Contract management capacity must always begin with subject matter expertise or access to that expertise.

2. What skills are needed to perform these tasks, and where do we find those skills? Once the contract manager understands the work that must be performed, the next step is to find the organizations with the experience and skills to do that work. This requires that the contract manager be skilled at developing and maintaining an informal network that will provide information on the best organizations for performing these tasks. This is not the job for an introverted, studious analyst. It also requires experience at understanding the disciplines and skills that are required to perform tasks. Sometimes a particular skill looks correct on paper but fails operationally. A successful contract manager needs to either possess or have access to operational experience with performing the work required by the contract.

3. How do we ensure that the work is done effectively but at the lowest possible price? This is the capacity to monitor and evaluate the work. It requires an understanding of formal program evaluation methods and results, but also skill at establishing informal feedback loops. The effective contract manager must establish informal communication with contractor staff members and customers. Are the outputs being produced the correct ones? Is the organization really producing those outputs in the best possible way? Are the mistakes being made and the waste that is produced within acceptable parameters? Communication and networking skills are required here, along with skill at quantitative measures and program evaluation. The ability to conduct or at least understand cost-effectiveness analysis is also critical here, as are bargaining and negotiation skills. A firm's perspective in setting a price for services is not shared by

the contracting organization. Therefore, government should expect that price is always negotiable. However, if the price is set too low, quality will suffer. If it is set too high, the public interest is not served.

4. How do we know the work has been completed? In addition to factors related to price and informal communication, the effective contract manager must have the capacity to develop, maintain, and utilize a set of performance measures that track contractor performance. These indicators must be linked to incentives, and they must be audited to assure accuracy. To ensure that the contract describes the work that needs to be done, provides incentives to stimulate the work, and tracks its accomplishments, the contract's provisions must be well crafted and enforceable. While the contract manager does not need to be capable of developing contract language, he or she must be able to work with and manage lawyers who develop RFPs and contract terms.

5. How do we know that the outcomes we've produced are the correct ones? This requires that the contract manager be able to measure outcomes and judge their usefulness. The measurement of outcomes is difficult, and assessing an outcome is inherently subjective. The capacity called for is that intangible known as judgment.

In sum, contract management is more complex than internal management. It requires all the functions of effective internal management with the additional requirement of managing the interorganizational relationship required to get work done by "outsiders." The management capacity needs are high, but so too is the potential payoff.

Contracting not only solves problems, it creates them as well. We must learn how to identify and solve the problems that contracting creates.

This chapter now turns to a discussion of twenty problems created by government contracting. We have identified twenty key problems that fall into five general categories:

1. Problems related to letting contracts
2. Communication issues
3. Contractor internal management issues

4. Government contract management issues
5. Environmental or external issues

Problems related to letting contracts
1. Flawed Request for Proposal (RFP) and/or contract language
2. Overly bureaucratic contracting procedures resulting in delays and high transaction costs
3. Too few bidders and/or contractor monopolies

Communication issues
4. Poor communication between government and contractor management
5. Poor communication between government and contractor staff
6. Inadequate direction from government to contractors

Contractor internal management issues
7. Contractors that give an agency's work a low priority
8. Insufficient contractor staffing, training, equipment, and facilities
9. Poor contractor management

Government contract management issues
10. Underestimating or overestimating resource needs for contractor-performed tasks
11. Insufficient or excessive profits
12. Inappropriate or outmoded performance measures and insufficient systems for communicating performance data
13. Incomplete methods for auditing performance reporting
14. Inadequate methods for incorporating performance data into government and contractor decision making
15. Misdirected or inadequate contract incentive provisions

Environmental or external issues
16. Political opposition to contracting
17. Political interference in contractor selection or management
18. Conflict of interest issues

19. Union opposition to contracting
20. Media and political attention to contractor failures

Problems Related to Letting Contracts

1. Flawed Request for Proposal (RFP) and/or contract language
When a service is being contracted for the first time, it is difficult for the staff working on the RFP (or on the actual contract) to develop contract provisions that anticipate all the tasks involved in the work and all the problems that may arise. Sometimes specifications in the RFP or the contract do not permit critical tasks to be performed. While contracts must provide a vendor with some predictability, there are a number of techniques that government can use to retain discretion over contract provisions and contractor work.

One common technique is to use a task order, mission contract. This large-scale, multipurpose contract provides a general description of the contract's anticipated tasks but does not release funding until a government client writes a specific task order directing the firm to perform particular tasks. Another practice for dealing with this problem is to let a short-term "trial" contract with explicit provisions for early and rapid renewal. Both these techniques are useful as the organization learns more about the work being contracted out. As this learning occurs the contract can get more specific. In the long run, it is best to translate these learning experiences into standard operating procedures and clearly delineated tasks, incentives, and expected outputs and outcomes.

Other techniques for improving an RFP or contract include a request for qualifications or request for information from perspective vendors. These requests to firms to either provide a demonstration of capability or evidence of qualifications can be used to narrow the field or develop the additional information needed to draft an appropriate RFP. Another strategy is to find one organization to work with and use sole-source procurement to pay that firm. Through this method the government can obtain some of the firm's time to learn more about how to define and measure the service being contracted. If this sole-source technique is used, it may be necessary to prohibit this firm from competing on the final contract in order to avoid conflicts of interest.

2. Overly bureaucratic contracting procedures resulting
in delays and high transaction costs
The rules governing contracting can be quite cumbersome and time-consuming. Some of the procedures are designed to combat waste and fraud; others are needed to allow for public comment and governmental transparency and accountability. Still other procedures are designed to enhance the power and leverage of senior administrators. Some of these procedures have a basis in law and some in regulation, and others are internal practices and standard operating procedures.

There are several approaches you can use to overcome this particular obstacle. The most common is to bundle a number of RFPs under a single, more general heading. A second is to find a colleague with a large contract vehicle that is not fully funded and add your contract dollars to your colleague's contract vehicle in return for access to the contractor or to subcontractors you are hoping to work with. This is not a cost-free option. The subcontractors must be qualified to work on the contract, the assignment must be related to the contract's purpose, and frequently your colleague who manages the contract will ask for funding for his or her own tasks in return for contract access.

Another approach is to go over the head of the procurement office staff and either ask to use emergency contracting procedures (if they are applicable) or put pressure on the procurement staff to move quickly. These strategies are also not cost-free, since they often lead to resentment and retaliation.

A final option is to advocate reforms in contracting procedures. This is a long-term strategy with some promise, although it will not help you get this contract out the door. The details of contracting are not simple and not without cost. The amount of time and effort expended in letting a contract must be factored into the overall cost of privatizing a function.

3. Too few bidders and/or contractor monopolies
Some of the work government performs is not performed by the private sector. It may be that there is no private market for the service or product.

It may be that it is not a product or service that governments have typically purchased from external sources. The contract may be seeking to purchase something that is available in some regions of the country but not in others. If privatization is critical or mandated and there are not enough bidders to generate competition, the agency must develop methods to entice private organizations into the bidding.

Private participation can be stimulated by providing grants or contracts for capacity building. Such participation can also be encouraged by permitting generous payment schedules, profits, and even payment of up-front capital and/or provision of facilities. The absence of bidders in a contract competition is a strong indication that the approach to privatization must be restructured. It is dangerous and foolish to proceed with a contracting process in the absence of competition. A monopoly will permit a vendor to raise prices unilaterally, and, even more damaging, a contractor can withhold service after the government has come to depend on it. If the service or product is essential, government simply cannot allow a vendor to hold a monopoly on its delivery.

There is a simple, commonsense method for determining whether a service can be purchased in a particular jurisdiction. This is the "yellow pages test." Simply look in the commercial phone directory in your area and see if there are any vendors who sell the goods or services you are hoping to buy. If you can't find it in the phone book, you probably need to make it or do it yourself.

Communication Issues

4. Poor communication between government and
contractor management
Some government officials think of contracting as a "turn-key operation." You set it up, turn the key, and it starts working. Unfortunately, most contracts do not work that way. Once a contract is in place and a vendor is providing a service, the work of government managers is ready to begin. A working relationship must be developed between the contract's managers and the vendor's management. This includes relationships with the program's substantive managers and their counterparts in the private firm, as

well as with the government's contract and financial management staff and their private sector counterparts.

Poor communication can result in late payments that save government no money but that require the vendor to pass along the increased cost of working capital in the contract's cost structure. Additionally, poor communication can result in poorly defined tasks and can lead to unacceptable performance. It can also result in conflict between government and contractor when projects fail. Management must set the tone for a cooperative and productive relationship.

Frequent formal and informal meetings, clear milestones, and mutual respect are fundamental requirements for effective interorganizational relations. Government managers need to make an effort to understand the constraints and forces driving the behavior of private sector managers. High transaction costs can erode savings that contracting may bring, and these costs must be recognized during the contract decision phase and not after a contract has been signed. The relationship between contractor and government should be seen as a partnership and an exchange relationship based on mutual benefit.

However, sometimes all the good will in the world does not result in effective management. In cases where private or nonprofit contractors exploit the relationship and fail to produce, or act unethically, government managers need to utilize contract penalty and termination clauses and end the working relationship. The possibility of such failure is reduced by frequent communication, but it is not eliminated. A formal performance measurement system, backed up by frequent communication, can provide government managers with early warning of performance problems. While a sound working relationship requires informal communication and interaction, the government manager must be careful not to be taken in by friendliness and must be certain that no gifts or free meals are provided. Contract managers should never accept anything of monetary value from a vendor.

5. Poor communication between government and contractor staff
Senior management communication and relationships are important, and so too are staff-level relationships between government and contractors. Very often, poor communication at the staff level reflects similar problems at higher levels of the organization. Sometimes staff members, seeing these

problems, work together to solve problems at the operational level. Other times they develop strategies for getting their bosses to talk to each other. Without regular communication at the staff level, it is difficult for contractor staff members to determine the definition and requirements of the assignment they have been given. When problems develop or choices must be made, contractors must make the choices themselves without the benefit of input from their government customers.

The solution here is to write frequent contact into the contract's requirements and to assign senior staff to work with contractors. The conversations should take place in formal meetings and in informal settings as well. For government to truly benefit from the communication process, contractors must be encouraged to be honest and they must be made to feel free to identify problems. Most businesses are reluctant to share operational problems with their customers, so eliciting such honesty is not easy or simple. Off-the-record conversations in informal settings can often uncover crucial information that would not surface through formal channels of communication.

6. Inadequate direction from government to contractors
Inadequate communication is one cause of inadequate direction. It's hard to know what to do if no one bothers to tell you. Inadequate direction also has several other causes:

- Conflicting or inconsistent goals. This can lead to multiple directions and deep confusion at the operational level.
- Inadequate knowledge. Sometimes a contractor is being asked to perform a task that no one in the government (or possibly anywhere else) knows how to do.
- Political gamesmanship, secrecy, and other obstacles to communicating direction.

Sometimes the government staff or management has a political reason to be vague about what a contractor is being asked to do. They may not want to leave a paper trail, or they are worried that by asking for "A" they are implicitly or explicitly rejecting "B," causing anger and political retribution from those advocating "B."

One solution to this problem is for contractors to recognize the danger from inadequate direction and actively seek direction when none is offered. The reality is that many contractors are content to bill hours if they can and make money while government decides what to do. This strategy may work for firms holding contracts for analysis and other less tangible services. When a facility's construction or its management is being contracted, it's a little more difficult to hide behind vague and inconsistent direction. Another solution is for government to delay the contracting decision until fundamental choices about direction are in place. Unfortunately, some bureaucratic players use the action-forcing characteristics of contracting as a tactic to facilitate decision making. Policy is made implicitly because the contractor is obligated to act in order to get paid, and therefore may act without clear direction from the government client.

Contractor Internal Management Issues

7. Contractors that give an agency's work a low priority

Small local governments sometimes find when contracting that the only time the huge national engineering or consulting firm pays attention to them is when the company is trying to win the contract. Sometimes a poorly managed firm simply decides to "punt" on a piece of work and tries to get by with an inadequate effort. A company may know that a contract is not going to be renewed and may decide to assign weak, or at least inexpensive, personnel to staff it. There are a variety of methods government can use to encourage a private firm to put more time and effort into a job.

Meeting with the firm informally and formally can alert senior management to problems and elicit attention for your concerns. Incentives and threats of punishment can be used to motivate the desired behavior. A particularly potent threat, one that even small jurisdictions can play, can be to publicize inadequate performance. The problem is that it forces you to admit that something you are responsible for is not working.

Contract mechanisms should be designed to include frequent reviews with specific sanctions for poor performance. Where you sense that your work is not getting the effort it deserves, you should make your views known to the firm and (if necessary) to its senior management as soon as possible. While it is not in your interest to be seen as a poor or whining client, it is also important that you signal your dissatisfaction as clearly as possible. If you are a small client but work in a large organization, you may want to call your problem to the attention of the contract management staff in your organization. They can threaten the contractor with being frozen out of the agency's, or even the jurisdiction's, contracts.

8. Insufficient contractor staffing, training, equipment, and facilities

If the RFP was not specific enough, or if the firm allocates its resources to other contracts, one result of being a low priority is that you find yourself with inadequate numbers of staff members, a poorly trained staff, inadequate facilities, and/or outmoded equipment. Sometimes the contract itself can be used to require specific resources. These requirements can then be subject to contract-mandated audits. Most contracts have cancellation clauses that allow the government to cancel or defund the contract if performance is deficient.

Contractors can experience startup problems and growing pains that are typical of new or quickly growing organizations. The government client must determine if the problem is one of poor management, inadequate resources, or simply an early place on the learning curve. Each issue calls for different strategies. It is vital that the government does not ignore the problem and has detailed information on specific shortfalls.

9. Poor contractor management

Some contractors are better at winning contracts than managing them. The incentives in many firms are often directed toward the "rainmakers," the people who bring in business. While a well-managed firm will understand the need to execute as well as win contracts, the problem we are discussing is not characteristic of a well-managed firm. A consultant friend of ours once divided consultants into three categories: finders (rainmakers), minders (project managers), and grinders (workers). Contract RFPs can be designed to elicit the management experience of the senior people in the firm that the contractor plans to use if they win the contract. However, there is no guarantee that these people will actually work on the contract or devote sufficient energy and attention to it. This may well be the most fundamental and difficult problem to solve in privatization.

The absence of competent contractor management makes it difficult to address other issues. If the government manager has no capable counterpart to communicate with in the firm, it is unlikely that the contract has any chance of succeeding. When faced with this type of situation, the best strategy is contract termination, as soon as possible.

Government Contract Management Issues

10. Underestimating or overestimating resource needs for contractor-performed tasks

When a function or program is being contracted out for the first time, it is difficult to project costs precisely. As a program moves from government to the private sector, the costs of capital and a variety of legal, administrative, reporting, and other costs must be included in cost estimates. Governments do not pay taxes on their supplies and facilities, but private for-profit organizations typically pay these taxes. There are often free and in-kind services that government agencies receive when delivering a service. These hidden savings become costs when a private firm assumes responsibility for performing a task. On the other hand, private firms do not have to deal with civil service protections and can motivate workers through both financial incentives and fear of unemployment. Private organizations are not independent of regulation and, like government, are subject to legal restrictions on hiring and firing and often must deal with unions, contracts, and work rules.

Moreover, the work being contracted out often involves tasks that the private organization has not performed before. It may have performed similar tasks, but possibly not at the scale required by the contract or to the same group of customers they now serve. All these factors can contribute to underestimating or overestimating the costs of performing a function. When a firm bids too low, it may cut corners and do a poor job on a contract. When they bid too high, it can create a problem if the media discovers they are "gouging" the public. In either case, the contract mechanism for a newly contracted out function needs to permit renegotiation of price based on experience. An agency's critics may see a change in the pricing structure of a contract as a method of getting around a sealed competitive bidding process. This is, of course, less of a problem if the contractor overestimated costs when bidding. Nevertheless, a well-structured mechanism for price adjustment is often needed to remedy this problem.

11. Insufficient or excessive profits

A related problem when contracting with a for-profit firm is the amount of profit generated by the contract. In some contracts, profit is a fixed fee that is figured as a percentage of the contract's costs. Through accounting manipulation, firms manage to increase real profits by charging overhead or other costs to a contract that are not generated by that contract. Still, if a private firm holding a contract does not generate an adequate return on the equity invested in it, investors will turn to other firms, and the contractor may become starved for capital.

Even if the profit to be made on the contract is sizable but lower than profits generated in other parts of the firm, government contract work will not be able to attract the firm's best and brightest staff members. These talented staff members will gravitate to more profitable work, leaving government contract work to mediocre staff members. While such a tendency can be countered by effective government management of a contract and by recruiting mission-driven contractor staff members, it is a factor that should be understood and addressed by government managers using contractors to get work done.

The problem of excessive profits is essentially one of perception. If a private firm can figure out a way to get the work done more efficiently and at a lower cost, shouldn't their ingenuity be rewarded with increased profits? The answer might be yes in some cases, but if the media learns that a contractor is profiting "at the public's expense," the reaction against the firm and the government agency involved in the contract can be severe. The issues around profit are an outgrowth of the fact that government and for-profit firms operate with different organizational cultures and often relate to different cues from their organizational environment. While all organizations are concerned about their public image, government organizations are more frequently subjects of media scrutiny. Private firms can pick up and operate in another jurisdiction and can drop unprofitable services. Governments, however, do not have the advantage of that flexibility.

An open and truly competitive process and a true market environment should work to prevent these problems. If profits are excessive, a lower-cost bidder should emerge when the contract is open to rebid. If profits are inadequate, a more efficient firm may develop a less expensive way to deliver the service and increase profit levels.

12. Inappropriate or outmoded performance measures and insufficient systems for communicating performance data
When some of the functions of a government program are contracted out, government managers become coordinators of interorganizational networks. To do this job effectively, government managers must have accurate and timely information about contractor performance. These performance measures must be carefully designed to provide information about the processes, outputs, and outcomes that matter the most to the government and its program. Since the program's activities are being implemented by another organization acting under contract, the performance measurement system must be explicitly designed into the contract's structure.

The performance measurement system must be allowed to evolve, but it should include specific indicators, reporting processes, and deadlines, along with mandatory periodic briefings and discussions. The data must be collected and reported, but the government client must have the opportunity to question the data and its analysis. The data must also be subject to independent audit. If these systems are not developed and maintained, it is impossible to monitor and manage the contract. You cannot manage something if you cannot measure its performance. Without measurement you cannot tell whether management decisions and actions are improving or impairing a service. The performance measurement system must be flexible and should be regularly revised to reflect new conditions, processes, outputs, or outcomes.

Related to the issue of measures is the compatibility and reliability of the computer hardware, software, and communication system used to transmit performance measures. For measures to be utilized, they must be easily accessible and frequently updated. Contracts must include specific provisions for adequate performance measures, but must also ensure that those inputting data and those receiving the data are capable of simple and rapid two-way communication.

13. Incomplete methods for auditing performance reporting
One of the fundamental problems with performance measurement systems in most organizations is that the people being measured also do the measuring. While we believe that most people are honest most of the time, performance measurement seems to bring out the creativity in some government managers. The best way to keep a reporting system honest is, not so coincidentally, the same way the IRS keeps us honest when filing our taxes—a real and credible threat that someone may go back and check the numbers and see if they were real. Most government performance measurement systems have no provision for audits. It may be that performance measurement is still quite new and some managers are simply happy to have any performance data they can obtain.

Unless information is checked and a credible audit system is in place, it is difficult to know if the performance data is real. This is not simply a matter of reporting nonperformance; credible data is also needed to demonstrate that management innovations have succeeded and that new initiatives are paying off. The cost of auditing such data is typically not factored into the cost of contracting, but it should be seen as a standard and necessary interorganizational transaction cost.

14. Inadequate methods for incorporating performance data into government and contractor decision making
Collecting and verifying performance data is interesting and potentially meaningful work, but it only makes a difference in the real world if performance data is used to influence management and organizational activities. In the case of contract relationships, performance measures need to be used to influence changes in contractor behavior and contract provisions.

There are many techniques that can be used to bring performance data into program management. However, to use these techniques the contract must allow for a change in activity based on an assessment of current performance. One method that can be used to increase the use of performance data in management decision making is to have a periodic meeting where managers are asked to explain current levels of performance and, when necessary, to identify the steps that are planned to improve performance. A related technique is to have managers demonstrate how they use performance data in day-to-day management as part of the process during which management performance is appraised. Periodic release of performance data to the public can also help focus attention on public management and government performance. In New York City government, this is accomplished through the annual release of the Mayor's Management Report—a massive collection of management indicators from every unit of city government.

15. Misdirected or inadequate contract incentive provisions

Contractors, like everyone else, work better when there are rewards associated with superior performance. Some government contracts reward performance with cash bonuses; others provide firms with advantages during contract renewal competitions. Since many government managers have not worked as private sector managers, they do not always understand the incentives that are most effective with private firms and that with constantly changing markets the incentives are also constantly shifting. Nonprofit organizations may be a bit closer to the government manager's field of understanding, due to the shared mission orientation of many government and nonprofit organizations. However, the entire matter of financial incentives for organizational performance can be difficult for government managers to fully understand unless they have excellent communication with their contractors.

We are strongly attracted to the use of incentive clauses in contracts. These work best when they are the result of the accomplishment of specific, verified performance measures. For example, when a firm that is installing subway tracks completes the work a month ahead of time, it is given a bonus for every day the project comes in ahead of schedule. In fact, an even better technique links a similar penalty clause to late completion. The point of an incentive is that it is only useful if it inspires the specific changes in behavior that improve organizational performance. If it doesn't motivate change or motivates the wrong change, it fails.

Managers should experiment with different forms of incentives and attempt to determine the independent impact of the incentive on performance. One problem with bonuses is that if they are given too easily, they are soon seen as a type of base pay and people come to rely on and expect them. When that happens, their impact on performance is significantly reduced.

Environmental or External Issues

16. Political opposition to contracting

Political opposition to the idea of contracting out or privatizing a function is a problem that agencies often face. Some of this opposition is simply fear of change. Some of it comes from people who benefit or receive privileged access with the current arrangement. Some political opposition is ideological and based on a belief that a certain function should not be performed by a private organization. The potency of the political opposition is a critical issue for a manager seeking to privatize. If the opposition is intense, privatization might be discouraged or even prohibited by elected officials or political appointees. In these cases, a strategic retreat may be necessary.

More typically, political opposition is not as clear-cut and may be counterbalanced by political support. There may be some approaches to contracting that can be used to address political issues. A fear of layoffs, for example, can be countered by a requirement that the contractor hire some or all of the current employees. It is also possible to initially contract on a pilot project basis and only gradually expand if the experiment works.

As part of an overall management strategy, a manager may decide to produce certain goods and services and buy others. Sometimes these decisions are interconnected, and being forced to contract one program or function may make it more difficult to privatize a function you consider more appropriate for outsourcing. Antigovernment ideology may lead to pressures to privatize functions that managers would rather retain direct control over and might even need control over in order to effectively privatize other functions.

In general, public managers must understand and seek to accommodate political factors. This can be accomplished the following two ways: first by paying attention to political issues and players and treating political input seriously; and second by developing a strategy for accommodating political input with the least possible damage to operations management. Where opposition to contracting is deep, ideological, and uncompromising, the manager will need to determine if the force of opposition can be overcome and if the cost of doing so is worth the benefit.

17. Political interference in contractor selection or management

While political opposition to the concept of contracting is a legitimate policy dispute, political involvement in contractor selection or contract management tends to be unsavory and should be resisted. This is easier said than done. Political influence will be expressed by elected officials through political appointees. Career employees must decide whether to disregard the advice (if not the commands) of their bosses. Appointed officials must decide if they can afford to resist the demands of their elected mentors.

Typically, this interference comes from efforts to reward campaign contributors and former government officials now working in private firms. Sometimes the pressure helps a firm that is well-qualified and might receive the contract without political influence. At other times it is used to help firms that are not capable of doing the work. Political influence can also originate with the contractor, mediated by politicos, then communicated to the unelected official. The influence can be used to obtain a contract, but it can also be used to influence contract oversight and performance management.

If a political person simply calls the firm to the attention of the contracting official or mentions how difficult the contractor's task has been, and how much so and so would appreciate some management leeway, such pressure is subtle and probably not illegal. But if pressure is exerted, the contracting official is placed in an ethically and possibly legally compromising situation. In those cases, public managers must resist political pressure for ethical reasons, regardless of the practical or managerial issues involved. Moreover, even the appearance of impropriety can taint the contracting out process and make it appear that privatization is being pursued for personal or political gain rather than as a method of improving public services. In extreme cases, reporting to the official ethics organization, resigning, or leaking the situation to the media might be necessary.

18. Conflict of interest issues

Another obstacle to contracting is that people who work in government organizations may have a history of work relations with counterparts in private firms. People in the private organizations may also have been political supporters of elected officials whose administrations are now seeking contractor assistance the private firms could provide. It is critical that government officials avoid both the reality and appearance of conflicts of interest. Government officials must bend over backwards to recuse themselves from any contract situation where such a conflict is possible. Moreover, government officials must be proactive in these situations and anticipate any potential problems. It is not enough to respond to an investigation or attack. Government officials must think through their past interactions and those of people they are close to and anticipate potential conflicts of interest.

A number of techniques have been developed to reduce the possibility of conflicts of interest. Sealed, competitive bidding is one such technique. So too is the use of panels of officials to review proposals and select winning bids. Panels can include people from outside the agency to ensure greater independence and objectivity. Still, the best technique is vigilance and sensitivity on the part of government officials involved in contracting. From the point of view of managers seeking to privatize a function, the issue of conflict of interest makes the contracting process more complicated and cumbersome. It is simply another constraint on the make-or-buy decision that makes contracting more difficult.

19. Union opposition to contracting

Public employee unions can be a significant source of opposition to contracting. It's quite simple—why should they support a practice that reduces employment or opportunities for its members? If the firms or nonprofits bidding on the contract are unionized, such opposition may be muted or even nullified. However, sometimes the issue is simply the economic survival of the union's elected and administrative staff. They need the money generated from members' dues for their own salaries and, consequently, oppose contracting because it reduces union revenues and their own pay.

Powerful unions can oppose contracting successfully through political influence and media campaigns as well as through the electoral power of their members. Unions opposing such contracts typically do not place concerns with the effectiveness or efficiency of public organizations ahead of their members' self-interest, nor should they be expected to. Some of the more sophisticated unions will argue that government operations will be harmed by contracting out, and they will maintain that they are also concerned with public service. In making the decision to contract, all the relevant stakeholders should be consulted both while deciding to contract and after the contract is in place. This includes unions, but also community-based groups, public interest groups, and business interest groups.

Union opposition to contracting can be addressed politically through deals negotiated between elected officials and union leaders. It can also be a subject of collective bargaining. In return for union support of contracting, the government could provide increased pay, job security, or other benefits. Alternatively, the contract could include severance pay, job placement, and other resources that minimize the effect of contracting out on current job holders. Where public employee unions are powerful, those interested in contracting functions must take unions seriously and see them as significant and legitimate stakeholders in the decision-making process. Unions cannot be ignored, and if they are not accommodated, they can generate substantial and costly conflict. A key step in the privatization process is to analyze and assess the position and influence of organized labor.

20. Media and political attention to contractor failures

When a government function has been privatized, it often generates a level of media scrutiny that government managers are often familiar with, but private managers have rarely seen. Nongovernmental organizations often find press inquiries, legislative oversight, audits, and all manner of citizen participation as unexpected and unwelcome additions to their lives and cost structures. Government officials are responsible for any failures and may find themselves blind sided by an unexpected exposé of a contractor failure.

Both government and contractors should act at all times as if their activities will be the lead story on the evening news. If things are not going well, it is better to proactively bring the information to oversight bodies than wait for an investigation to identify a problem. By anticipating issues, the contracting agency has the opportunity to define the way the problem is presented and can control and communicate a plan for solving the problem.

Nevertheless, the extra level of scrutiny that a newly contracted function faces must be seen as an obstacle to privatization. Most organizations make mistakes early in the process of taking on a new task, and making mistakes in public does not always speed up the process of organizational learning. Attention is paid to the placement of blame as well as to presentation and appearance, rather than on the issue of how to improve operational performance. This can make it difficult to successfully bring in a nongovernmental player and may impede success.

Conclusions

The process of contracting out a function is not easy or automatic. It brings significant transaction costs along with significant benefits. The procurement process requires skills and determination, and yet simply letting a contract may very well be the easiest part of the procurement process. The more difficult challenge for government involves managing leaders and staff members who work in a separate and private organization. To address this challenge, government must establish the formal mechanisms, incentive systems, and informal communication processes that stimulate appropriate contractor behaviors.

In many instances, contracting leads to superior results and the work and expense of establishing these complicated interorganizational relations is worth incurring. In other cases, contracting is a political or ideological decision that will bring more cost than benefit. The make-or-buy decision must be an integrated element of an organization's overall strategy. It must relate to the organization's definition of its own distinctive competence. It must be built on an understanding of private sector capacities and incentives. The government is getting better at working with nongovernmental organizations, but a great deal more must be learned.

At this point we have defined terms and asked fundamental questions about contracting ethics and accountability. We now turn to a series of operational issues about contract management:

- How do we approach the make-or-buy decision?
- If you decide to buy, how can you find the "right" contractor?
- Once you have the right contractor, how do you manage their work?
- What skills are needed and what mistakes should you avoid when managing contractors?

Chapter 8

Performance Measurement and Performance Management

CONTRACTED SERVICES require government workers to develop a whole new set of skills including contract design, negotiation, program monitoring, and evaluation. Sophisticated information systems are also needed to provide the performance measures and evaluation programs that are essential to effective contract management.

This chapter explores the theory and practice of performance management and information technology in the context of outsourcing public service delivery. We discuss the use of government strategic planning and information-based performance management to plan and manage private contractors performing public tasks. While information systems are critical to the management of in-house organizational activities and units, we believe they are even more important in managing the work of contractors.

Performance Management Challenges Posed by Organizational Networks

Although well-managed, dynamic organizations find themselves undergoing constant change, two factors do not change—the need for management direction and the demand for accountability. While mayors and commissioners might try to blame a bad result on an inadequate contractor, that argument is generally not accepted by the public, especially over the long term. When programs are implemented by a variety of organizations that form a network, issues of communication, coordination, and direction are generated.

Organizations within the network need to learn what tasks they are to perform, when they should perform them, the objectives they are attempting to achieve, the customers they are being asked to serve, and the information they must provide to the agency they are working for. This requires extensive contact and information exchange. When members of the network are contractors, the agency contracting for the work does not perform the tasks in question, but it should determine what tasks must be performed, by whom, at what time, and for what purpose. The agency must learn whether the tasks have been performed and what outputs and outcomes the tasks have generated. It must coordinate the actions of numerous contractors and, where contractors must interact, ensure that the interaction is working as designed. When noncontractual members of a network are involved in program implementation, the public agency may need to provide incentives and services to encourage network members to provide data to the performance measurement system.

Organizational networks, when they run well, can be more efficient and effective for some functions than can vertically integrated hierarchical organizations. However, they must be managed, and such management is not cost-free or easy. It requires an innovative type of management that relies on new and additional mechanisms for communicating to and influencing the behavior of external organizations. Often contract instruments must be used to exercise influence: for example, linking payment schedules and bonuses to performance. To receive these incentives, vendors must perform in certain specific ways, and they must also provide the lead agency with information on their performance. A performance-based contract cannot function without accurate and verified information about contractor performance.

Performance Management

In addition to the data we present in chapter 1, a number of researchers have noted the trend over the past decade for state and local governments to contract out, or outsource to private and particularly nonprofit organizations, many of the services previously delivered by civil servants (Sclar 2000; Cohen and Eimicke 2002; Avery 2000; Butcher 1995; Forrest 1993). Forrest notes that agencies have thus been transformed "from direct providers to monitoring, regulation, and contract-enforcing agencies" (1993,

51). He emphasizes the importance of new management skills necessary to guide these organizations that now have a networked contractor structure rather than the traditional hierarchical service delivery structure. Forrest regards the increase in emphasis on performance monitoring as part of the process of contract specification and oversight necessary in these new structures (1993).

Martin and Kettner cover the process of performance measurement in human service agencies and programs in some depth (1996). They define performance measurement as the regular collection and reporting of information about the efficiency (inputs/outputs), quality, and effectiveness (outcomes) of programs (1996, 3). They argue that the chief reason to adopt performance measurement in human services is to improve the management of those programs by supplying agencies with information about who their clients are: their demographic characteristics; their service requirements; the amount, quality, and level of service received; and the outcome of receiving the service. Performance measures keep managers informed about how their program is doing and assist in oversight.

Performance measures may be used to monitor the delivery of contractors' services in the same way they can be used to monitor agency performance. The advantage, according to Martin and Kettner (1996), is that once performance measures are in place, the agency can move to performance-based contracting, in which contractors are paid for meeting certain performance-based criteria. For example, payment to a job training and employment contractor is based on the number of people actually placed in a job, not on the number of people the contractor is currently training.

Performance Management and Contracting Out

Management of interorganizational networks and contracts means that leaders cannot depend on traditional hierarchical controls to influence the behavior of subordinates who are responsible for performing particular tasks. This means that management cannot directly use organizational culture, personnel promotion, demotion, termination, or authoritative command structures to influence behavior. In our view, many of those tools are of declining usefulness anyway. Given public employee due process rights, it is increasingly difficult to fire someone. In the professionalized environment characteristic of most government agencies, few professionals are responsive to direct command. They are more likely to behave as management requires in response to persuasion and positive incentives. Merit pay and other bonus systems can be effective in rewarding good performance, but few techniques are available to government to effectively punish poor performance.

In contrast, contractual relationships with private and nonprofit firms provide the surest way to punish poor performance: contract termination. While there are limits to the use of this technique—it is difficult to terminate contracts in midterm—it does send a message that is clearly understood by the people who work in the organizations holding the contract. Competition and the intense work environment it engenders can be created through contracting. Systems can be established with competing vendors, and contracts can be signed with incentive and penalty clauses. When the term of the contract is over, new bids are sought, and a poorly performing contractor can see its contract simply come to an end. In this sense, the contractor has some of the same attributes as an employee on a renewable term appointment.

One example of a contractual mechanism to enhance contractor performance was used in a 2007 San Francisco Bay Area emergency freeway repair project. A vital section of an interstate overpass feeding commuters into San Francisco was destroyed on April 29, 2007, when a gasoline tanker crashed, igniting a fire so hot it melted the freeway above. The contractor repairing the overpass received a $200,000 bonus for each day the project was finished ahead of schedule for a maximum of $5 million (and could have been fined $200,000 for each day it was late). The project was completed more than a month before the transit agency's deadline, and the contractor was paid the maximum bonus of $5 million (May 2007; Nelson 2007). To develop this incentive and disincentive clause in the contract, the government needed to know a reasonable deadline and the appropriate level to set the reward/punishment. They also needed an operational definition of "complete project" to put in the contract. Finally, they needed to find a way to confirm when the project was completed. These extensive information requirements place new demands on government managers that must be addressed if the contract mechanism is to work.

The challenge to management is to develop contract clauses that provide managers with tools to influence the behavior of the organization under contract. It is also important to ensure that the vendor does not develop a monopoly over the function it is performing. If the contractor is the only organization capable of performing the task, threats of termination can be easily ignored. We have seen this frequently in military procurement and, ironically, in the purchase of information technology hardware, software, and contracting services. In our view, functions that cannot generate competitive bids should be directly performed by government wherever feasible. If sole-source contracting is unavoidable, government managers must ensure that performance criteria are clear, well publicized, easily measured and understood, and that penalties for missing performance targets are severe.

Performance Management and Information Needs

Contract management requires that government receive timely, accurate information. When possible, contracts must be developed that require vendors to report input, process, output, and outcome measures on a frequent basis. However, self-reporting, while necessary, is not sufficient. When services are provided directly to the public, citizen service complaints and compliments can serve as a useful barometer of contract performance. It is also important to have all contract performance measures and payment generation actions verified and audited by independent third parties. This can be done directly by a government agency's performance measurement unit, or it can be done under contract to a consulting firm, think tank, or university.

Auditing requires access to information, and even those sent to verify data can be fooled by contractors intending to deceive the government. There is no foolproof system, and any effort to design a corruption-proof system will result in convoluted production and reporting processes and organizational paralysis. All an effective audit can do is increase the probability of honesty. It helps reinforce those who wish to be honest by raising the costs of deception. When corruption takes place in the presence of an audited measurement system, the legal system, not a management system, should be used to punish and reduce lying.

Some members of a program's implementation network are organizations that are not under direct contract to the government. Examples of these actors include nonprofit organizations and private firms with a similar mission. The Environmental Protection Agency (EPA) enforces underground storage tank standards, but the companies who own tanks are gas station owners who do not work for the EPA. Recently, the insurance industry was credited by the federal government with encouraging the automobile industry to voluntarily accelerate its compliance with government requirements for passenger protections in vehicle collisions. In this sense we see the public and private sectors playing complementary roles.

Similarly, a nonprofit organization that advocates for the government protection of abused children may also provide shelter for such children. The nonprofit is thereby part of a city's network for protecting and providing foster care for children, but it may not be a government contractor. In these cases, collection of important performance data may be difficult if not impossible. Despite these difficulties, information about performance must be collected if the government hopes to manage the program being implemented by the interorganizational network.

The Use of Performance Measurement Systems to Respond to Network Management Problems

The managers of government programs that utilize networks of organizations to perform critical tasks must obtain information about the performance of these organizations if they are to effectively manage these programs. This requires strategic thinking about what information they need and how they might obtain it. When dealing with private firms, government must overcome the issue of proprietary information. Some firms are reluctant to tell you what they are doing, as they consider their work processes and outputs to be part of the competitive edge they have over other organizations. If they are under contract to you, it is possible to use the contract as leverage to collect information. If the firm is simply in a business related to yours, information collection may require substantial effort.

However difficult the collection of information might be, the first key step is to decide what information is needed. This should be guided by the management needs of the program. What is the definition of success? What direct or surrogate measures can be used to determine whether progress is being made? The definition of success and the appropriateness of measures to that definition are critical. One cannot manage a program unless one can measure its performance. As we mentioned earlier, without a way to measure performance you cannot tell if your actions are leading you toward or away from success. You have no way of knowing if you are moving forward or backward.

Decisions on performance measures are critical management decisions. They are the ground-level, operational definition of policy. They provide real-world specificity to abstract ideas and policy and are therefore of great consequence. The information collected on performance must be an integral part of an agency's strategy for implementing a program. If the goals of a program change, the measures must change as well.

Once the information necessary to manage the program is known, a strategy is needed for collecting the information. A fundamental principle of management information systems is that people and organizations are more likely to provide accurate information to a system if they utilize the data themselves and they see a benefit to cooperation. If the organizations providing information think its provision can help sell the program and help them obtain additional resources, they will be more cooperative than if the data are only used to monitor and punish poor performance. The problems of collecting timely, accurate information can be overcome if care and strategic thought are given to developing and maintaining the performance measurement system. Information retrieval is not an automatic, mechanical process. It is a political process requiring the buy-in of those providing information.

Performance measurement is critical to overcoming the management challenges faced when using an interorganizational implementation network. The construction of a system of measurement is an important early task for a program's managers. It should not be off-loaded to a consulting firm or the organization's management information systems (MIS) shop. It is leaders who create partnerships and networks, not technical experts. As such, the system should be treated as a subject worthy of formal negotiations and either contractual agreement or memorandum of understanding (written or tacit) agreement. Below, we discuss in conceptual terms the types of measures that should be included in these performance measurement agreements.

Measures of Performance

Most performance measurement systems incorporate four types of measures: inputs, process, outputs, and outcomes. Traditional, budget-based performance measurement systems focus primarily on inputs: What are the resources available to address the priority problems faced by the organization? Input measures are relatively easy to identify and collect. Commonly used input measures include dollars appropriated and allocated, person-hours committed, equipment purchased, space provided, and/or length of time committed to the problem. Other less common but relevant input indicators are other funds or other organizations involved or leveraged as a result of the initial organization's actions or decisions; capital funds directly or indirectly committed as a by-product of the operating budget commitment; and external staff and consultant time dedicated to the preparation, operation, monitoring, and evaluation of the program being launched.

Input measures are frequently criticized because they tell you only how hard you are trying to do something about a problem or the extent of your commitment to reach a particular goal (e.g., how much are we willing to spend to find a cure for AIDS?). Input measures tell you very little about how well you are doing in reaching the objective—they measure effort much better than they assess results. But input measures should not be ignored. They provide an important barometer of the scope of activity and of the present and future demand on overall resources, serve as surrogates of the organization's priorities, and often reflect the organization's customer preferences as well.

The process of producing work is an increasing focus of performance management systems and indicators. Total quality management's lasting contribution to management practice may be its attention to the work steps involved in producing goods and services (Cohen and Brand 1993). Measurement of those activities facilitates organizational learning and improvement. Process measures include the delineation and definition of specific work steps, measures of the amount of time it takes to perform specific tasks, error rates, and similar indicators. Requiring organizational units to report process measures can signal government's concern for the quality and efficiency of an organization's internal operations and can compel attention to these fundamental management issues.

Output measures are the third type of performance measurement indicators. Output measures seek to quantify the amount of work accomplished with the input or resources provided. Output measures can seek to measure quantity, quality, or both. Typical output measures include customers or clients served, facility condition and cleanliness, miles of road paved, number of applicants trained, tons of garbage collected, wages earned, course work completed, certificates or licenses acquired, or number of products sold. In simple terms, output measures gauge the volume of activity generated by inputs. As with input measures, some outputs are more important than others. Utilizing a select number of indicators that have a direct impact on performance (particularly for customers and funding agencies) leads to a successful performance measurement system. A multiple indicator approach ensures that several dimensions of performance can be measured and permits a more nuanced analysis of outputs, allowing an assessment of the causal flow from outputs to outcomes. Just as basic social science research requires multiple indicators to enhance our ability to measure concepts, the multiple indicator approach provides more sophisticated measures of organizational performance.

From World War II until the early 1990s, most successful performance measurement systems were output-based. However since the 1990s, many experts have written about the weaknesses inherent in output-based systems. Output systems tend to measure and reward work accomplished on a milestone basis. For example, interim payments are doled out as a contractor achieves pre-established targets along the way toward a completed assignment or full service to a customer.

On the surface, output measures seem to provide exactly what senior management should want—simple categories designed to encourage the staff to accomplish the work desired by paying for milestones actually achieved. The key weakness of an output-based system is that it often pays more for the process toward the desired outcome than for the outcome itself. The ultimate objective ends up being underemphasized. For example, in the welfare-to-work reform efforts of the 1990s, we found that by the time employment and training programs are paid for outputs such as training, certification, resume preparation, and job interviews, only a small percentage of the contract amount remains to reward the contractor for actually placing clients in jobs, keeping them employed, or assisting them up the employment ladder (Cohen and Eimicke 1999a; 1998; 1996a).

This leads us to outcome or impact measures. Performance measurement experts are seeking to tie input and output measures to more meaningful program impacts and goal achievement (Eisenberg 2003; Kaestner, Korenman, and O'Neill 2003). For example, the performance of a police department is not best measured by the number of officers on the payroll (input), how many people are arrested (output), or even the reduction in the overall crime rate (output), but rather by how safe people feel and how safe they actually are (outcome). In New York City, a private think tank has constructed a "Quality of Life" index to measure the overall performance of its hometown city government (McMahon 2003).

An initial review might lead to the conclusion that properly designed outcome indicators are all a good performance management system requires. In practice, outcome measures have significant weaknesses. First, outcome data is usually the most difficult to identify and expensive to collect. H. George Frederickson argues that because performance measures are quantitative representations of some reality, they are necessarily never as neutral and objective as they are presented (2000). Rather, program supporters will use the same measures as program critics to come up with diametrically opposite conclusions regarding the efficacy of the initiative. In Washington, D.C., then mayor Anthony Williams initiated an extensive system of agency scorecards that even cynics agreed produced positive results. However, with persistent problems such as unsafe streets, high homicide rates, and poorly performing schools, critics questioned the importance of the scorecard improvements (Scott 2002).

Second, outcomes are ongoing and the long-term impacts, both positive and negative, often do not evolve quickly. So, while in theory outcome measures are supposed to measure long-term impact, annual budget cycles and biennial elections often lead to short-term definitions of the long term. Third, it is often difficult, if not impossible, to determine the independent effect of a program or government activity on a particular outcome (Eisenberg 2003). To compare the performance of government service providers with nongovernment service providers, common metrics can be helpful, but it is important that managers do not simply implement the same performance measurement system when they contract. Fourth, even outcome measures fail to answer the question of maximum potential—"How well are we doing? Compared to what?" Some sort of comparative benchmarking exercise is required to assess how well a program or organization is performing compared to other entities doing similar work (Morley, Bryant, and Hatry 2001).

Finally, in the early 1990s, creators of the so-called balanced scorecard argued that existing performance management systems were far too limited and failed to adequately account for the need for continuous improvement, innovation, and the needs and wants of customers (Kaplan 2002; Kaplan and Norton 1996; 1992). The balanced scorecard sets goals and measures from four perspectives—financial, internal business operations, innovation and learning, and customers. The challenge for managers is how to create a set of measures that is comprehensive and still limited enough to focus the organization on what is most important. In the case of government performance management, politics is often about which program goals are most important. Also, while most of the work of government resembles private organizations, some of the work of government is unique. In these instances, innovation and customer needs may very well be less important than accountability and transparency. In these cases, appropriate performance measurement is deliberately skewed and unbalanced. Still, the function of performance management remains the same: What are we trying to do, and are we succeeding in doing it?

Conclusions

What is striking about contemporary program management is the degree to which computer-based information systems are now fully integrated into organizational standard operating procedures. Even paper forms are now e-mailed, and the use of standard spreadsheets that are easily downloaded into off-the-shelf data systems has significantly reduced the costs of collecting, reporting, and analyzing data. Performance data is now routinely and rapidly collected from vendors and, when connected to a tangible reward system, is considered a central tool of contract management.

Performance is measured, and incentives are beginning to be based on the reports of performance. In the case of community-based, nonprofit organizations, the issue of staff capacity and resources used limits the ability of government to require participation in a particular electronic performance measurement system. Today, those limits have virtually disappeared in even the smallest nonprofit organizations.

As the technology of personal computers, networked both locally and through the Internet, expanded throughout society, ease of access to these systems made their use more commonplace. It is increasingly easy to construct performance measurement systems that connect and track the accomplishment of all the organizations involved in implementing a particular program. This in turn has increased the tendency for organizational networks to be constructed to deliver services such as parks and homeless services in New York City.

While the cost of information and communication is coming down, the organizational imperatives that make interorganizational communication difficult remain. While even the smallest nonprofit contractor can participate in a performance measurement system, they must be convinced to do so. This requires a system that provides them with benefits as well as costs and a contract that pays for and requires participation. In sum, if contract work is to be managed by government, a carefully thought through, well-designed, and audited system must be developed to measure contractor performance.

At this point we have identified and discussed the ethical, accountability, and management challenges created by government's growing tendency to outsource. To illustrate these challenges and further clarify a set of central concepts, we turn now to a set of case studies of government contracting.

Part IV

Case Studies in Contracting

Chapter 9

When Not to Contract
The U.S. Military and Iraq

UNDER WHAT conditions is the task best performed directly by your own organization? When should you develop the capacity in-house instead of purchasing it from another organization? The war in Iraq is the most contracted-out war in world history. It is clear that overcontracting was one of a number of strategic errors in this war. While some contracting is typical in military operations, it is the amount of contracting that is the issue here.

There are, of course, many other examples of contracted efforts that do not succeed and are replaced by development of in-house capacity. This book will review two cases of failed contracting with the aim of developing a deeper understanding of the factors that cause such failure. Our objective is not to argue against contracting, but to enhance our understanding of the factors that limit it.

Contracting for the War in Iraq

The use of contractors in combat raises a variety of issues related to democratic accountability. First, if their conduct does not adhere to military rules and priorities, they are not subject to military discipline. The need for strict adherence to orders from a chain of command is obviously more important for military and police officials who are authorized to take a person's freedom or even his or her life. In a democratic system, the need for such strict accountability is profound and absolutely necessary if the values of liberty and self-determination are to be preserved while security is maintained.

The modern American military has a set of contracts to provide private sector support services for all manner of operational logistics. Food services, communications, transportation, supplies, and even "security" are provided under contract to private firms. The size and scope of these contracts were indicated in a statement before Congress in June 2004 by William Reed, director of the Defense Contract Audit Agency (DCAA). As Reed reported at the time, "DCAA currently is responsible for providing Iraq-related contract audit services to both DOD and other Government organizations at 56 contractors holding more than 80 prime contracts with contract ceiling amounts of $34.6 billion and funding to date under those contracts of about $12.4 billion" (Reed 2004, 1). Several of those contracts were issued to Halliburton subsidiary Kellogg Brown & Root (KBR). Reed noted that "KBR has been awarded Iraq reconstruction contracts with ceilings totaling more than $18 billion under two major programs: Logistics Civil Augmentation Program (LOGCAP III) for $10 billion; and Restore Iraqi Oil (RIO) for $8.2 billion" (2004, 2). The scope of this work was so extensive that the DOD had established an extensive audit organization exclusively for Iraq. Reed testified, "To carry out the extensive and time-sensitive audit requirements, DCAA has implemented new planning and coordination procedures to effectively integrate audit work between the new Iraq Branch Office, opened in May 2003, and more than 50 DCAA CONUS Audit Offices with cognizance of companies performing contracts in Iraq. The Iraq Branch Office itself now has 22 auditors, and will increase to 28 auditors by the end of June.... During the first 8 months of FY2004, DCAA has issued 285 audit reports related to Iraq reconstruction contracts" (2004, 1).

Most of the contracted functions identified in these audits were standard and fairly prosaic support services, but some were not. Reed testified about the activities of one contractor, CACI, and observed,

> DCAA is expanding its audit coverage at CACI based on recent disclosure of additional contracts awarded to the Company. Since August of 2003, the Army has awarded 11 task orders under a GSA Supply Contract for Information Technology services for interrogation and intelligence gathering effort in Iraq. At least three of those tasks related to interrogation of Iraqi prisoners. Billed costs as of March 2004 under these task orders is $12.7 million, with a total funded contract value in excess of $60 million. DCAA is reviewing the potential misuse by CACI of the GSA schedule contract on this Depart-

ment of Interior contract that is funded by the Army, since "interrogator" type effort is not a function provided by CACI in their GSA schedule. (2004, 4)

The abuse of prisoners in the Abu Ghraib prison by contractor personnel was one of the issues that alerted the media to the unprecedented contracted effort underway in Iraq. Contracting with these organizations continues in Iraq, with four contracts totaling over $48 million to CACI and $4.5 billion in three contracts to KBR for fiscal year 2005 (Department of Defense 2005a).

Peter Singer of the Brookings Institution has written the definitive work on this new method of performing military tasks in *Corporate Warriors: The Rise of the Privatized Military Industry* (2003). Singer details the firms and services provided by this industry and discusses the management and political implications of outsourcing. More recently he focused his attention on the specific issue of contracting in Iraq. In "Warriors for Hire in Iraq," he discusses the use of this new form of military contractor in Iraq:

> Known as "private military firms" (PMFs), they range from small companies that provide teams of commandos for hire to large corporations that run military supply chains. This new military industry encompasses hundreds of companies, thousands of employees, and billions of revenue dollars. In Iraq, they're also accounting for a growing share of the force and the casualties. There are 15,000 private personnel carrying out mission-critical military roles, and they have suffered at least 30 to 50 killed in action. . . . The Bush administration was unwilling to enlist serious assistance from the United Nations or from most of our NATO allies, but thanks to the PMFs that employ private soldiers of more than 30 nationalities, it has been able to assemble an international coalition of sorts in Iraq. But it is more a "coalition of the billing" than of the "willing." Indeed, there are more private military contractors on the ground in Iraq than troops from any one ally, including Britain. One single company, Global Risks, has a reported 1,100 employees in Iraq, including 500 Nepalese Ghurka troops and 500 Fijian soldiers, ranking it sixth among troop donors (2004a).

Singer discusses the increased use of contractors in combat but also notes that elected officials and even senior Pentagon officials are either ignorant of the nature of the contractor role or in "denial" about it. The visibility of the private effort is not enhanced when casualties of the Iraq war are discussed in the media; only military personnel are listed, not those casualties suffered by private contractors supporting military operations. Further, there are clear costs associated with contracting that were not considered when the decision to contract was made. The loss of institutional memory and the idea that government soldiers are more committed to the "cause" could lead us to conclude that they will be more efficient in performing their duties in Iraq. Contracting, therefore, will not result in cost savings, but will replace highly motivated government soldiers with private contractors who have a motivation which may not be the "cause" for which the country is fighting.

Contracting Reconstruction

Another major use of contracting in Iraq has been rebuilding infrastructure destroyed by the war. In some ways the mistakes we see here are no different than those that characterized the federal government's post-Katrina reconstruction. What makes this different is that reconstruction is being undertaken while fighting continues. It is difficult to gauge the impact of the fighting on the efficiency and effectiveness of contracted reconstruction efforts. Continued fighting provides contractors with an all-purpose explanation for any mistakes made or resources wasted during reconstruction.

A major *New York Times* investigative piece in April 2006 analyzed contractor performance in rebuilding Iraq's oil infrastructure. The article focused on a project designed to allow an oil pipeline to cross the Tigris River. According to the article, experts believed the project was technically unsound:

> The project, called the Fatah pipeline crossing, had been a critical element of a $2.4 billion no-bid reconstruction contract that a Halliburton subsidiary had won from the Army in 2003. The spot where about 15 pipelines crossed the Tigris had been the main link between Iraq's rich northern oil fields and the export terminals and refineries that could generate much-needed gasoline, heating fuel and revenue for Iraqis.

For all those reasons, the project's demise would seriously damage the American-led effort to restore Iraq's oil system and enable the country to pay for its own reconstruction. Exactly what portion of Iraq's lost oil revenue can be attributed to one failed project, no matter how critical, is impossible to calculate. But the pipeline at Al Fatah has a wider significance as a metaphor for the entire $45 billion rebuilding effort in Iraq. Although the failures of that effort are routinely attributed to insurgent attacks, an examination of this project shows that troubled decision making and execution have played equally important roles (Glanz 2006).

The Corps of Engineers had difficulty managing the contractor. While its technical staff and the inspector general of Iraq reconstruction questioned the feasibility of the project, it proceeded anyway. According to Glanz, "[t]he Fatah project went ahead despite warnings from experts that it could not succeed because the underground terrain was shattered and unstable. It continued chewing up astonishing amounts of cash when the predicted problems bogged the work down, with a contract that allowed crews to charge as much as $100,000 a day as they waited on standby. The company in charge engaged in what some American officials saw as a self-serving attempt to limit communications with the government until all the money was gone" (Glanz 2006).

One issue in reconstruction contracting relates to the environment within which accountability must be established. Normal reporting and financial control systems are difficult to implement amidst the chaos and dangers of war. The work itself may be interrupted by fighting, as might deliveries of supplies. When the project involves construction, sabotage can destroy work before the project is completed. All these factors make accountability difficult even when the contractor is honest.

Despite all the difficulties that have come from ongoing fighting in Iraq, several questions have been raised about the "success" of reconstruction projects that have been completed. According to a report in the *New York Times* in April 2007, "inspectors for a federal oversight agency have found that in a sampling of eight projects that the United States had declared successes, seven were no longer operating as designed because of plumbing and electrical failures, lack of proper maintenance, apparent looting and expensive equipment that lay idle." The claims of success for projects that have serious problems could be construed as evidence of the political nature of the contracting process in Iraq.

A difficulty of a war like Iraq is that the conditions of war are less clear-cut than in more traditional conflicts between sovereign nations. Reconstruction is needed to demonstrate that "normalcy" has been re-established. However, since the mode of war tends to be terrorist and insurgent violence rather than combat between armed forces, it is difficult for contractors involved in reconstruction to do so in areas free of violence. This in turn subjects these private organizations to the same conditions that contractors face when directly supporting the work of the armed forces, which results in the same issues of accountability and exposure to hazards faced by these other contractors.

To summarize, we see three types of contracting related to the war in Iraq. The first is the traditional military support and logistics that seem to be part of the "head-count"-driven trend of contracting throughout the federal government. The amount of this contracted support is quite high but not without precedent. The second type of contracting and what is new, or at least newly discovered, is the use of contractors in combat roles. Whereas a certain amount of contracting is clearly needed in any military situation, the extent of contracting and the use of contractors in combat strike us as examples of practices that should be avoided. The third type of contracting relates to the rebuilding effort.

The decision to contract logistics and even military actions was a highly constrained make-or-buy decision. Political factors made it necessary to present the smallest possible military force for public consumption. This is not a phenomenon new to government, although it did come later to the military than to the civilian agencies. After the expansion of the federal government in the 1960s to fight the war on poverty and the war in Vietnam, government staff growth was halted while government contract funding continued to expand along with the nation's population and federal budget. Elected officials felt that if the number of full-time employees did not grow, then government did not grow. Paul C. Light has written the definitive work on this phenomenon in *The True Size of Government* (1999), and Cohen experienced this directly in two instances in the 1980s. In the Superfund program, as a relatively junior GS-13 employee, he had access to hundreds of thousands of contractor dollars and what was essentially a staff of about six or seven people in a D.C.-based consulting firm. Later, as a consultant to the Department of Energy's (DOE) nuclear waste program, he was part of a 150-person contractor team that reported to a DOE office of fewer than ten people.

The work done by these contractors could have easily been done by government employees, but the political pressure to keep the head count down and the relative ease of hiring nongovernment workers made it necessary to use contractors. This seems to be the case here as well. In Vietnam, there were four to five support troops for every soldier on the front engaged in combat. Of the 500,000 soldiers in Vietnam at the war's peak, no more than 150,000 were engaged in combat. This indicates that the scale of the U.S. commitment in Iraq is similar (in order of magnitude) to the level of commitment in Vietnam. This is a comparison that the Bush administration did not want to invite and with an official force deployment (or head count) of less than 200,000, they could avoid these comparisons (at least until the "quagmire" images reappeared). Although the violence in Iraq has not diminished as of this writing, President Bush continues to keep the number of active military personnel deployed in Iraq low with a total of 158,000 deployed as of March 19, 2008 (Fell 2008).

Contracting practices in Iraq raised a series of issues related to billing, contractor oversight by the military, and what the General Accounting Office, now the Government Accountability Office (GAO), termed issuing task orders for work that was "outside the contracts' scope of work" (Walker 2004). Walker's testimony dealt directly with the issue of maintaining sufficient distinctive competence to manage contractor work. He observed that "effective oversight of the diverse functions performed under the [Iraq] contracts requires government personnel with knowledge and expertise in these specific areas. DCMA [Defense Contract Management Agency] contract administrators are contracting professionals, but many have limited knowledge of field operations" (Walker 2004, 10). These contracting officials rely on the military field units to provide them with the knowledge of operations needed to manage contractors. However, this expertise was frequently lacking in Iraq, and contractors had very little real oversight.

In the case of dining services and transportation, the issue is one of placing civilians in harm's way—a duty that perhaps should be reserved for military personnel who have been recruited or drafted to take those risks and trained to minimize them. According to a GAO report on the rebuilding of Iraq, the security situation in Iraq had deteriorated to such a degree by September 2003 that "[a]ll international organizations and contractors, as well as Iraqis cooperating with the CPA [Coalition Provisional Authority] were potential targets of deliberate, direct, and hostile attacks" (United States General Accounting Office 2004, 46). As we know, these attacks continued through 2004, 2005, 2006, and 2007. While an argument can be made for contracting support services, the argument grows weaker in combat situations and weaker still when the contractor is expected to bear arms and participate in combat. While this is a relatively new issue in need of further research and analysis, Peter Singer, the scholar who has focused the most attention on this issue, concludes his analysis of military contracting in Iraq by stating the following: "We should also take a step back and examine the overall trend, rather than continue to breathlessly outsource. Just because we can turn something over to the private market does not always mean we should. Two basic questions must always be asked before handing over any public function, most particularly to private military firms: Is the function being privatized in symmetry with national security and the public interest? If so, how will this privatization save money and promote efficiency?" (2004b)

For purposes of this analysis, even ignoring issues of cost and efficiency, the larger issue of accountability is a clear indicator that these practices should be avoided. How can a contractor be held accountable when it is unclear who they are accountable to? Contractors in Iraq adhere to the laws of their parent country, not the laws of Iraq, as declared in June 2004 by the Coalition Provisional Authority (Avant 2004, 24; Coalition Provisional Authority 2004). Although the contractors are performing many military duties, they are not subject to the Uniform Code of Military Justice because the war in Iraq was officially declared over in May of 2003 (Avant 2006, 338). The U.S. laws, which private contractors may be subject to, are the Military Extraterritorial Jurisdiction Act and the Patriot Act, but these laws are new and full of uncertainties (Avant 2006, 338–39). In a broader view, private military contractors are hard to legally define under international treaties. They cannot be defined as mercenaries under the 1989 UN Convention on Mercenaries; if they are captured by enemy forces they are not likely to receive prisoner of war status, and they cannot be easily placed into the categories of combatants, noncombatants, and civilians laid out by the Geneva Conventions (Avant 2004, 2006). Given such status, it is difficult to hold these private contractors accountable for crimes committed. The scandal at Abu Ghraib provides a clear example of this. Although the military personnel who were involved with the abuse of prisoners at Abu Ghraib have been charged and tried, the private contractors who participated in prisoner abuse have not been charged and their companies deny any allegations.

Lessons

While there is precedent for some of the contracting that has been done in Iraq, the outsourcing of private military contractors is clearly something that should be avoided. Some of the contracts that were let may have been awarded for political reasons, something we have recommended against. The make-or-buy decision should be based upon a manager's weighing of cost and benefits and not constraints placed upon him or her by politicians. Additionally, the importance of management control during wartime is essential, and, as we have discussed, the management of contractors and through networks is not the same as internal management, and communication can be difficult, two things that would be highly undesirable in a war zone.

A yellow pages test in this instance could possibly show a few contractors for the type of work being done in Iraq, but many of the contracts awarded during Operation Iraqi Freedom had little competition, eroding the financial benefits of contracting. Some of the largest contracts, including sole-source contracts, have also been awarded to Halliburton, formerly run by Vice President Cheney. As we have mentioned earlier, it would have served the vice president well to recuse himself from the situation to avoid even the appearance of favoritism. While we are certain that he would argue that he had done so, the appearance of impropriety was still overwhelming. What was needed was an overt and visible step that ensured that he was in no way involved in the contracting decision.

The contracting in Iraq has been the subject of many questions regarding corruption and profiteering. Questions have been raised about whether the "best" contractors were selected for the job. The selection of contractors for work in Iraq should have been held in an open and transparent way. Competition should have been required where feasible, and no-bid or sole-source contracts should have been avoided. In situations where this was not possible, contracting should have been avoided.

Our questions about the use of private military contractors extend to the use of contractors for reconstruction as well. Unfinished, substandard, and ill-conceived projects serve to highlight the failure of contractors to complete the job. It is difficult to apportion blame for these failures among contractor negligence, poor government oversight, or the obvious difficulties of operating in a war zone. If the failure of contractors to deliver upon their agreements was due to negligence and inability, fault lies not just with the contractor but also with the contracting agency and its failure to properly negotiate and manage the contract.

As we write this, Iraq is in the midst of an anti-American insurgency and a full-blown civil war, creating a difficult environment for a contractor to build infrastructure. Despite these conditions, transparency, honesty, competition, and a proper cost-benefit analysis would have gone a long way to prevent many of the problems seen in Iraq.

Conclusions

One hopes that the experience of cost overruns, corruption, and inadequate accountability will influence future contracting practices by the military and the government. It is unlikely that the political dynamic leading to a war with a smaller military and no draft will fade soon. There is little question that the war in Iraq was characterized by overcontracting as well as poor contract management practices. The key lesson is that the extent of contractor effort and the management of contractor behavior must be subject to at least as high a level of strategic analysis as any other military activities. Democratic considerations must also be taken into account when considering the use of private military contractors who have the authority to take lives.

Chapter 10

When Contracting Really Works
Welfare-to-Work in Philadelphia

THE TRANSITIONAL Work Corporation is a nonprofit corporation that was created to help welfare recipients comply with the time limits incorporated into the federal welfare reform legislation of the mid-1990s. This chapter focuses its analysis of government contracting with a nonprofit organization that was designed to serve as a government contractor. The nature of the Transitional Work Corporation and the challenges it faces were shaped by the evolution of the welfare-to-work philosophy, legislation, and policy in Pennsylvania. The Commonwealth of Pennsylvania enacted enabling legislation that reinforced the philosophy of work-first for welfare recipients. In practical terms, this meant that current welfare recipients had two years to find an average of twenty hours a week of work or lose their welfare benefits.

In most states, the welfare-to-work funds were managed by state agencies, and then Pennsylvania governor Tom Ridge decided that the Pennsylvania Department of Public Welfare (DPW) should manage his state's federal allocation and matching funds. The DPW therefore had to manage the welfare-to-work grant program as well as the newly designed Temporary Assistance for Needy Families program (TANF), the successor to the long-established AFDC program (Aid to Families with Dependent Children). Since the federal law required that the grants go in part to local workforce boards, the DPW would need to work with localities such as Philadelphia in developing its program (Greenwald 2002, 3).

Work requirements presented a major new challenge for social services departments across the country. Philadelphia faced a particularly difficult assignment as more than half of the welfare population of Pennsylvania lived in the city. There was virtually no private sector job growth in the city, and the suburban job market could not be easily accessed through public transportation. Among the cities with the largest public assistance population at the time—New York, Chicago, Detroit, and Philadelphia— Philadelphia was the only one with negative overall job growth (Hughes 1996). Finally, Pennsylvania did not have a long history of experimentation in the field of welfare-to-work. The new federal and state requirements initially overwhelmed and confused both recipients and the city's welfare department workers.

The situation was complicated by a basic philosophical disagreement between the city and the Commonwealth of Pennsylvania. The commonwealth took a strong stance: work means real employment in paying jobs, primarily in the private sector. The strong economy across most of Pennsylvania led state officials to believe their firm stance was reasonable and could be achieved.

In Philadelphia, the economy was not nearly as strong as the rest of the state, and there were many welfare recipients to place. City officials and social service advocates favored a broader definition of work activities to meet the twenty-hour requirement, including work readiness training, basic education, job search, and supported work opportunities. By the spring of 1997, the city and the commonwealth discussions were stalemated.

A new and creative idea helped break the stalemate. Mark Alan Hughes, vice president of a Philadelphia-based, innovative nonprofit called Public/ Private Ventures, wrote an op-ed for the major local newspaper, *The Philadelphia Inquirer*. Hughes proposed that the city and commonwealth create a transitional jobs program to meet the federal works requirement. Hughes argued that this approach was superior because it would enable recipients to meet work requirement and also remain eligible for TANF benefits, participants would end up with more income at the end of the month, participants would be eligible for the Earned Income Tax Credit (EITC), and working would enable participants to build a work history and contacts to help obtain a permanent job (Hughes 1997).

Under the Hughes plan, a nonprofit organization would be created to develop transitional job opportunities in nonprofit and government agencies. Willing participants would be placed in these six-month, transitional jobs. Welfare grants would be channeled through the nonprofit job developer who would convert the grant into a wage. These transitioning welfare recipients would thereby become paid employees of the nonprofit organization that placed them in the transitional job. At the same time, Philadelphia mayor (and subsequent Pennsylvania governor) Ed Rendell and his staff concluded that the transitional work option could work for Philadelphia.

Donald Kimelman, manager of the Venture Fund at the Pew Charitable Trusts, read the Hughes op-ed and decided to invite Hughes and state and city officials to a meeting. The trusts are a major force in social policy nationally and command substantial respect in their Philadelphia hometown. City officials believed the transitional work mechanism would help recipients meet federal work requirements in a difficult local economy (Greenwald 2002, 3).

Kimelman was able to engage commonwealth DPW secretary Feather O. Houston in developing the plan. The fund wanted to test new ideas that would help welfare recipients meet the requirements of the new federal welfare law. While months of negotiations followed, all key players were now involved, a program known as Philadelphia@Work would soon emerge, and a nonprofit agency that was to be called the Transitional Work Corporation (TWC) would be created to carry out its objectives.

The trusts provided a planning grant to support the ongoing discussions and program development. As important, the trusts served as an honest broker and nudge. Government officials and advocates came to rely on the trusts as a force for results that also respected the positions of all sides involved in the negotiations. In the end, the federal, state, and city governments would provide most of the funds for participant salaries, benefits, and training. The trusts would provide substantial support for the administrative structure of the new nonprofit managing entity as well as support for innovation and expansion. Without the good faith cooperation of all three key stakeholders, the TWC would not have been possible.

The TWC Experiment Begins

In September 1998, the TWC opened for business. As part of the complex negotiations that led to its creation, TWC was founded to operate a program called Philadelphia@Work. The program design sought to strike a balance between work experience, skill building, and support services. Richard Greenwald, head of the TWC, characterizes the organization's philosophy as "everyone should work. But you cannot expect self-sufficiency for all participants. The clear message is that you learn to work by working. At the same time, people who have never worked, and who have children and a wide range of problems cannot succeed without support during a transitional stage" (Greenwald 2006).

TWC competes with other city- and commonwealth-funded welfare-to-work providers, faith-based providers, for-profit employment agencies, and direct recruitment by employers for participants. To recruit participants, TWC advertises in local newspapers, seeks positive news coverage in the local media, partners with community-based organizations and faith-based organizations, and benefits from positive word-of-mouth endorsements from alumni now working full-time in jobs with benefits. Many participants come to TWC after failing with competing providers.

The Philadelphia@Work program planning group correctly anticipated that the clients TWC would serve face multiple obstacles to work, including criminal records, domestic violence, substance abuse, mental health issues, lack of experience with workplace expectations, inadequate child care, and spotty work histories. TWC clients have little or no work experience, and few have high school diplomas. The majority of TWC participants are at a fifth-grade math level and a sixth-grade reading level, but the range is from below first grade to above twelfth grade. Many clients lack the fundamental hard or soft skills needed to perform a basic job search. Those who have been successful in finding work in the past have trouble with long-term job tenure, moving from job to job frequently (Greenwald 2002, 5).

Most clients have failed to complete at least three other welfare-to-work programs. After failing in so many other programs, many new clients lack confidence that any program will lead to success in the job market. These individuals need intensive career counseling to ensure job retention and advancement. To address the comprehensive needs of these clients, TWC follows three core principles:

- put clients on payroll the first day they enroll and place them in transitional jobs so they can build a work history, get a job reference, and

take advantage of all the benefits that come with receiving a paycheck instead of a welfare check;
- train and support people during the work experience so they become more marketable to employers and have a better chance of retaining a job than before they came to TWC;
- help place people in unsubsidized jobs and support them in those jobs so they stay employed.

From the beginning, TWC focused on the long-term effects of their program on the participants' ability to retain a job and stay attached to the labor market. TWC structures a more active engagement in real work that provides workers with marketable skills. Tailored professional development training, job placement services, and retention services enhance paid work experience. TWC implements this model through the two main components of Philadelphia@Work—orientation and employment.

An orientation team prepares new clients for a transitional job, starting with the identification of (and plan for overcoming) any barriers to employment. Facilitators build a relationship with participants and find ways to motivate and encourage them to stick with the program. Many clients emphasize that they feel supported and motivated to stay in this program; they realize the people and the services at TWC are different from many of the other programs that they failed to complete. Using this relationship-based model throughout the program, clients are more willing to disclose information about issues they might be dealing with that are obstacles to job retention. During this time clients:

- attend twenty-five hours of orientation for two full weeks;
- are paid $5.15 per hour by TWC and receive a wage subsidy (equal to half of the welfare check they were getting) from DPW;
- receive child-care and transportation subsidies from DPW;
- develop many skills including interviewing, resume writing, and professional etiquette;
- interview for and are placed in a transitional job at a nonprofit organization or government agency.

After orientation comes transitional and finally permanent employment. During the transitional phase clients learn how to work by actually working. To that end, all participants:

- work for twenty-five hours each week—TWC is the employer of record and pays each client $5.15 per hour;
- attend ten hours per week of professional development training at TWC;
- are mentored by a work partner at their work site;
- are eligible for child-care and transportation subsidies for up to six months;
- receive support from the entire in-house TWC employment team.

Participants interview for transitional jobs requiring twenty-five hours per week. Usually entry-level positions in city government or nonprofit offices in Philadelphia, these jobs are similar to paid internships. Transitional positions provide participants with the hands-on work experience they lack, eliminating one barrier to their future employment. Participants are given site mentors and TWC staff to help them build their work history and develop a track record.

Comprehensive professional development is an integral part of the program. This training focuses on employment goals and career advancement in health care, hospitality, professional services, child care, or data-intensive careers. All clients receive basic reading, math, English, and computer training based upon their skill level. After assessing the unique needs of each individual, career advisors work one-on-one with clients to develop an Employment Development and Retention Plan (EDRP) that outlines employment and career goals. While each person's transitional training schedule is designed to fit his or her educational and professional needs, every client is encouraged to pursue a GED.

To help participants take the next step toward permanent employment, TWC employs a sales team to match qualified participants to unsubsidized employment and local employers. TWC serves entry-level employees through the region and a secondary human resources office for all of its unsubsidized employers, following each placement to ensure that both the participant and employer are satisfied.

The sales staff begins work with participants about four months into the transitional employment phase by assessing each one's skills and interests. TWC sales staff members have built relationships with employers, enabling them to provide participants with "live" job leads in for-profit, nonprofit, and government organizations in the Greater Philadelphia region. At the same time, the sales representatives encourage clients to take ownership of their own job search.

After placement in a "permanent" job, TWC continues to support their "graduates" for up to six months. These graduates also continue to receive transportation and child-care subsidies and are eligible to receive retention bonuses (a payment to reward ongoing employment) from TWC of up to $800. It costs about $7,000 for TWC to take a participant from the first day of orientation to placement in a market job. This is higher than the less-comprehensive workfare programs, but few of those programs are able to match TWC's high job placement and retention rates.

From orientation through six months after placement in a market job, TWC helps its participants overcome the substantial obstacles they face to self-sufficiency. They help with transportation subsidies, child-care subsidies, clothing allowances and used but serviceable professional attire, income tax and EITC filing assistance, and school books for their children.

Growing Pains—The Contract Creates Challenges

A great deal of thought and discussion among a wide array of experts and policymakers went into the development of the TWC model. It was initially conceived of as a three-year experiment. The early outcomes substantially exceeded the expectations of the board and the senior staff, as well as those of many outside observers. Yet, after only nine months of operation, TWC leadership was already convinced that the organization's operating model could be improved.

Beginning in the summer of 1999, TWC conducted the first in a series of annual retreats. TWC retreats involve every staff member in both the planning and the event itself. Retreats include sessions to build spirit and unity and are designed to focus the organization on key issues for improvement.

In 1999, the issue was communication. TWC was a huge effort, developing on the fly, with little time to build consensus or keep everyone informed. The consequences included feelings of exclusion and lack of respect. Also, not everyone was carrying out the organization's standard operating procedures. Therefore, the first retreat sought to find better ways to communicate management policies throughout the organization and to communicate back what TWC staff members learned on the front lines. In what was to become a TWC tradition, the retreat ended with a list of action items and a strategy for implementation and follow-up.

The results seemed to meet most staff members' and participants' expectations. TWC committed itself to a major upgrade of its computer, telecommunications, and information processing systems. Overall, the general view was that the retreat had been a complete success.

Next, TWC committed to greater staff involvement in policymaking. Numerous committees were established. Some committees accomplished the follow-up tasks from the retreat and were retired. Some committees accomplished the retreat tasks and identified an ongoing mission and new tasks. They continue to operate. Other committees did not attract sufficient interest and were terminated. The option to create new committees remains open should the need arise.

As 1999 came to an end, the TWC board, management, and staff were able to celebrate a very successful first full year of operation. More than a thousand participants were enrolled in the program. About 250 "graduates" had been placed in permanent jobs paying an average hourly wage in excess of $7.00. TWC had become one of the largest transitional work programs in the country. However, there were also areas where improvements seemed possible.

Performance-Based Contract Leads to Management Issues

Prior to coming to TWC, Richard Greenwald had worked at America Works, a for-profit employment agency for those with significant barriers to employment. America Works was an early advocate of pay-for-performance contracts. Greenwald saw firsthand the business advantage of getting paid for results rather than activities, for the customer, the employee, and the bottom line of the organization, and he worked hard to make the TWC contract performance based. By the end of TWC's first year, the performance targets incorporated into the contract were already creating problems for the organization.

To ready participants for the world of work, TWC strictly enforces attendance requirements, appropriate work behaviors at TWC and at the transitional work sites, and a policy of no drugs or alcohol at work. As a result, more than five hundred participants had to be terminated in the first year for failure to meet attendance requirements, discipline issues, or substance abuse. This strict enforcement policy led to participation rates that were not sufficient for TWC to meet contractual targets for permanent placements—that is, there were not enough candidates active in the program to meet the job placement goals of the contract.

For 2000, the TWC board and senior management decided to focus on improving communications between its departments and developing a comprehensive yet manageable set of performance indicators. The plan was to recruit more participants, inform them better, and build support for the participant behavior requirements and thereby enable TWC to meet the permanent placement requirements of the contract. TWC was able to increase enrollments and permanent placements significantly in 2000, but advocates and outside forces (including TWC funding sources) were pressuring TWC to do even better.

In part, TWC was the victim of its own success, and this is the challenge of a performance-based contract. If you set the performance standards too low, you can be paying vendors top dollar for less than their best work and bonuses for what is really average performance. However, if you set the bar too high, you can make excellent performance look bad and force good contractors to drop out.

Government contract details are also subject to public disclosure. In Philadelphia, there were other organizations with similar missions who were jealous of the funding TWC received and the media attention it attracted. These competitor agencies were quick to criticize TWC for anything less than superior performance or any downturn in a measure of workload or outcome.

After much discussion, the senior staff at TWC decided to focus on what they found meaningful to measure their own performance, including but not limited to the targets incorporated into their contract:

- Enrollments—people who sign up for the program;
- Participants who successfully complete the program;
- Participants placed in permanent jobs;
- Participants that receive longevity bonuses for staying in their permanent jobs.

A new performance management system was implemented that featured these four factors but also incorporated a large number of workload indicators and progress measures designed to help everyone at TWC assess their progress week by week and month by month. An inclusive strategic planning process produced a three-tiered performance indicator system—one set for the board, funding sources, interested observers, and the media; a second, more detailed, set for senior management; and a third set tailored to each division and focused on key aspects of their responsibilities in the overall TWC mission.

The new system had the desired impact. Performance improved. At the same time, as a whole, the three-tiered system with dozens and dozens of indicators was confusing, labor intensive, and time consuming to maintain and use.

Key indicators for 2000 were substantially better than for 1999. Enrollments were up by more than 300, totaling more than 1,500. Permanent placements more than doubled. Average hourly wages were up from an average of $7.11 in 1999 to $7.24 in 2000. The retention rate for permanent placements exceeded 70 percent.

Raising the Bar—What's Good and Not So Good about Pay for Performance Contracts

As 2001 began, TWC was becoming known as an effective program. Representatives from governments and nonprofit organizations from all over the United States were visiting TWC and asking for technical assistance and even requesting TWC to set up shop in their community. TWC had assisted hundreds of inexperienced, long-term welfare recipients to move into private sector, market wage jobs within a year of entering the TWC system. Despite this initial success, the organization's leadership thought improvements were needed.

The most substantial challenge faced by the corporation was its inability to succeed with the more difficult and less willing participants. Senior management and the board moved aggressively to involve outside observers, consultants, evaluators, critics, and other providers to assess the effectiveness of its programs. The contract treats all placements equally even though the successful placement of "hard to place" participants is generally more difficult and expensive for the contractor and probably of greater benefit to society.

This commitment to focus on the harder to place was compromised when management noted a substantial dip in permanent placements. If that trend continued, TWC would not meet its placement goals for 2001. In addition, some staff members were not being held accountable for their performance by management, lowering key indicators and seriously affecting the morale of others working well above management's expectations.

As TWC grew, the departments became separate and competitive rather than integrated and cooperative. Placements were dropping because participants were falling between the cracks of departments. Organizational units drifted apart; orientation, transitional placement, professional development training, and placement had become separate and independent activities. The transitional placement division might view a participant as an outstanding candidate for permanent placement while the training division was ready to expel the person for failure to attend class. No one group took full responsibility for a participant, and few people in the organization knew what was happening with a participant unless they were in direct contact. These problems were exacerbated by the rapid growth in the size of the TWC staff combined with the normal amount of staff turnover.

In response, a new structure was put into place with the following characteristics:

- The elimination of most existing departments of TWC and the restructuring of the organization into functional, task-based teams, emphasizing the performance targets in the contract.

- Refocusing the central program of the organization on two major functions—orientation and employment, also reflecting the two key performance indicators in the contract (participation and placement).
- Restructuring of the employment function into multidisciplinary teams that serve the same group of participants throughout their career at TWC.
- Better communication and more emphasis on the need to reach and exceed performance targets, particularly job placements.
- Enhancing the governmental and community relations activities of TWC so that the organization receives more public funds for longer periods and so that the organization achieves a more positive image in the inner-city community of competing and complementary nonprofit companies.
- Expanding the activities of TWC to encompass a program to include participants with limited English proficiency and to focus more intently on activities to ensure retention and advancement in the participants' permanent jobs.
- Redesigning the physical space, creating an open, bullpen design with low partitions and placing team members in close proximity to each other.

Everyone in the organization became a member of a team. Each team focused on an important function of the organization: senior management, finance and administration, orientation, retention services, or employment. The orientation and employment teams were focused directly on participants.

The largest unit was the employment division, and it was organized into five teams, known as pods. Each pod took full responsibility for approximately 100 participants during their entire time with TWC until they were placed or separated. Each pod included career advisors, retention specialists, a sales representative, a job match coordinator, and facilitators. This structure provided a one-stop, full-service environment for the participant and a comprehensive picture of the participant for the multiple service specialists at TWC attempting to assist those participants.

Contract-Driven, Measurable Success

From the time that the first clients were enrolled in the fall of 1998 until June 2006, 15,853 participants entered the program. More than 95 percent completed the transitional employment program, and more than 50 percent were hired in market-rate jobs. The average wage was $7.50 an hour for thirty-five hours, and more than 68 percent had benefits within the first year of employment. Nearly 45 percent were still employed six months later. This performance should be viewed in context. Nearly 37 percent of those enrolled at TWC did not have high school diplomas, and nearly 25 percent had criminal records. Compared to remaining on Temporary Assistance for Needy Families (TANF), the net savings to the state for those participating in the TWC was more than $6.4 million per class.

Unlike workfare, transitional work enables workers to pay into Social Security and take advantage of the Earned Income Tax Credit (EITC). Transitional work enables participants to gain work experience and obtain professional references while receiving support services such as child-care and transportation subsidies. Independent evaluations of transitional jobs programs have found that these programs significantly improve the employment rate of the participants compared with other options such as job search, pre-employment training, and workfare (Klawitter 2001). Other studies support the conclusion that hard-to-serve participants need the flexibility, supportive services, and balance of work and training that programs such as the TWC provide (Kirby et al. 2002).

These are all good results, and the contract with the local government authority in Philadelphia helped drive these outcomes. At the same time, it also forced TWC to focus on permanent employment and on those participants that had a reasonable chance of moving into permanent employment as quickly as possible, certainly within the one-year term of its contract (which was renegotiated annually). Inevitably, the transitional work phase received less emphasis over time, and those participants that could make slow progress through the transitional phase received less and less attention. The good and the bad of performance-based contracts is that you get what you pay for.

A Contract Document Focused on Accountability

The funds that supported TWC came primarily through a contract with the Philadelphia Workforce Development Corporation (PWDC), a quasi-governmental entity, nominally controlled by the mayor of the City of Philadelphia but directed by an independent board of prominent citizens from the community. The PWDC is similar to the private industry councils and workforce investment boards created across the country to run job training and placement programs funded by the U.S. Department of Labor. As previously discussed, TWC was created to operate a program called Philadelphia@Work. The PWDC receives the federal and state funds allocated for welfare-to-work initiatives and then contracts with TWC to operate Philadelphia@Work.

The PWDC entered into a series of one-year contracts with TWC that provided a mixture of cost reimbursement and performance-based payments. An annual contract without an option to renew under similar terms kept the contractor under tight control. However, it also made it difficult for the contractor to develop long-term plans and retain good employees. This was particularly true in this case, when the contract terms were not finalized until well into the first or second quarter of the contract year. That is, TWC did not know the final contract goals until three or more months of the one-year contract term had passed.

The TWC contract for 2005–2006 was representative (Philadelphia Workforce Development Corporation 2005). The maximum compensation due to TWC was $9,500,000. PWDC reimbursed TWC for 100 percent of the cost of paid work experience, client fringe benefits, supportive service, and incentive payments made directly to clients—a total of $1,732,500. The rest of the contract was divided into cost reimbursement (60 percent, or $4,270,800) and performance (40 percent, or $2,847,200).

The performance portion was then subdivided into three categories—a successful completion payment (50 percent, or $1,423,600), a placement payment (30 percent, or $854,160), and a six-month retention payment (20 percent, or $569,440). To earn these performance payments, TWC needed to enroll 1,500 participants. For TWC to earn the full successful completion payment, 85 percent of those enrolled had to meet minimum attendance at transitional worksites, achieve satisfactory or better performance as determined by their career advisor and the workplace partner, and complete the state-mandated Employment Development Retention Plan.

The full job placement payment was earned if 70 percent of those achieving successful completion obtained twenty hours per week of permanent unsubsidized employment or thirty hours per week of subsidized employment with an average wage of $7.00 per hour with health benefits. The job retention payment was earned when 65 percent of the job placements maintained employment for six months.

In the scope of services, the contract specified that TWC would train work partners (employers) to provide participants with a quality work experience. The contract also specified that work partners would serve as on-site supervisors and mentors for participants and would sign off on all participant time sheets. It also permitted TWC to compensate work partners "to encourage their continued support of the P@W participant for as long as the participant is on the work site" (Philadelphia Workforce Development Corporation 2005, Scope of Services). Finally, TWC was directed to design and deliver orientation and regular follow-up sessions to ensure that work partners demonstrated effective methods for developing the skills and enhancing the proper work attitudes and behaviors of their participants.

The contract also pays TWC to establish relationships with private businesses so they can place and help retain participants in unsubsidized jobs. To achieve these objectives, the contract stated that TWC career advisors "will help the participant to maximize childcare and transportation supports and will make referrals to any other support services that are appropriate" (Philadelphia Workforce Development Corporation 2005, Scope of Services).

Section one of the contract stated, "Nothing in this Agreement shall be construed to create a partnership or joint venture between the Philadelphia Workforce Development Corporation and Contractor" (Philadelphia Workforce Development Corporation 2005, 1). The Philadelphia Workforce Development Corporation may not consider its relationship with TWC a partnership, but it clearly required TWC to develop an extensive, ongoing network of for-profit and nonprofit employers, social service providers, and governmental agencies to successfully implement its contract and earn the incentives for job placement and retention. During its first eight years of operation, TWC established strong ties with a wide array of transitional employers who supervise multiple participants on a regular basis. Some of the largest and longest lasting transitional employers include the Academy of Natural Science; the City of Philadelphia's Department of License and Inspection, Department of Health, and Department of Records; Drexel University; the First Judicial District; the Free Library of Philadelphia; Jefferson Hospital; Philadelphia Corporation for the Aging; TWC itself; and the YMCA.

TWC was able to place multiple "graduates" in a wide range of permanent jobs with major employers at wage rates often well above the minimum wage, with full benefits. Organizations that provided permanent employment included the City Department of Public Health, Prudential Insurance, Avis Rent a Car, Wachovia Bank, Hilton Hotels, the IRS, Kelly Services, Mercy Hospital, the City Department of License and Inspection, the First Judicial District, H&R Block, Aramark, Thomas Jefferson Hospital, and Edison High School. A number of transitional employers were satisfied with their transitional placements and decided to hire them as regular employees at the end of the transitional period. To achieve and maintain these permanent placements, TWC worked with a regular group of child-care agencies, the public transportation system, legal aid, the courts, substance abuse agencies, and domestic violence service providers.

The Philadelphia Workforce Development Corporation can be seen as a node in a network that extends back to the office of the mayor of Philadelphia, the Pennsylvania Department of Welfare, the governor's office, and the federal departments of Health and Human Services and Labor. The Pew Charitable Trusts and Public/Private Ventures continue to play an important role in the funding and shaping of the TWC model. This complicated, multisector network has developed and improved its carefully measured outcomes over eight years.

Conclusion

A key lesson of this case for contract management is that in many cases, the contractor is not simply a neutral repository of government policy, but in fact is a policymaker in its own right. The Transitional Work Corporation was certainly a government contractor, providing critical services to the city of Philadelphia and the Commonwealth of Pennsylvania. However, it was also an independent, mission-driven, nonprofit organization with multiple sources of revenue. One source of its funds was a major grant from the Pew Charitable Trusts. Pew is not simply a granting agency, but a powerful force in the governing network that rules Pennsylvania. The management techniques adopted by the contractor may very well have been more sophisticated than those employed by the government agencies they worked for.

The decision to outsource transitional work was ultimately made by governments in Philadelphia and Pennsylvania, but it was a highly constrained make-or-buy decision. Government was not seen as a likely implementer of a transitional work program. The program's inception, funding, and political support were closely connected to the organizational form that was developed. If the Transitional Work Corporation had not had sound leadership, it might have failed when the first signs of difficulty emerged. How can government identify excellent nonprofit leadership and distinguish it from mediocre or even lower quality management? This is a critical factor to be considered by the effective government contract manager, but it is a difficult factor to assess.

The city embraced annual performance-based contracts because they can be an effective way for government to hold vendors accountable. However, if the government contract managers are not thoroughly familiar with the work of the contractor and do not actively engage the contractor in developing the performance measures, they may end up emphasizing the wrong measures, setting thresholds that are too high or too low, and providing a lower value of service to the citizen/consumer. In the case of TWC, the city did not discuss the performance measures with TWC in advance, and the contracts were not finalized until several months into the one-year term of the contract.

Paying for performance also raises other issues in the relationship between government and its contractor. The city of Philadelphia emphasized placement and retention in permanent jobs as the key payment point for TWC. This led to several negative, unintended consequences. First, it created serious cash flow issues for TWC since placement and retention are the last steps in the many months that it works with its participants through orientation, ready-for-work training, transitional work, skill building, interviewing, and support services. All these critical, expensive activities are only indirectly rewarded by the contract. Other important services, such as helping participants qualify for the Earned Income Tax Credit, are not rewarded at all. In such circumstances, the responsible contract manager may wish to consider a contract with both pay for performance and cost reimbursement compensation components.

Chapter 11

When Contracting Really Doesn't Work
Atlanta's Water Contract

WE ALL need between twenty and fifty liters of water free of contaminants every day to live a healthy and productive life (UNESCO 2006). Water's importance is rising as population densities and climate change interact to create more regions with acute water shortages (Sachs 2005, 283). Indeed, water has been called "the oil of the 21st Century" (CBC News 2004).

According to the U.S. Environmental Protection Agency (EPA), the United States has one of the safest water supplies in the world (U.S. Environmental Protection Agency 2006). However, water quality varies from state to state. In Georgia, where Atlanta is located, there were no water systems violating maximum containment levels or treatment levels according to a recent report of the U.S. EPA (2003, 4). Atlanta decided to privatize its water services in an attempt to solve a fiscal crisis rather than to deal with a water supply or quality problem (although there was a potential environmental crisis looming in the background).

Atlanta was not alone in dealing with water- and sewer-system-related fiscal challenges. In 2005, the U.S. EPA reported to the Congress that the U.S. public water system infrastructure investment needs would total $276.8 billion over the next twenty years (U.S. Environmental Protection Agency 2005, 1). What makes Atlanta notable is that it sought to solve its water infrastructure challenges through a large and comprehensive agreement with a multinational, for-profit corporation.

Private operation of public water and sewer systems was not prevalent in the United States during the late 1990s, but it was hardly unusual. In 1990 there were private operations in twelve countries serving fifty million people; a little more than a decade later, there were private systems in fifty-six countries serving 300 million people (Carty 2003; Marsden 2003). Among the largest companies are France's Suez Lyonnaise des Eaux Group and Vivendi Environment, and British-based Thames Water (owned by Germany's RWE AG). These firms operate in every region of the world (Marsden 2003). Saur of France and United Utilities of England (working with the U.S. Bechtel) have also secured major contracts (Marsden 2003).

On January 9, 1998, the Suez Lyonnaise des Eaux Group proudly announced that its United Water Services subsidiary was selected to take over management and operation of the drinking water system for the 1.5 million residents of Atlanta, Georgia (Suez Lyonnaise 1998). At the time, the contract was estimated to be worth more than $400 million, the largest of its kind ever awarded in the United States (*New York Times* 1998). In the press release announcing the contract signing, then Atlanta mayor Bill Campbell said that "this day really marks the beginning of a partnership which will result in tremendous savings that will reduce the amount our water customers will have to pay in the future. Our citizens and ratepayers will benefit by improved technology and more efficient and innovative approaches to management. This will be a win-win situation for all involved" (United Water 1998).

Mayor Campbell was not a privatization advocate. At the time of the water contract he was "philosophically opposed to privatization." He also maintained that "privatization is a government's admission of failure. Government ought to be able to accomplish projects as efficiently as business" (Ramage 1998). In fact, early in his tenure as mayor, Campbell signed an agreement with municipal workers that he would not contract out city jobs unless faced with a fiscal emergency (Savas 2005, 87).

Campbell turned to privatization in the case of water because he faced a budget deficit, a water system in need of major overhaul, and the opportunity to save the city about $30 million a year in operation and maintenance costs by contracting with a private entity (Ramage 1998). He also faced mandates to upgrade the city's three wastewater treatment plants totaling $1 billion in capital expenditures, which would translate into a near doubling of water and sewer rates for consumers (Savas 2005, 88). After careful analysis and a two-year battle with opponents, the city entered into a twenty-year partnership with United Water Services.

Mayor Campbell was not alone in supporting the move to privatization. The public water agency did not have a great reputation. According to then City Council member Lee Morris, "I personally agreed with the concept of turning it over to a private operator because the water department had been a poster child for government inefficiency, where politicians would dump their friends and relatives when they needed a job. It was not a well-run department and it was a very costly department" (Koller 2003).

Despite the early promise, privatization failed. In August 2002, the new mayor, Shirley Franklin, presented United Water with a detailed report charging that the company would default on its twenty-year contract in ninety days if major improvements were not made, and she instituted a performance scorecard to monitor the contractor on a daily basis.

The city charged that due to understaffing, the contractor was providing poor water quality, not fixing leaks, not maintaining or reading meters on a timely basis (leading to revenue losses), and failing to provide the city with the information it needed to monitor the contractor. The government assumed that the contractor kept staffing at low levels to keep costs low and inflate its bottom line. Past supporters such as former council member Morris reported dozens of constituent complaints of brown water and advisories to boil the water before drinking.

The contractor initially responded that it had not been cited with water quality violations. They also argued that the city had underestimated the maintenance workload in the original contract. Nevertheless, the contractor agreed to be accountable to the city through a performance scorecard for a ninety-day re-evaluation period. Both the city and the contractor affirmed their commitment to continue the relationship (Rubenstein 2002). Yet on January 24, 2003, United Water Services Atlanta and the City of Atlanta announced that they had reached a mutual dissolution agreement for the contract they signed in 1999 (Suez 2003).

In departing Atlanta, the contractor cited recent independent performance reviews rating its performance at 97 out of 100 and noted its successful operation of more than a hundred similar contracts for cities across the United States, Canada, and Puerto Rico. But the citizens of Atlanta, the city government, and independent sources told a different story of brown water, delayed maintenance, recurring leaks leading to collapsed roads, and billing irregularities. Additionally, an independent audit showed that the city saved only about half what the company had promised when the contract was approved (The Center for Public Integrity 2003).

So in early 2003, the city of Atlanta, coming off an $82 million budget deficit, began the process of recreating a public utility with the Department of Watershed Management to run the city's water system. The city faced the prospect of increasing the charges to ratepayers for the real cost of service with no obvious way to pay for $800 million worth of short-term repairs and as much as $3 billion in long-term infrastructure investment (Jehl 2003). While the Atlanta case is important in and of itself, it might also provide lessons for communities around the country (indeed around the world) that are considering the privatization of their water system.

What Went Wrong?

The process of determining what went wrong in Atlanta began in 2003 and continues as we write this chapter. Soon after canceling the contract, city officials blamed the contract itself—"There were too many gray areas," said the new manager of the city water system (Mariani 2003). For example, there was no timetable for fixing leaks in the system.

Second, the numbers didn't add up. The contract initially promised annual savings of $20 million a year to the city, but the independent audit before the cancellation showed actual savings closer to $10 million. The city estimated it could operate the system for about $1 million more than it was paying United (Mariani 2003). And since United reported losing $10 million a year running the system, it appears that there were few real efficiencies and a lot of complaints about water quality, maintenance, and management (Arrandale 2003). United attributed its higher than projected costs to the city's failure to disclose the poor shape of its infrastructure, but, as Elizabeth Brubaker of Environmental Probe, an environmental research group based in Toronto, said, "[i]t looks like they didn't take a close enough look at the system before taking on the contract" (Simpson 2003).

According to Public Citizen, a Ralph Nader–affiliated group, the "ugly realities" of the privatization were clear early on—a cutback of employees from more than seven hundred to just above three hundred, a system-wide backlog of work orders, $16 million paid for "additional repair and maintenance costs," and improper billing for work done by the contractor outside of Atlanta (Public Citizen 2003). United Water claimed the city grossly underestimated the basic repairs and maintenance that would be required—1,171 water meter repairs per year estimated versus 11,108 actual, 101 main breaks estimated versus 279 actual, and 734 hydrant repairs estimated versus 1,633 actual (Segal 2003, 7).

The gap between the estimates and actual experience was the result of the absence of good data to establish a baseline. The city had either failed to keep proper records or to collect the required data in the first place. Nevertheless, even privatization advocates acknowledge that United Water and other private bidders knew about the data problems before they bid and they all had experience with large, older systems. The firms should have adjusted their bid based on past experience with similar systems and also included a contingency factor for uncertainty (Segal 2003, 8).

And then there is the Mayor Campbell factor. On August 21, 2006, former Atlanta mayor Bill Campbell entered a federal correctional institution in Miami to begin serving two and a half years on three tax charges (Scott 2006; Associated Press 2006; CNN.com 2006). A five-year investigation of corruption in the Campbell administration in Atlanta resulted in ten criminal convictions, including Campbell's top two deputies (Whitt 2004). According to the indictment, Campbell and his COO Larry Wallace accepted a $12,900 trip to Paris from United Water in 1999. Campbell later signed an $80 million increase in the contract, which was subsequently disallowed (Whitt 2004; *New York Times* 2004).

The benefits of privatization are often linked to competition—private companies will use cutting-edge technology, cost control, and superior management to win customers with the best product or service at the lowest price. The more competitive the market, the better it is for consumers. In the case of Atlanta's water system, the intense competition among private companies may have actually worked to the detriment of the people of Atlanta. To win the contract, the contractor may have lowballed the bid and provided an unsustainable price to the city. In the late 1990s, the Atlanta water contract was the largest water contract open to private operators, and it was therefore viewed as a major advantage in competing for other city deals where there were aging, cash-strapped public utilities. Five major companies spent millions competing for the deal, and according to Lee Morris, then chair of the Utilities Commission, "[w]e certainly heard that it was important to all of these large companies, that this was going to be the first one, the toe hold if you will, and it was important for them to land it even if it meant they did not necessarily make a lot of money or maybe even any money. So certainly it took deep pockets" (Koller 2003).

Some believe that United Water was so intent on getting the contract that it wrongly consented to every demand the city made. To begin with, United's bid was $2 million less per year than the next lowest bidder (Savas 2005, 88). The contractor also agreed to hire former city employees regardless of their prior performance record and take on subcontractors that were promoted based on local connections and minority status rather than competence (Koller 2003). United initially demanded that the city make warranties regarding the physical and financial soundness of the water system, but the city refused and United conceded the point in contract negotiations (Segal 2003, 7).

Is the Atlanta Experience Representative?

Unlike other core utilities such as electricity, gas, and telecommunications, water has been and remains primarily a government monopoly—more than 80 percent of the United States population receives its water from a public agency (Wallsten and Kosec 2005, 1). In poor countries, the percentage is even higher, about 97 percent, and those same countries are home to the more than one billion people who do not have access to clean and safe water (Segerfeldt 2005, 1). In France, the situation is quite different, with 75 percent of the population receiving water services from private companies (Wallsten and Kosec 2005, 1).

While there is much disagreement regarding whether water services should be privatized, there is general consensus that there is a global crisis in terms of access to safe drinking water and that a significant investment is needed to improve the situation. One of the key Millennium Development Goals of the United Nations is to halve the number of people without access to clean water (United Nations 2006). In the United States, the American Water Works Association has estimated that $250 billion will be needed to upgrade U.S. water systems over the next thirty years (Wallsten and Kosec 2005, 2).

There are strong advocates for public and for private operation of water systems, but available research indicates that both public and private systems generally comply with water quality regulations and that the cost of the private operation may actually be, on average, slightly lower than the cost of publicly provided water (Wallsten and Kosec 2005, 3). While there are many successful private water systems, there have also been spectacular failures. In Cochabamba, Bolivia, Bechtel abandoned its water contract and left the country in the face of massive riots in protest of huge increases in water bills and alleged corruption (Watson 2003).

In Cochabamba, privatization resulted in a 43 percent increase in water rates. However, the increase raised the price of water for the poorest citizens to 5.4 percent of income, a common level for this income group in the region and around the world, regardless of whether the operator is public or private. The mayor of Cochabamba also demanded the inclusion of a new dam in the privatization, which inflated the necessary price increases, and it is charged that the mayor expected to reap illegitimate personal profits from the dam. Some observers charge that vested interests in the status quo helped foment the riots to get Bechtel out of their way (Segerfeldt 2005, 84–88).

To put the problems with the Atlanta water contract in perspective, there are more than 25,000 privately operated water systems in the United States and tens of thousands of others around the world that operate without notable issues, suggesting that the Atlanta case may be an "outlier" (Wallsten and Kosec 2005, 7). Indeed, in Indianapolis, Indiana, a partnership including Suez Lyonnaise (the owner of United Water Atlanta) won the contract to operate the city's wastewater treatment plant. That private partnership cut costs and workforce, reduced energy consumption, and returned more than $11 million a year to the city compared to the public operator—more than a 30 percent savings. The private partnership also dramatically improved environmental standards and compliance (Goldsmith 1997, 199–221).

What is typical of the Atlanta case are the problems that led the city to turn to a private operator in the first place. Underinvestment and a lack of preventive maintenance left the system in poor condition, leading to frequent leaks, damage to streets and infrastructure, waste, interruption of service, and reduced water quality. The administration was characterized by slow decision making, lack of performance incentives, and politically influenced hiring and promotion practices. Meter repairs were slow, and billing and collection practices were lax (Segerfeldt 2005, 18–27).

Advocates of the privatization of water argue that private companies are well equipped to deal with the problems faced by Atlanta in the late 1990s. Large multinational companies have ready access to capital, possess cutting-edge technology, and are focused on cost control. Private companies are also driven to maximize the number of individuals and businesses receiving services, streamline billing and collection procedures, and seek optimal pricing to yield maximum profits (Segerfeldt 2005, 77).

As for the problems typically associated with privatization, some apply to the Atlanta case and some do not. A major concern associated with the privatization of water management is that prices will rise, making water unaffordable for the poor. This was not a major problem in Atlanta.

Second, privatization frequently involves substituting a private monopoly for a public one, losing the benefits of competition. This was less of a problem in Atlanta because the bidding for the contract was highly competitive, so Atlanta received an excellent price. However, once United Water took over, they did not face ongoing competition, which may have led to deterioration in the quality of service provided. It could also be argued that the city failed to carry out its regulatory responsibilities and monitor and enforce the terms of its contract with United Water.

What Has Happened Since the City Cancelled the Contract?

Water and sewer services returned to Atlanta city government in 2003 under the supervision of the Department of Watershed Management (DWM), and they remain a city responsibility as of this writing. It is too soon to say that the city administration is succeeding where United Water failed. It is true that water is generally off the front pages of the local newspapers and is seldom a topic for television and radio investigative reporters.

A 2006 report by the DWM to the Atlanta City Council highlights the progress on mandated combined sewer overflow capital projects, water main replacement, and sewer rehabilitation projects; the on-time, on-budget completion of the Nancy Creek Tunnel and Pumping Station; and a more efficient and customer-friendly billing system (Department of Watershed Management 2006, 3). The DWM reports no Safe Drinking Water Act violations since taking over in 2003, only three boil water advisories, and 100 percent of water quality complaints responded to within twenty-four hours (Department of Watershed Management 2006, 7). The agency also reports an increase in meters read, rising from 60 percent in 2003 to 97 percent by March 2006. Rate collections had increased to an annual rate of 99.36 percent, compared to a target of 98.5 percent (Department of Watershed Management 2006, 18).

DWM administration has not been all good news. In January 2004, faced with a court-ordered moratorium on water and sewer hookups, the City Council and Mayor Shirley Franklin agreed on a five-year package of rate increases that raised the average consumer bill from $49.60 to $107.57, a 117 percent increase, by 2008 (Tagami 2004a, B1). A significant portion of the rate increase was necessary to pay for more than $1 billion in court-mandated sewer work. Nevertheless, Mayor Franklin commented, "We should compliment ourselves for turning the corner on clean water for the first real time in 30 years" (Tagami 2004a, B1). Not everyone in Atlanta shared the mayor's enthusiasm. John Sherman, head of the Fulton County Taxpayer Association, said, "We feel these water rate increases . . . will result in an exodus of moderate and middle class income families from the city of Atlanta and Fulton County" (Hendrick 2004, JN1).

A 2004 city internal auditor report found that the Department of Watershed Management was doing a worse job of collecting water and sewer bills than United Water had, with $81.3 million uncollected, up $26.6 million since the city took over in April 2003 (Tagami 2004b, D3). DWM commissioner Rob Hunter blamed the problem on a lack of employees, saying he expected the number to rise from four to forty by the end of 2005. He commented, "It takes awhile to turn around the ocean liner" (Tagami 2004b, D3).

Two DWM employees were arrested in 2005 and charged with cheating the city out of $1 million in water bill revenues, using computer expertise to clear indebted accounts in return for kickbacks from customers

(Tagami 2005, B1). During 2005, ten DWM employees were charged with insurance fraud for claiming injuries they did not suffer, and an erosion control inspector was charged with bribery (Tagami 2005, B1). Clearly, the ethical challenges related to water administration did not end with the Campbell administration and the United Water contract.

The city's progress on the court-mandated $3.2 billion in water and sewer infrastructure has been a series of ups and downs since it resumed management of the system. Mayor Shirley Franklin called herself the "sewer mayor" and has raised the sales tax and water and sewer rates to pay for work. In 2005, ten years after the Upper Chattahoochee River-keeper advocacy group filed its first federal lawsuit to force the city to fix its sewers, its executive director Sally Bethea said, "This mayor has dealt with the problem head-on. . . . The river is definitely better when it comes to the impact of the city of Atlanta" (Shelton 2005, B1).

Only a year later, the mayor reported that the $3.2 billion overhaul would now cost $3.9 billion and that water and sewer rates would have to go even higher. Those increases alone will double the rates from where they were when the city resumed management of the system in 2003 (Tagami 2006, B6). The higher costs were blamed on higher construction costs due to the economic growth of China and the post-Katrina cleanup along the Gulf Coast. The aforementioned Chattahoochee River project had fallen behind schedule and would not meet the November 7, 2007, completion date required by the consent decree. The city blamed the drilling contractor and the drill manufacturer for a twenty-seven-foot drill bit that broke. Even before the breakdown, the contractor was making only half the expected daily progress (Pendered 2006, B1).

In the three years since taking back management of the water and sewer system, the city of Atlanta has encountered all the problems that led them to seek an outside contractor to operate the system in the late 1990s. Water and sewer rates have been raised substantially. The public payroll for the department has increased dramatically. The capital construction costs have continued to rise, and key project completion dates are being missed. At the same time, the new mayor's willingness to accept responsibility for the system has seemed to keep public and media criticism to a level well below the anger directed at the Campbell administration and United Water.

Why Did Contracting Work Better in Indianapolis Than in Atlanta?

Stephen Goldsmith, the former mayor of Indianapolis, is perhaps best-known for his pursuit of competition rather than privatization, permitting city agencies to compete with private companies to deliver city services (Osborne and Plastrik 1997; Osborne and Hutchinson 2004; Savas 2005). While city agencies won back about half of the services Indianapolis put out to bid, one of Indianapolis's most successful contracts with a private vendor involved the city wastewater treatment facility. The winning bidder in 1993–1994 was a private partnership that included Suez Lyonnaise des Eauz/United Water, the same company that failed in Atlanta.

United Water has continued to participate in the operation of the Indianapolis facility through the time of this writing, with positive results. When the privatization of the sewer collection system occurred in the late 1990s, the public employee union, AFSCME, which had bitterly opposed the first contract, decided to partner with United (Center for Civic Innovation 1999). The city saved $72 million under the first contract through 1999, more than the $65 million promised by the United partnership, pollution control standard violations dropped by 60 percent, time lost from accidents decreased by 91 percent, wages and benefits increased from 9 to 28 percent over comparable city job titles, and sewer rates were held constant (Savas 2005, 56). The number of employees did drop significantly, from 321 to 196, as a result of the application of state-of-the-art technology and automation (Savas 2005, 56–57). No employees were laid off as a result of the transaction. The city and the contractor used a series of banked job vacancies at the city to manage down the staffing levels without laying off existing utility employees.

Indianapolis's contracting out of wastewater services is frequently cited by proponents of privatization, outsourcing, and reinvention because it was a well-run public service that became substantially better and cheaper under private management. Atlanta entered into its contract with United within a year of Indianapolis's renewing its contract with the same vendor. How is it possible for two American cities to get such different results using the same contractor at the same time?

In late 2006, Goldsmith observed, "When a government administration is inept and ethically challenged, it is highly unlikely that they will be able to build an effective partnership with a private vendor. Was the Atlanta water debacle a failure of contracting or a failure of government?" (Goldsmith 2006) Goldsmith further noted that "[w]hen Atlanta began the process of outsourcing their water and sewer system, we [Indianapolis] volunteered to donate the information we had learned about the contracting of wastewater treatment over the past six years. Atlanta did not want the help." As Mayor Goldsmith told us, "[w]hen we started out, we tried to copy the best practices we could find in other governments and in the private sector. It seemed very odd to me that Atlanta administration did not even want to talk to us" (Goldsmith 2006).

What were the key elements of the wastewater project in Indianapolis? According to Goldsmith, the keys to their success were a strong team of inside experts reporting directly to the mayor and empowered to speak with his authority, a commission of private sector entrepreneurs to oversee all competitions, a sense of urgency based on the belief that if the city did not do more with less it would lose its tax base to the surrounding suburbs, and a clear recognition that tradeoffs are inherent in all decision making. Regarding tradeoffs, Goldsmith noted that the success of the wastewater contract involved a conscious balancing of price with service and quality considerations (Goldsmith 2006).

On the contract itself (which Atlanta pointed to as part of their problem), Goldsmith noted that the Indianapolis team had negotiated a good contract, but a good contract is only the beginning. A good working relationship is the key to success—"A great contract cannot make up for a bad relationship and if the relationship is solid, the contract document itself matters much less" (Goldsmith 2006). Atlanta and United point to the data problems in their deal regarding the initial condition of the system. Goldsmith told us that when he began as mayor, Indianapolis had very little management data and much of the data the city had was incomplete or inaccurate. "You have to make educated guesses, use benchmarking and your past experience. And both sides have to act in good faith and recognize they are dealing with imperfect data" (Goldsmith 2006).

Uncertainty is always a part of multiyear projects and agreements, which is why Goldsmith stressed the need "not to take every dollar off the table," "set reasonable expectations," don't overpromise, and build in reserve funds to deal with unanticipated problems (Goldsmith 2006). In the end, Goldsmith argued, "[i]t's all about the people—on both sides. We put our best people on the wastewater project and we demanded that the United Partnership do the same. And we did not hesitate to let them know if we felt strongly about the need for reassignments, from time to time" (Goldsmith 2006).

As to the proposition that contracting increases the danger of corruption, Goldsmith was strong and firm in his disagreement. "Honest people behave honestly, whether they are direct employees or contractors. Corruption comes from the individual and from the work environment, whether it is the public or the private sector" (Goldsmith 2006). Goldsmith (1997) also identified some other important lessons from the United contract. For example, it marked the first time the city brought legislators in early in the process and made it a practice to "overcommunicate" with all stakeholders, including the council and the general public (1997, 210).

In Atlanta, Mayor Campbell kept the details private, and the process was more of a war with stakeholders than a collaboration. Indianapolis carefully analyzed vendor proposals to help determine whether they were realistic in terms of price, service, and quality, based on their work in other places (Goldsmith 1997, 210). Had the Campbell administration carefully examined the work of United in other places, they might have realized that their price and service demands were unrealistic and that they were forcing the vendor into an agreement that could not be sustained, thereby creating unrealistic expectations among stakeholders.

Conclusion

More than any other make-or-buy decision, turning over the management of water services to private companies is fraught with ideological considerations. Many believe water is a right and, as such, water service provision is best carried out by the government (Bailey 2005). Another way to view it is that government is responsible for ensuring that all citizens have easy access to pure, safe, and affordable water. Government may determine that it is more efficient and effective to employ private organizations to deliver the water service. In the case of Atlanta, the failure of the United Water contract is as much a story of a government failing to properly execute its contract management and regulatory responsibilities as it is the failure of a private company to provide the water services it promised the people of Atlanta.

Despite the best efforts of governments around the world, a billion people lack access to sufficient, affordable drinking water. One analyst has estimated that to meet this unmet need, the financial resources devoted to water infrastructure would have to double (Payen 2006, 25). Public-private partnerships, private and public investments, increases in water rates, and new technologies will all be used to meet these needs. Improved contracting processes and better contracts for water services will be needed for privatization to succeed. Government will also need to do a better job of monitoring and enforcing the terms of those contracts.

Part V

Conclusions

Chapter 12

Contracting, Representative Democracy, and Public Ethics

THIS VOLUME has attempted to explain the contracting phenomenon in modern government, place it in context, assist in its improvement, and discuss the opportunities and problems it presents. The cases in the preceding chapters highlight the difficulties—in Iraq and Atlanta—and the promise—in Philadelphia and Indianapolis. While the cases are filled with stories of contracting advocates and opponents, we reiterate the point that we are neither. While we of course recognize the relationship between public administration and politics, we see contracting as purely instrumental—we see it as a tool. We recognize that ends and means are interconnected and that the design of a policy is never neutral, any more than the design of an administrative process is ever free of politics and values. Still, while ends and means are related, they are not the same thing. Where the bus stops is a matter of political choices, the design of the bus's engine must remain an issue of engineering. The politicization of contracting is unfortunate and something that, of course, must be dealt with by all public administrators. However, we feel that decisions about contracting should not be ideological but rather should be managerial. We could no more advocate for contracting than we could advocate for the use of hammers. They are useful for driving nails and less useful for cutting wood. Opposition to contracting strikes us as equally silly. Contracting is a fact. It is increasing. It is not going away. It provides both problems and opportunities for representative government and accountability, for public ethics, and for organizational management.

Key Lessons from the Case Studies

What can we learn from the cases presented in the previous section? These cases were not selected as typical cases, representative of the "average" contracting experience. Rather, we selected them for the richness of the lessons they could provide to contract managers and governmental policymakers. At the most practical level, the cases provide evidence of both the complexity of contracting and its growth in the public sector here in the United States. In the Iraq war and the attempt at reconstruction we see a case study of overcontracting—in this instance our government needed to make more and buy less. The full range of contract failure is on display: corruption, incompetence, and unethical, unaccountable behavior. If this is what we mean by contracting—let's just forget about it and try something else. In the Atlanta water case, we see a contractor operating on familiar turf—a privatized water system. This is a service that has been successfully contracted out in other places but failed in Atlanta. The contract provisions were unrealistic, the overall environment was plagued with political corruption, and an effective relationship between the government and the contractor could not be established. This stands in sharp contrast to Indianapolis, where the local government employed the same contractor with far better results. Finally, we have the Transitional Work Corporation in Philadelphia. Here we saw government and contractor learning over time to work together effectively. While the case illustrates many ups and downs, the overall contracted effort to move people from welfare to work succeeded. Both government and contractor learned how to improve their performance in a new environment.

Three cases can only provide illustrations and examples, and even if we had sought "representativeness," one should never generalize from so few data points. We selected these cases for the lessons they could teach us, and they certainly provide an indication that we have a great deal to learn about effective contract management. In our view, we need to get beyond these discussions of the value of contracting and move on to a more robust discussion of effective contract management. We need to develop best practices on the make-or-buy decision. We need to be sensitive to political environments, like Atlanta's, and learn when to defer privatization. Most important, we must identify a set of government tasks that should never be contracted—like the war in Iraq.

Smaller-scale and more prosaic examples of contracting can easily be found throughout government: the cafeteria run by a private food service, the park benches inspected and replaced by a street furniture company, the high school teacher training program run by the local teacher's college. Over the next decade we need to collect best, typical, and worst practices from all these experiences, analyze this data, and develop a more sophisticated set of contract management practices.

Contracting and Representative Government and Accountability

The sections in this book that are the most conceptual and rooted in theory are those that deal with representation and accountability. As government and our economy have become more complicated and technical in content, we have come to rely on more and more expertise to accomplish government's work. This means that the work of government must be translated for the public to influence its conduct. It means that to represent the public we must now link public preferences for policy and programs first to its elected leaders, then to its unelected officials, and then to the acts of private organizations under contract to government.

While contracting extends the chain of accountability by one more link, these links are not purely additive. Each additional link does not create an equal problem for political linkage. In this case it is a link that has the burden of stretching from the public sector to the private sector. This makes linkage more difficult, but we would argue that the more profound difficulty was the one that was created when we increased the technical complexity of government's work. At that point the average citizen could no longer even understand the behaviors and policies he or she needed to influence.

Policy is harder to influence if you don't understand its content. It is also harder to influence if you require money to have your views heard. This brings us to the growing role of money in politics. The U.S. Supreme Court has ruled that an individual's right to spend money on politics is a First Amendment free speech right. This means that the firms who benefit from the public's purse have a right to pay for the political campaigns of elected leaders who vote on the appropriations that the firms live off of. This creates, in operational terms, a representative system of weighted votes—since those who pay tend to have a higher probability of being asked to play. As contracting increases and the cost of political campaigns increases, it is easy to see that contracting will continue to grow in part to fund the growing cost of political campaigns. These trends will have a negative impact on the institutions of representative government.

Still, private organizations can bring some clear benefits to the public. With the exception of huge firms such as Bechtel and Halliburton, private contractors tend not to be large, impersonal (government-style) bureaucracies. Although they may see people as customers with money rather than citizens with rights, that orientation may result in better treatment and greater responsiveness than consumers would get from public organizations. Of course these images are not uniform—our cell phone company (who shall remain nameless) makes the post office look efficient, and some government organizations are superb at serving the public. We raise the issue to note that accountability to the public also includes responsive service—a phenomenon that varies within and between the public and private sectors. We also acknowledge the problems that a host of public administration scholars point to when one uses the term customer and citizen interchangeably.

The issue of money and politics is more clear-cut. Political participation and turnout of people without financial means could be reduced, and political agenda setting will be increasingly dominated by money interests. Of course the key is how one measures "increasingly." Policy in the United States has always been dominated by wealthy elites. Virginia's plantation owners and New England's traders, not its workers, dominated the constitutional convention. Moreover, due to the Internet, the possibility of mass fundraising has become more common, and the costs of some forms of political communication and most access to information continues to go down.

Another element of accountability is that a private contractor is not in the same organization as government and is governed by different rules and norms. The issue is influence and control of the behavior of the private individual and/or organization. If that behavior cannot be controlled, or at least made subject to government authority, how can the agency assure that its actions are controllable? If these actions are not controllable then accountability is made more difficult.

One could make the point that intergovernmental relations and interorganizational relations within government are also subject to similar problems of influence and control. Managing influence and control is difficult within hierarchical, vertically integrated organizations, and so networked organizations are bound to be more difficult to influence. When we wrote the first draft of this chapter, the New York City Police Department, a vertically integrated, hierarchical, and well-managed organization, faced a crisis due to the behavior of undercover detectives who fired fifty shots at a car of unarmed men leaving a bachelor party, killing the groom. These officers violated the department's own procedures and created a political crisis for the department and the mayor. While the chain of accountability is clear and response from the chain of command was instantaneous, this incident only reinforces the difficulty of accountability. The people in the field did not adhere to pre-established policy and procedure. This a problem identified by Herbert Kaufman in his classic study of administrative behavior, *The Forest Ranger*. The need for operating staff to adhere to "preformed" decisions is a fundamental challenge of management. The challenge is made more important by the need for democratic accountability and is made more difficult by public organizational networks that cross into the private sector.

The contrast between the immediate accountability in the New York City police case with the prisoner abuses at Abu Ghraib is of course worth noting. Just as acts of the police in New York would be subject to organizational and legal review, the military at Abu Ghraib faced military discipline. However, the private contractors who worked with the military did not receive the same level of scrutiny. As reported by Joanne Mariner:

> The soldiers responsible for the disgraceful physical and sexual abuse of Iraqi prisoners may face court-martial proceedings, at least if the military justice system functions as it should. One soldier has already been charged, and six others are likely to be brought to court soon. Although no military officers have yet been prosecuted—and Secretary of Defense Donald Rumsfeld has not resigned [an event that took place in December 2006]—at least six officers have received career-ending reprimands.
>
> But what of the civilian contractors who worked hand in glove with the military at Iraq's Abu Ghraib prison? Will the atrocities they committed be, at most, bad for their careers—a source of negative letters in their employment files? Or will the civilians who shared

responsibility for the criminal abuse meted out to detainees at Abu Ghraib be tried, convicted, and sent to prison? The most likely option, under the rules crafted by the U.S. occupation authority, is prosecution in U.S. civilian courts. (Mariner 2006)

Despite prosecutions of military personnel, civilians have largely gone free for the abuses at Abu Ghraib. According to Mark Follman and Tracy Clark-Flory, "U.S. investigators have determined that the CIA and civilian contractors also bear some responsibility for crimes committed at Abu Ghraib and elsewhere, including the murder of at least one detainee at Abu Ghraib and the deaths of three others in Iraq and Afghanistan. Yet despite the fact that Pentagon and CIA investigators have referred 20 cases to the Department of Justice, only one civilian—a CIA contractor—has been prosecuted. Not a single military contractor or CIA officer has been charged" (Follman and Clark-Flory 2006).

Despite the clear abuses by civilians, there appears to have been only one prosecution. The need for military justice in the face of this behavior was clear and obvious, but the laws for civilians in this instance are more ambiguous. The different notions of accountability could not be more graphically portrayed. Nevertheless, it is possible to develop a legal framework, coupled with an organizational culture, that reinforces responsibility and accountability in private organizations. While private justice cannot equal its military version in this instance, it may very well be that a stricter set of rules could be enforced, reducing the dangers to accountability. However, at present we see a clear contrast in rules, organizational culture, behavior, and accountability.

Accountability and responsiveness to public control are critical to the work of government in a representative democracy. Contracting presents challenges to the goals of accountability and responsiveness. However, as we indicate in chapter 1, contracting continues to grow. We don't expect that trend to end. Complaining about the increased interaction of the public and private sectors strikes us as a waste of time. Government is subject to the same facts of modern organizational production that have led to massive outsourcing and globalization in the private sector. To ensure accountability and the health of our representative democracy, we must develop effective methods for influencing the behavior of private government contractors. That is a management task we devoted substantial attention to in this volume, and it is one we will again address at the end of this chapter.

When we discuss representation and accountability, as we have throughout this volume, we inevitably address the issue of capacity. We must devote attention to the political system's capacity, as evidenced by representatives who are responsive stewards, and the management of contractors whose behaviors public administrators understand and can steer. We turn next to our conclusions on contracting and political representation, while the final section of this chapter provides conclusions on the issue of contractor management.

We do not believe that the ability of representatives to act as responsive stewards is compromised by the presence of contractors working for unelected government officials. To the extent that contracted work enhances government's capacity and performance, it connects representatives to a more effective and efficient administrative system. This enhances the efficacy of representation and reinforces the stewardship function. In a formal sense, policy decisions flow from elected leaders to unelected government officials and from these public officials to private organizations under contract to the government. The reality, of course, is that contractors are in direct communication with elected leaders. Contractor behavior is influenced by contractor perceptions of the policy intent of elected leaders. Contractors lobby and make campaign contributions to influence those policies. The policy intent of these elected representatives is mediated and made operational by regulations, guidance, and contract provisions developed by unelected officials. All these factors influence the behaviors that make the policy pronouncements of elected leaders real.

The probability that private contractors will independently thwart the policy intent of elected officials is probably lower than the probability that unelected officials will resist policy. The mission orientation of unelected officials could stimulate such resistance. Nonprofit contractors might be similarly mission-driven and could pose a risk to policies promulgated by elected officials. Private, for-profit contractors, more motivated by profit, would be least likely to develop an independent approach, unless it clearly led to larger and more certain profit.

In sum, contracting presents new challenges to accountable, representative government. However, these challenges are simply part of a series of difficulties arising from modern technology, globalization, and new cultural norms in the world. Contracting, properly managed, should not impair accountability and representative democracy. Poorly managed, contracting can pose new threats. A well-managed contract with effective performance measures and clear limits on contractor behavior is no threat.

Contracting and Public Ethics

Earlier we provided a definition of public ethics and discussed the ethical issues raised by contracting. The potential for conflict of interest issues and corruption are a clear danger given the complexity, size, and duration of the contracting process. Staff members may be hired from time to time, but contracts are renewed all the time. The financial stakes are high, and the pressure on often poorly paid government staff members can be intense. Moreover, we frequently see a clash of cultures as the values of the private sector and those of the public intersect.

Of central concern is the issue of corruption. When government was kept relatively distinct from the private sector, a separate public service ethos and culture could develop that reduced the probability of corruption. With network management and multisectoral careers, this separation becomes more difficult. The lure of private riches becomes more likely and with it the probability of corruption. While we wish it were not the case, people who work in bars drink more and people who work at casinos gamble more. Environment matters, and environment influences organizational culture.

The issue in many respects is not simply contracting, but interaction with the private sector when the potential financial stakes are high. For example, in late 2006, the media renewed its focus on the Department of Interior's program for leasing the rights to drill for oil and natural gas on federal lands. In a *New York Times* investigative piece titled "Blowing the Whistle on Big Oil," Edmund Andrews reported on the culture in the Department of Interior that enabled massive underpayment of royalties due the government. Andrews noted that:

The Interior Department's own inspector general [inquired] into whether the agency properly collects the money for oil and gas pumped from public land. Investigators say they have found evidence of myriad problems at the department: cronyism and cover-ups of management blunders; capitulation to oil companies in disputes about payments; plunging morale among auditors; and unreliable data-gathering that often makes it impossible to determine how much money companies actually owe.

In February, the Interior Department admitted that energy companies might escape more than $7 billion in royalty payments over the next five years because of errors in leases signed in the 1990s that officials are now scrambling to renegotiate. The errors were discovered in 2000, but were ignored for the next six years and have yet to be fixed. (Andrews 2006).

This is not an example of contracting but of the effect of an agency in a regular relationship with a part of the private sector that has a huge profit stake in its interaction with government. The problem as we see it in this instance is essentially a clash of organizational cultures. It is also a result of an ideology that venerates the private sector and denigrates the public sector. Without vigilance, self-awareness, and strict oversight, the potential for corruption can be easily realized.

In many respects it is difficult to predict where and when corruption will take place. At the beginning of the twentieth century in New York City, we see Plunkitt of Tammany Hall distinguishing between honest graft and dishonest graft (Riordan 1994). Honest graft is "[s]eeing your opportunities and taking them," for example buying land adjacent to a site about to be developed as a park. Dishonest graft was melting the gold from the dome of a city building and selling it. During this period, Boss Tweed and his cohorts stole a breathtaking amount of money from the city treasury. In New York City at that time, the Tweed Courthouse was a famous monument to corruption and a constant conduit of funds from government to the private sector (and Tweed's bank accounts) through construction contracts. To some degree, the corruption was tolerated because the machine provided services and material benefits to poor people. However, Boss Tweed and the politicos of Tammany did not need large-scale contracting to develop and implement a culture of corruption. Their corruption did not result from the temptation of private riches—rather it was simply a way of life. It was a lubricant to the city's economic and governing machine. Similarly, today, the officials in nations characterized by government as kleptocracy will always find ways of exacting tribute and stealing money. In this sense, we argue that contracting does not cause corruption. A society, political culture, and organizational culture that tolerates corrupt government officials encourages corrupt behavior. Like the New York City stockbrokers who jumped subway turnstiles in the 1970s to avoid paying the fare "because they could," and as the broken window theory hypothesizes: In some environments, corruption and crime are contagious. We don't believe that the presence of the private sector inevitably stimulates corruption. In our view, it is possible to prevent corruption with well-understood policies, clear communication of values, and swift and public punishment of violators.

The corrosive effect of money in politics and a society that celebrates increased consumption over many other values creates an environment that could lead to increased corruption. However, the ease of communication resulting from cellular communications and the World Wide Web has increased the probability that there will be an outlet for reports of corruption. We have seen no data that indicate that increased contracting has led to increased corruption. Of course corruption itself has become more subtle and less overt in some of its modern variants than in the overt and sometimes visible method we saw in late nineteenth-century and early twentieth-century local American politics or in the contemporary kleptocracies we see today in parts of the developing world.

Contracting creates new patterns of spending and management and therefore provides new avenues of corruption. These avenues must be understood, monitored, and then countered. In that respect, countering corruption through contracting becomes another management issue presented by the increased use of this old tool of public management.

Contracting and Public Management

Several parts of this book focused on the issues of ethics, accountability, and democratic representation. We are concerned about the fundamental challenges that contracting poses to our political system and values. We hope this volume increases understanding of those challenges and suggests methods for meeting potential threats. In addition to these fundamental issues, contracting presents a series of practical challenges to public managers. Since the authors of this volume are first and foremost interested in understanding and improving public management, it is appropriate that we end this work with our conclusions about contract management.

Effective contract management requires skill at the use of all the tools of standard and innovative management: Managers must understand human resource, financial, organizational, information, performance, strategic, political, and media management. They also need experience with quality management, benchmarking, re-engineering, and team management. But the effective contract manager must do more. In addition to deploying those tools in problem solving, today's effective public manager must learn how to elicit contract bids that result in appropriate and well-priced services and goods. They must learn to monitor contractor performance and write contracts that allow them to perform this monitoring function. Contract managers must learn how to develop informal networks that reach deep into contractor organizations, just as they have done within their own organizations.

As the preceding chapters indicate, this is not easy to do. We devoted an entire chapter to problems that might arise in the contracting process. However, that chapter also included a discussion of methods for overcoming those obstacles. Contracting raises a number of issues, but they can be addressed with thought and effort. The first step in this process is understanding that a contract in a networked organization must be seen as a method for extending the organization. The distinction between internal and external is critical for issues of accountability and representation, but effective operations management requires that the manager learn to cut through organizational boundaries.

That is of course both the heart of the craft and the greatest potential danger posed by public sector contract management. The contractor is an external and private organization, but for the purpose of the project being managed, the contractor must be treated as a part of government's team. The most dangerous element of contract management is not the danger of corruption or lack of accountability, but the concept of a "turnkey" operation: "We've contracted that job out and now it's somebody else's headache." If only that were true. There are no handoffs in organizational life. You may be able to pay less attention to contracted operations, but you must still shape, measure, and manage contractor activities.

The management theme of this volume is that the responsible and effective contract manager must extend management's reach to the actions of contractors. They must do this while being careful not to violate regulations limiting their influence on the actions of private firms. The influence must flow *from* government and *to* government. Contractors must be involved in government management discussions and provide input to decisions and feedback on the impact of those decisions. The problem is of course that only government officials are permitted to make policy, so sometimes government officials believe they must exclude contractors from "confidential" discussions. In reality, contractors and networks frequently make policy, so it is all the more important to ensure that they are included in information and management discussions. We sometimes think this is as much about status as it is about meeting the needs of governmental decision making. Contractors often earn more money and may be better connected politically than the government bureaucrats they are working for. One way for the government officials to reinforce their status in these relationships is to distinguish roles more sharply than they need to.

The craft is to understand and influence the informal dimensions of the contracted organization enough to influence its behavior. In particular this requires recruiting contractor management into the agency's mission: obtaining meaningful buy-in. This doesn't mean that contractors will abandon their organization's own self-interest; it means they will work to find a way to wed their interests with the government's. This requires interpersonal connections between government managers and staff members and contractor managers and staff members. These relationships must be developed and maintained without the lubricant of contractor dollars; government buys the sandwiches for the meetings, and individuals pay for their own project T-shirts. Government officials must avoid the appearance of impropriety while developing a close relationship with the people who work for the firms they are contracting with.

These relationships make work life more pleasant, but they also provide the informal communication and information paths so essential to organizational management. These relationships must be established in the face of the substantial constraints posed by the formality of contract instruments, separation of space, and distinct organizational interests. However, in our view, this is simply a variant of normal organizational management. The tasks of external management and internal management are the same—the constraints are different. Managing within a government agency involves understanding highly regulated human resource and budget processes and the political environment of the organization. Managing from government to private organizations requires an understanding of rules governing conflict of interest and fraternization.

We strongly believe that effective contract management is an essential part of effective public management. Contract management raises new issues for accountability, representation, and ethics, but they are issues that can be addressed. We hope the preceding pages will increase the probability that these issues will be addressed.

References

Agranoff, Robert. 2006. Inside collaborative networks: Ten lessons for public managers. *Public Administration Review* 66: 56–65.

Allison, Graham T. 1971. *Essence of decision: Explaining the Cuban missile crisis.* Boston: Little, Brown & Company.

Altshuler, Alan A. 1968. *The politics of the federal bureaucracy.* New York: Dodd, Mead & Co.

Andrews, Edmund. 2006. Blowing the whistle on big oil. *New York Times,* December 3 (accessed December 27, 2006). www.nytimes.com/2006/12/03/business/yourmoney/03whistle.html.

Arrandale, Tom. 2003. Cities that tap private companies to run water systems often are hiring overseas firms. Some find that hard to swallow. *Governing Magazine,* June.

Associated Press. 2006. Ex-Atlanta mayor to begin prison sentence. August 4: A5. www.washingtonpost.com.

Avant, Deborah. 2004. Mercenaries. *Foreign Policy* 143 (July/August): 20–28.

———. 2006. The privatization of security: Lessons from Iraq. *Orbis* 50 (2): 327–42.

Avery, George. 2000. Outsourcing public health laboratory services: A blueprint for determining whether to privatize and how. *Public Administration Review* 60 (4): 330–37.

Babcock, Charles, and Jonathan Weisman. 2005. Congressman admits to taking bribes, resigns. *Washington Post,* November 29: A01. www.washingtonpost.com.

Bachrach, Peter, and Morton S. Baratz. 1963. Decisions and nondecisions: An analytic framework. *American Political Science Review* 57 (September): 632–42.

Bailey, Ronald. 2005. Water is a human right. August 17. Reason Foundation, www.reason.org/phprint.php4.

Bardach, Eugene, and Cara Lesser. 1996. Accountability in human services collaboratives: For what? And to whom? *Journal of Public Administration Research and Theory* 6 (April): 197–224.

Barnard, Chester I. 1938. *The functions of the executive.* Cambridge, Mass.: Harvard University Press.

Barzelay, Michael. 1992. *Breaking through bureaucracy: A new vision for managing in government.* Berkeley: University of California Press.

Beard, Charles A., and John D. Lewis. 1932. Representative government in evolution. *American Political Science Review* 26 (April): 223–40.

Behn, Robert D. 2001. *Rethinking democratic accountability*. Washington, D.C.: Brookings Institution Press.

Bertelli, Anthony, and Laurence Lynn. 2006. Public management in the shadow of the constitution. *Administration and Society* 8 (March): 31–57.

Bingham, Lisa Blomgren, and Rosemary O'Leary. 2006. Conclusion: Parallel play, not collaboration: Missing questions, missing connections. *Public Administration Review* 66: 161–67.

Bingman, Charles, and Bernard Pitsvada. 1997. The case for contracting and privatization. *Challenge* 40 (6): 99–116.

Blachly, Frederick F., and Miriam E. Oatman. 1934. *Administrative legislation and adjudication*. Washington, D.C.: Brookings Institution Press.

Boyer, William W. 1964. *Bureaucracy on trial: Policy making by government agencies*. Indianapolis, Ind.: Bobbs-Merrill.

Bowman, James S., ed. 1991. *Ethical frontiers in public management: Seeking new strategies for resolving ethical dilemmas*. San Francisco: Jossey-Bass.

Boyne, George A. 1998a. Bureaucratic theory meets reality: Public choice and service contracting in U.S. local government. *Public Administration Review* 58 (5): 475.

———. 1998b. The determinants of variations in local service contracting: Garbage in, garbage out? *Urban Affairs Review* 34 (1): 150–63.

Brown, Trevor, and Matthew Potoski. 2003. Contract-management capacity in municipal and county governments. *Public Administration Review* 63 (2): 157–64.

———. 2004. Managing the public service market. *Public Administration Review* 64 (6): 656–68.

Brudney, Jeffrey L., Sergio Fernandez, Jay Eungha Ryu, and Deil S. Wright. 2005. Exploring and explaining contracting out: Patterns among the American states. *Journal of Public Administration Research and Theory* 15 (3): 393–419.

Buchanan, William P., and Nancy McCarthy Snyder. 2001. Contracting with nonprofits: Reaganomics made me do it. *Public Management* 83 (3): 10–13.

Butcher, Tony. 1995. *Delivering welfare: The governance of the social services in the 1990s*. Buckingham, UK: Open University Press.

Cahlink, George. 2005. Former Air Force Acquisition Chief begins prison term. *Government Executive*, January 5: 1. www.govexec.com/.

Campbell, Gordon J., and Elizabeth McCarthy. 2000. Conveying mission through outcome measurement: Services to the homeless in New York City. *Policy Studies Journal* 28 (2): 338–52.

Carty, Bob. 2003. Water for profit—backgrounder Q and A. February 4. CBC News, www.cbc.ca/news/features/water/qanda.html.

CBC News Online. 2004. INDEPTH: WATER—Selling Canada's water. August 25. www.cbc.ca/news/background/water/html.

Center for Civic Innovation. 1999. The Entrepreneurial City. New York, Manhattan Institute.

The Center for Public Integrity. 2003. Water privatization becomes a signature issue in Atlanta. www.publicintegrity.org/water/report.aspx?aid=55 (accessed on October 24, 2006).

Christopher, Martin. 2005. *Logistics and supply chain management: Creating value-added networks.* 3rd ed. New York: Financial Times Prentice Hall.

Clynch, Edward. 1999. Contracting and government: Some further thoughts. *Public Administration and Management: An Interactive Journal* 4 (2). http://pamij.com/99_4_2_Clynch.html.

CNN.com. 2006. Atlanta's former mayor sentenced to prison. www.cnn.com/2006/LAW/06/13/mayor.sentenced (accessed on October 10, 2006).

Coalition Provisional Authority. 2004. Order number 17 (revised): Status of the Coalition Provisional Authority, MNF—Iraq, certain missions and personnel in Iraq. June 27. http://www.cpa-iraq.org/regulations/20040627_CPAORD_17_Status_of_Coalition__Rev__with_Annex_A.pdf (accessed June 19, 2006).

Cobb, Roger W., and Charles D. Elder. 1972. *Participation in American politics: The dynamics of agenda-building.* Baltimore: Johns Hopkins University Press.

Cohen, Steven. 2001. A strategic framework for devolving responsibility and functions from government to the private sector. *Public Administration Review* 61 (4): 432–40.

———. 2006. Review of *Government by network: The new shape of the public sector* by Stephen Goldsmith and William D. Eggers. *Journal of Policy Analysis and Management* 25 (1): 232–35.

Cohen, Steven, and Ron Brand. 1993. *Total quality management in government.* San Francisco: Jossey-Bass Publishers.

Cohen, Steven, and William Eimicke. 1995. Ethics and the public administrator. *Annals of the American Academy of Political and Social Science* 537 (1): 96–108.

———. 1996a. *Assessing the cost effectiveness of welfare-to-work programs.* New York: Columbia University SIPA Occasional Paper.

———. 1996b. Is public entrepreneurship ethical? *Public Integrity Annual.* Lexington, Ky.: Council of State Governments.

———. 1998. *Tools for innovators: Creative strategies for managing public sector organizations.* San Francisco: Jossey-Bass.

———. 1999a. *The Indianapolis independence initiative.* New York: The Rockefeller Foundation.

———. 1999b. Is public entrepreneurship ethical? A second look at theory and practice. *Public Integrity* (Winter): 54–74.

———. 2000a. Assuring public ethics in privatized public programs. Paper presented at the 61st annual meeting of the American Society for Public Administration, San Diego, Calif.

———. 2000b. Using strategic information systems to improve contracted services and assess privatization options. In *Handbook of public information systems*, ed. G. David Garson, 43–58. New York: Marcel Dekker Inc.

———. 2000c. The need for strategic information systems planning when contracting out and privatizing public sector functions. In *Handbook of public information systems*, ed. G. David Garson, 99–112. New York: Marcel Dekker, Inc.

———. 2002. *The effective public manager: Achieving success in a changing government*. 3rd ed. San Francisco: Jossey-Bass.

Connecticut Office of State Ethics. 2005. Plain language summary of state ethics laws for current and potential state contractors. November 30. www.ct.gov/ethics/cwp/view.asp?a=2313&Q=301720&ethicsNav=| (accessed November 30, 2005).

Considine, Mark. 2001. *Enterprising states: The public management of Welfare-to-Work*. Cambridge, UK: Cambridge University Press.

———. 2005. Partnerships and collaborative advantage: Some reflections on new forms of network governance. Paper to be presented at the Center for Public Policy of the University of Melbourne's 2006 international conference, Governments and Communities in Partnership: From Theory to Practice, Melbourne, Australia. www.public-policy.unimelb.edu.au/conference06/Considine_Background_Paper.pdf.

Considine, Mark, and Jenny M. Lewis. 1999. Governance at ground level: The frontline bureaucrat in the age of markets and networks. *Public Administration Review* 59 (6): 467–80.

———. 2003. Bureaucracy, network or enterprise? Comparing models of governance in Australia, Britain, the Netherlands, and New Zealand. *Public Administration Review* 63 (2): 131–40.

Cooper, Phillip J. 2003. *Governing by contract: Challenges and opportunities for public managers*. Washington, D.C.: CQ Press.

Cooper, Terry L. 2004. Big questions in administrative ethics: A need for focused, collaborative effort. *Public Administration Review* 64 (4): 395–407.

Corporation for Public Broadcasting. 2004. *Code of ethics and business conduct for employees of the Corporation for Public Broadcasting*. Washington, D.C.: Office of the General Counsel.

Denhardt, Kathryn. 1988. *The ethics of public service: Resolving moral dilemmas in public organizations*. Westport, Conn.: Greenwood Press.

Department of Defense. 2005. FY 2005 contract summary $25,000 or greater—place of performance. DOD procurement. http://siadapp.dior.whs.mil/procurement/2005_data/performanceDOD200509.pdf.

Department of Watershed Management. 2006. "Operations & Reference Report." Prepared by the Atlanta City Council.

Dimmock, Marshall E. 1936. The role of discretion in modern administration. In John M. Gaus, Leonard D. White, and Marshall E. Dimmock, *The frontiers of public administration*, 45–65. Chicago: University of Chicago Press.

Drucker, Peter F. 1999. *Management challenges for the 21st century*. New York: Harper Business.

Dunleavy, Patrick. 1991. *Democracy, bureaucracy and public choice: Economic explanations in political science*. New York: Harvester Wheatsheaf.

Eimicke, William. 1974. *Public administration in a democratic context*. Beverly Hills, Calif.: Sage Publications.

———. 2000. *San Diego County's innovation program: Using competition and a whole lot more to improve public services*. Washington, D.C.: IBM Center for the Business of Government.

———. 2005. Eliot Spitzer: The people's lawyer. *Public Integrity* 7 (4): 353–72.

Eimicke, William, Steven Cohen, and Mauricio Perez Salazar. 2000. Ethical public entrepreneurship: Common dilemmas from North and South America. *Public Integrity* (Summer): 229–45.

Eisenberg, Daniel. 2003. Evaluating the effectiveness of policies related to drunk driving. *Journal of Policy Analysis and Management* 22 (2): 249–74.

Else, John F., Victor Groze, Helaine Hornby, Ronald K. Mirr, and Julie Wheelock. 1992. Performance-based contracting: The case of residential foster care. *Child Welfare* 71 (6): 513–26.

Fairlie, John A. 1940. The nature of political representation, I. *American Political Science Review* 34 (April): 236–48.

Fell, Ben. 2008. Bush defiantly defends high cost of Iraq War, says 'World is better' for it. Associated Press, March 19.

Ferris, J. M. 1986. The decision to contract out: An empirical analysis. *Urban Affairs Quarterly* 22 (2): 289.

Fleishman, Joel L. 1981. Self-interest and political integrity. In *Public duties: The moral obligations of government officials*, ed. Joel L. Fleishman, Lance Liebman, and Mark Moore, 52–91. Cambridge, Mass.: Harvard University Press.

Follman, Mark, and Tracy Clark-Flory. 2006. Prosecutions and convictions. *Salon.com*. March 14 (accessed July 16, 2007). Available at: www.salon.com/news/abu_ghraib/2006/03/14/prosecutions_convictions/index.html.

Forrest, R. 1993. Contracting housing provision: Competition and privatization in the housing sector. In *Markets and managers: New issues in the delivery of welfare*, ed. Peter Taylor-Gooby and Robyn Lawson, 38–53. Buckingham, UK: Open University Press.

Framer, Ralph M. 1994. Voluntary agencies and the contract culture: "Dream or nightmare?" *Social Service Review* 68 (1): 33–60.

Frederickson, H. George, ed. 1993. *Ethics and public administration*. Armonk, N.Y.: M. E. Sharpe.

———. 1997. *The spirit of public administration*. San Francisco: Jossey-Bass.

———. 2000. Measuring performance in theory and practice. *PA Times* 23 (8): 8, 10.

Friedrich, Carl J. 1937. *Constitutional government and politics*. New York: Harper and Brother.

———. 1968. *Constitutional government and democracy: Theory and practice in Europe and America*. 4th ed. Waltham, Mass.: Blaisdell Publishing.

Frumkin, Peter. 2002. *Service contracting with nonprofit and for-profit providers: On preserving a mixed organizational ecology*. Washington, D.C.: Brookings Institution Press.

Ganeshan, Ram, and Terry Harrison. 1995. An introduction to supply chain management. http://lcm.csa.iisc.ernet.in/scm/supply_chain_intro.html.

Gaus, John M. 1936. The responsibility of public administration. In John M. Gaus, Leonard D. White, and Marshall E. Dimmock, *The frontiers of public administration*, 26–44. Chicago: University of Chicago Press.

Gerth, H. H., and C. Wright Mills, eds. 1958. *From Max Weber: Essays in sociology*. New York: Oxford University Press.

Gilbert, Charles E. 1959. The framework of administrative responsibility. *Journal of Politics* 21 (August): 373–407.

Gilmour, Robert S., and Laura S. Jensen. 1998. Reinventing government accountability: Public functions, privatization, and the meaning of "state action." *Public Administration Review* 58 (3): 247–57.

Glanz, James. 2006. Rebuilding of Iraqi pipeline as disaster waiting to happen. *New York Times*, April 25.

Globerman, Steven, and Aidan R. Vining. 1996. A framework for evaluating the government contracting-out decision with an application to information technology. *Public Administration Review* 56 (6): 577–84.

Goldsmith, Stephen. 1997. *The twenty-first century city: Resurrecting urban America*. Washington, D.C.: Regnery.

———. 2006. Telephone interview with William Eimicke. October 31.

Goldsmith, Stephen, and William D. Eggers. 2004. *Governing by network: The new shape of the public sector*. Washington, D.C.: Brookings Institution Press.

Goodon, Vincent. 1998. Contracting and negotiation: Effective practices of successful human service contract managers. *Public Administration Review* 58 (6): 499–509.

Gore, Al. 1993. *Creating a government that works better & costs less*. Washington, D.C.: U.S. Government Printing Office.

Gray, Cheryl W., and Daniel Kaufmann. 1998. Corruption and development. *Finance and Development* 35 (March): 7–10.

Greene, Jeffrey D. 1996. How much privatization? A research note examining the use of privatization by cities in 1982 and 1992. *Policy Studies Journal* 24 (4): 632–40.

Greenwald, Richard C. 2002. *Transitional jobs: The Philadelphia story.* Washington, D.C.: The Brookings Institution Center on Urban and Metropolitan Policy.

———. 2006. Telephone interview with William Eimicke. September 13.

Gulick, Luther. 1937. Notes on the theory of organization. In *Papers on the science of administration*, ed. Luther Gulick and L. Urwick, 3–44. New York: Institute of Public Administration.

Hanly, G. 1995. Probity in public sector contracting. *Australian Construction Law* (August): 34–40.

Harrison, Kathryn, and W. T. Stanbury. 1990. Privatization in British Columbia: Lessons from the sale of government laboratories. *Canadian Public Administration* 33 (2): 165–97.

Hart, David K. 1992. The moral exemplar in an organizational society. In *Exemplary public administrators: Character and leadership in government*, ed. Terry L. Cooper and N. Dale Wright, 9–27. San Francisco: Jossey-Bass.

Heinrich, Carolyn J. 1999. Do government bureaucrats make effective use of performance management information? *Journal of Public Administration Research and Theory* 9 (3): 363–93.

Hendrick, Bill. 2004. Water bills will ripple across rest of economy. *The Atlanta Journal-Constitution*, April 29: JN1.

Hibbing, John R., and Elizabeth Theiss-Morse. 2002. *Stealth democracy: Americans' beliefs about how government should work.* Cambridge, UK: Cambridge University Press.

Hill, Carolyn J., and Laurence E. Lynn Jr. 2005. Is hierarchical governance in decline? *Journal of Public Administration Research and Theory* 15 (2): 173–95.

Hirsch, Werner Z. 1995. Contracting out by (US) urban governments: A review. *Urban Affairs Review* 30 (3): 458–72.

Hirschman, Albert O. 1970. *Exit, voice, and loyalty: Responses to decline in firms, organizations, and states.* Cambridge, Mass.: Harvard University Press.

Hughes, Mark Alan. 1996. Facing the welfare reform storm: Philadelphia better start bailing. Opinion Editorial. *The Philadelphia Inquirer*, December 16.

———. 1997. Philadelphia, state should strike deal to make welfare reform work. Opinion Editorial. *The Philadelphia Inquirer*, May 14.

Hyneman, Charles S. 1950. *Bureaucracy in a democracy.* New York: Harper and Brothers.

Institute of Public Administration. 2005. Government integrity. www.theipa.org/programs/eac.html (accessed November 29, 2005).

Jehl, Douglas. 2003. As cities move to privatize water, Atlanta steps back. *The New York Times*, February 10.

John F. Kennedy School of Government. 1995. Organizing competition in Indianapolis. Cases C18-95-1269.0 (case A); C18-95-1270.0 (case B); and C18-95-1270.1 (sequel).

Johnston, Jocelyn M., and Barbara S. Romzek. 1999. Contracting and account-ability in state Medicaid reform: Rhetoric, theories, and reality. *Public Administration Review* 59 (5): 383–99.

Kaestner, Robert, Sanders Korenman, and June O'Neill. 2003. Has welfare reform changed teenage behaviors? *Journal of Policy Analysis and Management* 22 (2): 225–48.

Kalu, Kalu N., 2003. Entrepreneurs or conservators? Contractarian principles of bureaucratic performance. *Administration and Society* 25 (5): 539–63.

Kamarck, Elaine. 2004. Applying 21st-century government to the challenge of homeland security. In *Collaboration: Using networks and partnerships*, ed. John Kamensky and Thomas Burlin, 103–46. Lanham, Md.: Rowman & Littlefield.

Kamensky, John M., Thomas J. Burlin, and Mark Abramson. 2004. Networks and partnerships: Collaborating to achieve results no one can achieve alone. In *Collaboration: Using networks and partnerships*, ed. John M. Kamensky and Thomas J. Burlin, 3–20. Lanham, Md.: Rowman & Littlefield.

Kamensky, John M., and Albert Morales, eds. 2005. *Managing for results 2005.* Lanham, Md.: Rowman & Littlefield.

Kaplan, Robert S. 2002. *The balanced scorecard and nonprofit organizations.* Cambridge, Mass.: Harvard Business School Publishing.

Kaplan, Robert S., and David P. Norton. 1992. The balanced scorecard—measures that drive performance. *Harvard Business Review* 70 (1): 71–79.

———. 1996. Using the balanced scorecard as a strategic management system. *Harvard Business Review* 74 (1): 75–85.

Karabell, Zachary. 2004. *Chester Alan Arthur.* New York: Henry Holt and Company.

Kaufman, Herbert. 1956. Emerging conflicts in the doctrines of public administration. *American Political Science Review* 50 (December): 1057–73.

———. 1960. *The forest ranger: A study in administrative behavior.* Baltimore, Md.: Johns Hopkins University Press. Later editions: Washington, D.C.: Resources for the Future, 1986.

Kettl, Donald F. 1993. *Sharing power: Public governance and private markets.* Washington, D.C.: Brookings Institution Press.

———. 2000. *The global public management revolution: A report on the transformation of governance.* Washington, D.C.: Brookings Institution Press.

Kettner, Peter M., and Lawrence L. Martin. 1994. The purchase of service at 20: Are we using it well? *Public Welfare* 52 (3): 14–20.

Key, V. O. 1942. Politics and administration. In *The future of government in the United States: Essays in honor of Charles E. Merriam*, ed. Leonard D. White, 146. Chicago: University of Chicago Press.

Kirby, Gretchen, Heather Hill, LaDonna Pavetti, Jon Jacobson, Michelle Derr, and Pamela Winston. 2002. Transitional jobs: Stepping stones to unsubsidized employment. Princeton, N.J.: Mathematica Policy Research, Inc.

Klawitter, Marieka. 2001. *Effects of work first activities on employment and earnings.* Seattle: University of Washington Press.

Koller, Frank, 2003. No silver bullet: Water privatization in Atlanta, Georgia— a cautionary tale. February 5, 2003, CBC Radio. www.cbc.ca/news/features/ water/atlanta.html.

Krislov, Samuel, and David H. Rosenbloom. 1981. *Representative bureaucracy and the American political system.* New York: Praeger.

Landis, James M. 1938. *The administrative process.* New Haven, Conn.: Yale University Press.

Langton, Stuart, ed. 1978. *Citizen participation in America: Essays on the state of the art.* Lexington, Mass.: Lexington Books.

Leirson, Avery. 1942. *Administrative regulation.* Chicago: University of Chicago Press.

Lewis, Carol W. 1991. *The ethics challenge in public service: A problem-solving guide.* San Francisco: Jossey-Bass.

Light, Paul C. 1999. *The true size of government.* Washington, D.C.: Brookings Institution Press.

———. 2001. From Pentagons to pyramids: Whacking at bloat. *Government Executive* 33 (9): 100.

———. 2003. Government by the numbers. *Government Executive* 35 (15): 80.

Lippmann, Walter. 1955. *The public philosophy.* New York: New American Library.

Long, Norton E. 1952. Bureaucracy and constitutionalism. *American Political Science Review* 46 (September): 808–18.

Lowi, Theodore J. 1969. *The end of liberalism: Ideology, policy, and the crisis of public authority.* New York: W. W. Norton.

———. 1979. *The end of liberalism: The second republic of the United States.* 2d ed. New York: W. W. Norton.

Luttbeg, Norman R., ed. 1974. *Public opinion and public policy: Models of political linkage.* Rev. ed. Homewood, Ill.: The Dorsey Press.

Mainzer, Lewis C. 1973. *Political bureaucracy.* Glenview, Ill.: Scott Foresman & Co.

Mariani, Michele. 2003. Getting hammered: Atlanta's water contract is kaput. *Governing Magazine,* April.

Mariner, Joanne, 2006. Private contractors who torture. *CNN-Findlaws,* June 17 (accessed on December 27, 2006). www.cnn.com/2004/LAW/06/17/mariner .contractors/index.html.

Marsden, Bill. 2003. Cholera and the age of the water barons. *The Center for Public Integrity,* February 3. www.publicintegrity.org/water/report.aspx? aid=44.

Martin, Lawrence L., and Peter M. Kettner. 1996. *Measuring the performance of human service programs.* Thousand Oaks, Calif.: Sage.

Martin, Lawrence. 2002. Performance-based contracting for human services: Lessons for public procurement? *Journal of Public Procurement* 2 (1): 55–71.

———. 2003. Making performance-based contracting perform: What the federal government can learn from state and local governments. In *The procurement revolution*, ed. M. Abramson and R. Harris III. Lanham, Md.: Rowman & Littlefield Publishers, Inc.

Mathur, Navdeep, and Chris Skelcher. 2007. Evaluating democratic performance: Methodologies for assessing the relationship between network governance and citizens. *Public Administration Review* 67 (2): 228–37.

May, Patrick. 2007. Schwarzenegger salutes rapid repair of MacArthur Maze. *San Jose Mercury News*. May 26 (accessed May 29, 2007). www.mercurynews.com/ci_5994233.

McConnell, Grant. 1967. *Private power and American democracy*. New York: Alfred A. Knopf.

McDavid, James C., and Eric G. Clemens. 1995. Contracting out local government services: The British Columbia experience. *Canadian Public Administration* 38 (2): 177–93.

McGuire, Michael. 2002. Managing networks: Propositions on what managers do and why they do it. *Public Administration Review* 62 (5): 599–609.

———. 2006. Collaborative public management: Assessing what we know and how we know it. *Public Administration Review* 66: 33–43.

McMahon, E. J. 2003. City Journal's quality-of-life index. *City Journal* (Summer): 82–85.

McMahon, E. J., Adrian Moore, and George Segal. 2003. *Private competition for public services: Unfinished agenda in New York State*. New York: Center for Civic Innovation at The Manhattan Institute 41.

Miller, Jason. 2006. Report: DHS contracting lacks accountability, controls. *Washington Technology*. www.washingtontechnology.com (accessed August 1).

Milward, Brinton. 1994. Nonprofit contracting and the hollow state. *Public Administration Review* 54: 73–77.

———. 1996. Symposium on the hollow state: Capacity, control and performance in interorganizational settings: Introduction. *Journal of Public Administration Research and Theory* 6: 193–95.

Milward, Brinton, and K. G. Provan. 2000. Governing the hollow state. *Journal of Public Administration Research and Theory* 10 (2): 359–79.

Milward, H. Brinton, and Jörg Raab. 2002. Dark networks as problems. *PA Times* 25 (11): 5.

Miranda, Rowan, and Karlyn Andersen. 1994. Alternative service delivery in local government, 1982–1992. In *Municipal Year Book*. Washington, D.C.: International City Management Association.

Moe, Ronald C. 1994. The "Reinventing Government" exercise: Misinterpreting the problem, misjudging the consequences. *Public Administration Review* 54 (2): 111–22.

Morley, Elaine, Scott P. Bryant, and Harry Hatry. 2001. *Comparative performance measurement*. Washington, D.C.: Urban Institute Press.

Mosher, Frederick C. 1968. *Democracy and the public service*. New York: Oxford University Press.

MTA (Metropolitan Transportation Authority of the State of New York). 2005. Vendor code of ethics. www.mta.nyc.ny.us/mta/procurement/vendor-code.htm (accessed November 29, 2005).

Nadler, Judy. 2005. Ethics and public contracting. *Markkula Center for Applied Ethics*. http://www.scu.edu/ethics/publications/ethicalperspectives/ethics-public-contracting.html.

Nelson, Erik. 2007. MacArthur Maze contract awarded. *San Jose Mercury News*. May 8 (accessed May 29, 2007). http://origin.mercurynews.com/news/ci_5843809.

Neustadt, Richard E. 1976. *Presidential power: The politics of leadership, with reflections on Johnson and Nixon*. Rev. ed. New York: John Wiley & Sons.

———. 1990. *Presidential power and the modern presidents: The politics of leadership from Roosevelt to Reagan*. New York: Free Press; Toronto: Collier Macmillan.

The New York Times. 1998. Company news; United Water and Suez Lyonnaise win Atlanta contract. *The New York Times*, August 29.

The New York Times. 2004. Atlanta ex-mayor is indicted after corruption investigation. *The New York Times*, August 31.

NYCDSBS (New York City Department of Small Business Services). 2006. Government contracts/procurement outreach. www.nyc.gov/html/contracts.html (accessed February 20).

NYC.gov. 2006. General information for vendors. www.nyc.gov/html/selltonyc/html/new_vendors.html (accessed February 20).

Olsen, Johan P. 2006. Maybe it is time to rediscover bureaucracy. *Journal of Public Administration Research and Theory* 16 (1) (January): 1–24.

Osborne, David, and Ted Gaebler. 1992. *Reinventing government: How the entrepreneurial spirit is transforming the public sector*. Reading, Mass.: Addison-Wesley Longman.

Osborne, David, and Peter Hutchinson. 2004. *The price of government: Getting the results we need in an age of permanent fiscal crisis*. New York: Basic Books.

Osborne, David, and Peter Plastrik. 1997. *Banishing bureaucracy: The five strategies for reinventing government*. Reading, Mass.: Addison-Wesley.

Page, Stephen. 2004. Measuring accountability for results in interagency collaboratives. *Public Administration Review* 64 (5): 591–606.

———. 2005. What's new about the new public management? Administrative change in the human services. *Public Administration Review* 65 (6): 713–27.

Palmer, Kimberly. 2005. Acquisition panel considers ethics in contracting. *Government Executive*. February 28: 1. http://www.govexec.com/.

Panet, Philip de L., and Michael J. Trebilcock. 1998. Contracting out social services. *Canadian Public Administration* 41 (Spring): 21–50.

Payen, Gerard. 2006. Water Business. *OECD Observer*, Number 254, March.

Pendered, David. 2006. City can't meet sewer fix deadline. *The Atlanta Journal-Constitution*, October 26: B1.

Perry, James L. 1993. Public service motivation: Construct, content and reliability. Paper presented at the National Conference of the American Society for Public Administration, July 19, Washington, D.C.

Peters, B. Guy. 1978. *The politics of bureaucracy: A comparative perspective.* New York: Longman.

Peters, Thomas J., and Robert H. Waterman Jr. 1982. *In search of excellence: Lessons from America's best-run companies.* New York: Harper & Row.

Philadelphia Workforce Development Corporation. Contract #TW06-076 with Transitional Work Corporation. December 2, 2005.

Pitkin, Hanna F. 1967. *The concept of representation.* Berkeley and Los Angeles: University of California Press.

POGO (Project on Government Oversight). 2004. The politics of contracting. http://www.pogo.org/p/contracts/c/co-040101-contractor.html.

Powell, Norman J. 1967. *Responsible public bureaucracy in the United States.* Boston: Allyn & Bacon, Inc.

Prager, Jonas. 1994. Contracting out government services: Lessons from the private sector. *Public Administration Review* 54 (2): 176–84.

Public Citizen. 2003. The water privatization "model": A backgrounder on United Water's Atlanta fiasco. March 13. www.publiccitizen.org.

Radin, Beryl A. 1998. The Government Performance and Results Act (GPRA): Hydra-headed monster or flexible management tool? *Public Administration Review* 58 (4): 307–16.

Ramage, Stephanie, 1998. Campbell keeps battling. *Atlanta Business Chronicle,* September 4.

Reed, William H. 2004. *Statement before the House Committee on Government Reform given on June 15.* June 9. http://reform.house.gov/UploadedFiles/ DCAA%20-%20Reed%20Testimony.pdf.

Rehfuss, John. 1991. The competitive agency: Thoughts from contracting out in Great Britain and the United States. *International Review of Administrative Sciences* 57 (3): 465–82.

Riordan, William L., ed. 1994. *Plunkitt of Tammany Hall: A series of very plain talks on very practical politics with an introduction, by Terrence J. McDonald.* Boston: Bedford Books of St. Martin's Press.

Roberts, Nancy. 2004. Public deliberation in an age of direct citizen participation. *American Review of Public Administration* 34 (4) (December): 315–53.

Rohr, John. 1989. *Ethics for bureaucrats: An essay on law and values.* 2nd ed. New York: Marcel Dekker, Inc.

Romzek, Barbara S., and Jocelyn M. Johnston. 1999. Reforming Medicaid through contracting: The nexus of implementation and organizational culture. *Journal of Public Administration Theory and Research* 9 (1): 107–39.

———. 2005. State social services contracting: Exploring the determinants of effective contract accountability. *Public Administration Review* 65 (4): 436–49.

Rosenbloom, David H., and Robert S. Kravchuck. 2002. *Public administration: Understanding management, politics, and law in the public sector.* 5th ed. Boston: McGraw-Hill.

Rourke, Francis E. 1976. *Bureaucracy, politics, and public policy.* 2nd ed. Boston: Little, Brown and Company.

Rubenstein, Sarah. 2002. City blasts United Water. *Atlanta Business Chronicle,* August 9.

Ryan, Neal. 1999. A comparison of contracting arrangements in Australia, Canada and New Zealand. *The International Journal of Public Sector Management* 12 (2): 91–104.

Sachs, Jeffrey. 2005. *The end of poverty: Economic possibilities for our time.* New York: Penguin Press.

Salmon, Lester. 2003. *The resilient sector.* Washington, D.C.: Brookings Institution Press.

Sanger, M. Bryna. 2003. *The welfare marketplace: Privatization and welfare reform.* Washington, D.C.: The Brookings Institution Press.

Savas, E. S. 2002. Competition and choice in New York City social services. *Public Administration Review* (62) 1: 82–91.

———. 2005. *Privatization in the city: Successes, failures, lessons.* Washington, D.C.: CQ Press.

Schattschneider, E. E. 1960. *The semisovereign people: A realist's view of democracy in America.* Hinsdale, Ill.: The Dryden Press.

Schmid, Hillel. 2003. Rethinking the policy of contracting out social services to non-governmental organizations. *Public Management Review* 5 (3): 307–23.

Sclar, Elliott D. 1994. Public-service privatization: Ideology or economics? *Dissent* 41 (3): 329–36.

———. 2000. *You don't always get what you pay for: The economics of privatization.* Ithaca, N.Y.: Cornell University Press.

Scott, E. 2002. *Mayor Anthony Williams and performance management in Washington, DC.* Cambridge, Mass.: Kennedy School of Government Case Program.

Scott, Jeffry. 2006. Campbell begins prison term. August 22, 2006. www.palmbeachpost.com (accessed October 25, 2006).

Segal, Geoffrey. 2003. Issue analysis: The Atlanta water privatization: What can we learn? Georgia Public Policy Foundation, January 24. www.rppi.org/atlantawaterprivatization.html.

Segerfeldt, Frederik. 2005. Water for sale: How business and the market can resolve the world's water crisis. Washington, D.C.: Cato Institute.

Selznick, Phillip. 1957. *Leadership in administration: A sociological interpretation.* Berkeley: University of California Press.

Sharkansky, Ira. 1989. Policy making and service delivery on the margins of the government: The case of contractors. In *Services for sale: Purchasing health and human services*, ed. Harold W. Demone Jr., and Margaret Gibelman, 81–96. New Brunswick, N.J.: Rutgers University Press.

Sharpe, Murem. 1997. Outsourcing, organizational competitiveness, and work. *Journal of Labor Research* 18 (Fall): 534–49.

Shelton, Stacy. 2005. City's response to river lawsuit widely praised ten years later, Chattahoochee in better health. *The Atlanta Journal-Constitution,* October 10: B1.

Simpson, Jeffrey. 2003. Cleanup contract goes down the drain. *Halifax Herald Limited,* June 21.

Singer, Peter W. 2003. *Corporate warriors: The rise of the privatized military industry.* Ithaca, N.Y.: Cornell University Press.

———. 2004a. Warriors for hire in Iraq. Salon.com, April 15. www.brookings .edu/views/articles/fellows/singer20040415.htm (accessed September 11, 2004).

———. 2004b. Outsourcing the war. Salon.com, April 16. www.brookings.edu/ views/articles/fellows/singer20040416.htm (accessed September 11, 2004).

Smith, Martin. 2005. Private warriors. *Frontline* on PBS, June 21. www.pbs.org/ wgbh/pages/frontline/shows/warriors/interviews/cerjan.html.

Smith, Steven Rathgeb. 2005. Managing the challenges of government contracts. In *The Jossey-Bass handbook of nonprofit leadership and management,* ed. R. Herman & Associates. San Francisco: Jossey-Bass.

Spicer, Michael. 2004. Public administration, the history of ideas, and the reinventing government movement. *Public Administration Review* 64 (3): 353–62.

Steel, Brent S., and Carolyn Long. 1998. The use of agency forces versus contracting out: Learning the limitations of privatization. *Public Administration Quarterly* 22 (2): 229–51.

Stokes, Donald E., and Warren E. Miller. 1962. Party government and the salience of congress. *Public Opinion Quarterly* 26 (Winter): 531–46.

Suez Lyonnaise des Eaux. 1998. With Atlanta, UWS is awarded the largest private drinking water contract in the United States. Press Release of January 9, 1998, found at www.waternunc.com/gb/lyon7gb.html on October 10, 2006.

Suez, 2003. Suez and Atlanta reach a mutual dissolution agreement for the city's drinking water services contract. Press Release of January 24, 2003, found at www.waternunc.com/gb/Suez_eng01_2003.html on October 18, 2006.

Sullivan, John L., and Robert E. O'Connor. 1972. Electoral choice and popular control of public policy: The case of the 1966 House elections. *American Political Science Review* 66 (December): 1256–68.

Swabey, Marie Collins. 1969. A quantitative view. In *Representation*, ed. Hanna F. Pitkin, 90. New York: Atherton Press.

Tagami, Ty. 2004a. City Council OKs water rate increases. *The Atlanta Journal-Constitution*, January 6: B1.

———. 2004b. City lags in sewer bill collection, United Water did better job, Atlanta's internal audit says. *The Atlanta Journal-Constitution*, December 1: D3.

———. 2005. Watershed scam ends in arrests: Ex-employees allegedly cheated city of $1 million. *The Atlanta Journal-Constitution,* November 23: B1.

———. 2006. Atlanta's sewer fixes to cost more, may mean higher rates. *The Atlanta Journal-Constitution*, March 29: B6.

Thompson, Fred. 2006. "Netcentric" Organization. *Public Administration Review* 66 (4): 619–22.

Transparency International. 2005a. Integrity pact and public contracting. www.corisweb.org/article/archive/264.

———. 2005b. Preventing corruption in public contracting. www.corisweb .org/article/archive/322.

Turpin, Colin. 1972. *Government contracts*. Harmondsworth: Penguin.

UNESCO. 2006. The UN World Water Development Report: 2006. www.unesco .org/water/wwap/facts_figures/basic_needs.shtml.

United Nations. 2006. The Millennium Development Goals Report 2006. New York: UNDESA, June.

United States Environmental Protection Agency. 2003. Water on tap: What you need to know. Office of Water, EPA 816-K-03-007, October.

———. 2005. Drinking water infrastructure needs survey and assessment: Third report to Congress, Washington, D.C.: US EPA Office of Water, EPA 816-R-05-001, June.

———. 2006. Drinking water and health: What you need to know. www.epa.gov/ safewater/dwh/index.html (accessed on October 26).

United States General Accounting Office. 2001. Contract management: Trends and challenges in acquiring services. May 22. www.gao.gov/new.items/d01753t.pdf.

———. 2003. Federal procurement: Spending and workforce trends. April. www. gao.gov/new.items/d03443.pdf.

———. 2004. Rebuilding Iraq: Resource, security, governance, essential services, and oversight issues. June. www.gao.gov/new.items/d04902r.pdf.

United States House of Representatives Committee on Government Reform. 2006. *Waste, abuse, and mismanagement in Department of Homeland Security contracts*. Washington, D.C.

United States Office of Government Ethics. 2005. Impartiality in performing official duties. www.usoge.gov/pages/common_ethics_issues/common_ethics _issues_pg2.html#Anchor--Impartiali-23629 (accessed December 28, 2005).

United States Small Business Administration. 2006. *Contracting 101*. www.sba .gov/gcbd/newsletter/contracting101.html, accessed February 22.

United Water. 1998. 20-year agreement will save city taxpayers over $400 million. Press Release of November 10, 1998, found at www.unitedwater.com/atlantasing.html on October 10, 2006.

Vaughan, Diane. 1996. *The Challenger launch decision: Risky technology, culture, and deviance at NASA*. Chicago: The University of Chicago Press.

Verba, Sidney, and Norman Nie. 1972. *Participation in America*. New York: Harper and Row.

Waldo, Dwight. 1952. Development of theory of democratic administration. *American Political Science Review* 46 (March): 81–103.

Walker, David M. 2004. *Testimony before the House Committee on Government Reform*. June 15. www.gao.gov/new.items/d04869t.pdf.

Wallsten, Scott, and Katrina Kosec. 2005. Public or private drinking water? The effects of ownership and benchmark competition on U.S. water system regulatory compliance and household water expenditures. Washington, D.C.: AEI-Brookings Joint Center for Regulatory Studies, Working Paper 05-05, March.

Watson, Connie. 2003. Sell the rain: How the privatization of water caused riots in Cochabamba, Bolivia. CBC Radio, February 4. www.cbc.ca/news/features/water/bolivia.html.

Waugh, William L. Jr., and Gregory Streib. 2006. Collaboration and leadership for effective emergency management. *Public Administration Review* 66: 131–40.

Weber, E. P. 2000. A new vanguard for the environment: Grass-roots ecosystem management as a new environmental movement. *Society & Natural Resources* 13 (3) (April–May): 237–59.

Welch, Jack. 2005. *Winning*. New York: Harper Business.

Whitt, Richard. 2004. Former mayor Campbell indicted—Feds allege bribery, fraud at City Hall, August 30. www.waterindustry.org found on October 25, 2006.

Wilson, James Q. 2003. James Q. Wilson on John Ogbu: Convincing black students that studying hard is not "acting white." *The Journal of Blacks in Higher Education* 39 (Spring 2003): 85–88.

Witte, Griff. 2005. Former KBR worker admits to fraud in Iraq. *Washington Post*, August 23: A11. www.washingtonpost.com/.

World Bank. 2005. Glossary of key civil service terms. *Administrative & Civil Service Reform*. http://web.worldbank.org/WBSITE/EXTERNAL/TOPICS/EXTPUBLICSECTORANDGOVERNANCE/0,,contentMDK:20201644~pagePK:210058~piPK:210062~theSitePK:286305,00.html.

Worthen, Ben. 2002. The ABCs of supply chain management. *CIO Magazine*, January 22. www.cio.com/research/scm/edit/012202_scm.html.

Wulczyn, Fred, Britany Orlebeke, and Elan Melamid. 2000. Measuring contract agency performance with administrative data. *Child Welfare* 79 (5): 457–74.

Index

Figures are indicated by "f" following the page number.

Defense Contract Management Agency
(DCMA), 165
Defense Department (DOD): Acquisition University curriculum revision, 48; military contracting in Iraq, 41, 92; spending by, 12–13, 14*f*, 15; unethical behavior in, 25
demand articulation, 67
democratic governance principles, 61–68, 85–87, 159. *See also* representation
Denhardt, Kathryn, 37
Department of. *See specific department name*
descriptive representation, 63–64, 80
Dimmock, Marshall, 71, 87*n*7
direct linkage, 75
discretionary powers, 71, 74
disincentive clauses, 148. *See also* penalty clauses
distinctive competence, 93–96
divestiture, 34
Drucker, Peter, 45–46, 92
Druyun, Darleen, 27–28
Dunleavy, Patrick, 6–7

Earned Income Tax Credit (EITC), 170, 181, 186
EDRP. *See* Employment Development and Retention Plan
education: system management, 98–99; vocational, 116; and welfare-to-work programs, 174
e-file initiative (IRS), 48
Eggers, William D.: on capacity gap, 109; on evolution of contracting, 5; on network management, 30, 38, 40, 48; on performance measurement, 111
Eimicke, William, 73, 84
eligibility of contractors, 105–8
emergency contracting procedures, 128
emergency discretionary power, 71
Employment Development and Retention Plan (EDRP), 174, 183
Energy Department, 163
enterprise model of service delivery, 25
entrepreneurial public managers, 20
environmental contracting problems, 139–43
Environmental Probe, 190
Environmental Protection Agency (EPA), 93–94, 150, 187
estimation of resource needs, 134–35, 190–91
ethics. *See* public ethics
The Ethics Challenge in Public Service (Lewis), 23–24

Europe, 61
Executive Office of the President, 70
expertise: bureaucratic, 70; of contract manager, 124; retention of, 94
external contracting problems, 139–43
external influences, 77, 77*f*, 82–83

FedBizOpps, 106
Federal Acquisition Regulation (FAR), 106
federal government contracting, 8–13, 9*f*, 11*f*, 17–18. *See also specific departments and agencies*
federalism, 53
Fleishman, Joel, 32
Follman, Mark, 208
food services: military contracting for, 159–60, 165–66; at universities, 93
food stamp program, 116
Ford, Henry, 44
The Forest Ranger (Kaufman), 207
Forrest, R., 146–47
framing skills, 56
France, water services contracting, 192
Franklin, Shirley, 189, 195, 196
fraud. *See* corruption; public ethics
Frederickson, H. George: on fraud and corruption, 38, 42; on government contracting, 30; on need for selfless public servants, 32; on performance measurement, 154; on privatization, 25
Friedrich, Carl, 72, 84
Frumkin, Peter, 114
Fulton County Taxpayer Association, 195
"functional matching" approach, 122

Gaebler, Ted, 121
GAO. *See* Government Accountability Office
Gaus, John, 79
Geneva Conventions, 167
gifts, improper, 27, 33, 130
Gilbert, Charles E., 75–77, 84, 88*n*9
Gilmour, Robert S., 122
Giuliani, Rudolph, 85
Glanz, James, 163
globalization, 40
Globerman, Steven, 121
Golden Gate National Recreation Area, 48
Goldsmith, Stephen: on Atlanta vs. Indianapolis contracting experiences, 198–99; on capacity gap, 109; on evolution of contracting, 5; as

Printed in the USA
CPSIA information can be obtained
at www.ICGtesting.com
LVHW091312161123
763810LV00091B/540